东盟五国
海事管理法律研究

广东海事局　　广东省律师协会 ◎编著

**DONGMENG WUGUO
HAISHI GUANLI FALU YANJIU**

·广州·

版权所有　翻印必究

图书在版编目（CIP）数据

东盟五国海事管理法律研究/广东海事局，广东省律师协会编著 . —广州：中山大学出版社，2020.12

ISBN 978 – 7 – 306 – 07079 – 1

Ⅰ. ①东… Ⅱ. ①广… ②广… Ⅲ. ①海事法规—研究—东南亚国家联盟—汉、英　Ⅳ. ①D993.5

中国版本图书馆 CIP 数据核字（2020）第 255933 号

出 版 人：	王天琪
策划编辑：	蔡浩然
责任编辑：	蔡浩然　陈文杰
封面设计：	曾　斌
责任校对：	杨文泉
责任技编：	何雅涛
出版发行：	中山大学出版社
电　　话：	编辑部 020 – 84110283, 84111996, 84111997, 84113349
	发行部 020 – 84111998, 84111981, 84111160
地　　址：	广州市新港西路 135 号
邮　　编：	510275　　　传　真：020 – 84036565
网　　址：	http://www.zsup.com.cn　E-mail:zdcbs@mail.sysu.edu.cn
印 刷 者：	佛山市浩文彩色印刷有限公司
规　　格：	787mm×1092mm　1/16　18.125 印张　408 千字
版次印次：	2020 年 12 月第 1 版　2020 年 12 月第 1 次印刷
定　　价：	89.00 元

如发现本书因印装质量影响阅读，请与出版社发行部联系调换

《东盟五国海事管理法律研究》编委会

主　　　编：陈毕伍
副 主 编：肖胜方　杨　文
执 行 主 编：李华文　陈　方　邓　捷　林翠珠
编　　　委：刘　锋　杨运福　徐锦堂　张　敏　林俏媛　沈燕咪
　　　　　　　邝力飞　毕亚男　宋家艳　温望望　杨耀龙　梁子亮
　　　　　　　黄竞博　苏晓军

内 容 提 要

新加坡、马来西亚、印度尼西亚、菲律宾和越南等东盟五国，都是海上丝绸之路的重要节点和必经之地。为了进一步了解东盟五国海事管理法律、进一步提升我国与东盟五国海事管理国际合作的效能，本书课题组成员分别前往东盟五国实地考察，收集了大量的第一手海事管理法律法规、案例、机构设置和制度设计等资料，在此基础上研究分析了东盟五国之间在海事管理体制与法律的异同及各自优点，并对东盟五国海事管理法律的完善提出了一些有益的建议。

本书适合海事部门、司法部门以及高等院校法学专业人士阅读。

序　言

长期以来，新加坡、马来西亚、印度尼西亚、菲律宾、越南等东盟国家都是海上丝绸之路的重要节点和必经之地，也是"一带一路"合作倡议的重要参与国。基于地理优势和海上经济贸易发展优势，东盟五国在海事管理方面积累了丰富的经验，许多管理体制值得我们研究和借鉴。目前，我国尚未对这方面开展过系统的研究工作，这是我了解到国家交通部、广东海事局启动"东盟五国海事管理法律研究"课题研究的动因。

本书具有重要的学习借鉴意义和历史价值。此项课题是我国首次对东盟五国海事管理体制及相关法律制度展开的研究项目，也是广东海事局与广东省律师协会首次联合开展的课题研究项目。课题组深入东盟国家走访或书面调研了新加坡、马来西亚、印度尼西亚、菲律宾、越南等国家的海事管理部门、律师事务所、航运企业、中资企业等机构，收集整理了许多海事管理第一手资料，形成翔实的课题报告并以书籍形式出版，这将对我国海事部门、高等院校、航运企业、海事专业律师等起到重要的学习借鉴作用，并具有一定的历史价值。

研究素材新、数据全、内容实用，推动海事管理机制完善，促进依法行政。本书许多素材是首次掌握，着重对东盟五国的海事部门机构设置、管理体制和涉及的法律法规进行收集研究，尤其是聚焦研究海事安全调查机制和服务海员的经验做法，将为我国海事管理法律法规的修改完善提供了重要的参考，也将促进海事管理工作规范开展，推动依法行政。

借助律师专业优势开展研究，有助于解决实际问题。参与本书课题研究的课题组成员都是一线的海事管理实务人员和海事专业律师，具有丰富的海事工作经验和海事法律服务经验，对所研究的内容有着深切体会，通过东盟五国海事管理体制及法律的对比研究，更有助于吸收好的经验，提高水上交通安全监管水平，解决工作中的具体问题。

相信本书的成功出版将成为海事管理体制和法律研究工作的新起点，希望往后海事部门和法律行业搭建更多合作平台，加强课题研究和实务交流，推动依法行政，共同服务"海洋强国""交通强国"的国家战略实施，为"一带一路"建设和航运经济发展作出新的更大贡献。

广东省司法厅　陈旭东

2020 年 12 月

目　　录

前　言 ……………………………………………………………………………… (1)

第一章　新加坡海事管理法律研究 …………………………………………… (1)
　　一、海事管理体制与机构设置 ………………………………………………… (1)
　　　　（一）海事与港务局 ……………………………………………………… (1)
　　　　（二）交通安全调查局 …………………………………………………… (3)
　　　　（三）海岸警卫队 ………………………………………………………… (4)
　　二、海事法律 …………………………………………………………………… (5)
　　　　（一）国内法 ……………………………………………………………… (5)
　　　　（二）国际条约 …………………………………………………………… (9)
　　三、小结 ………………………………………………………………………… (9)
　　四、附录：新加坡海事法律（国内法）文件 ………………………………… (10)
　　　　（一）附录1：新加坡海事及港务管理局法 …………………………… (10)
　　　　（二）附录2：海上货物运输法 ………………………………………… (116)

第二章　马来西亚海事管理法律研究 ………………………………………… (130)
　　一、海事管理体制与机构设置 ………………………………………………… (130)
　　　　（一）海事局 ……………………………………………………………… (130)
　　　　（二）海事执法局 ………………………………………………………… (132)
　　　　（三）海员教育培训与服务管理体制 …………………………………… (133)
　　二、海事法律 …………………………………………………………………… (135)
　　　　（一）国内法 ……………………………………………………………… (135)
　　　　（二）国际条约 …………………………………………………………… (138)
　　三、小结 ………………………………………………………………………… (143)
　　四、附录：马来西亚海事法律（国内法与国际条约）文件 ………………… (143)
　　　　（一）附录1：1984年商船（避碰规则）法令 ………………………… (143)
　　　　（二）附录2：1953年船舶条约 ………………………………………… (147)
　　　　（三）附录3：515号法案——1994年商船（油类污染）条例 ………… (154)

第三章 印度尼西亚海事管理法律研究 (188)
一、海事管理体制与机构设置 (188)
（一）海事管理体制 (188)
（二）海运总局 (189)
（三）海事安全局 (191)
二、海事法律 (192)
（一）国内法 (192)
（二）国际条约 (194)
三、小结 (194)
四、附录：印度尼西亚海事法律（国内法）文件 (194)
（一）附录1：1998年船舶事故调查的1号政府法规 (194)

第四章 菲律宾海事管理法律研究 (208)
一、海事管理体制与机构设置 (208)
（一）海事局 (208)
（二）海岸警卫队 (211)
（三）海事调查委员会 (212)
（四）海员教育培训与服务管理体制 (213)
二、海事法律 (214)
（一）国内法 (215)
（二）国际条约 (219)
三、小结 (220)
四、附录：菲律宾海事法律（国内法）文件 (220)
（一）附录1：菲律宾海警关于船舶安全执法检查的06—12号通函 (220)

第五章 越南海事管理法律研究 (228)
一、海事管理体制与机构设置 (228)
（一）海事局 (228)
（二）海警司令部 (229)
（三）海事调查体制 (231)
二、海事法律 (231)
（一）国内法 (231)
（二）国际条约 (233)
三、小结 (234)
四、附录：越南海事法律（国内法）文件 (234)
（一）附录1：海警条例 (234)

（二）附录2：2012年越南海洋法 ……………………………………（240）

第六章　东盟五国海事管理法律对比思考 ……………………………………（259）
　一、海事管理体制对比思考 ……………………………………………………（259）
　　（一）海事管理体制的相同点 ………………………………………………（259）
　　（二）海事管理体制的不同点 ………………………………………………（259）
　　（三）海事管理体制的思考 …………………………………………………（260）
　二、海事调查体制对比思考 ……………………………………………………（260）
　　（一）主要特点 ………………………………………………………………（260）
　　（二）关于海事调查体制的思考 ……………………………………………（261）
　三、海员服务管理体制对比思考 ………………………………………………（262）
　　（一）主要特点 ………………………………………………………………（262）
　　（二）关于海员服务管理体制的思考 ………………………………………（262）
　四、海事法律对比思考 …………………………………………………………（262）
　　（一）主要特点 ………………………………………………………………（263）
　　（二）关于完善海事立法的思考 ……………………………………………（263）

第七章　东盟五国海事管理体制改革建议 ……………………………………（264）
　一、加强航运安全监管工作 ……………………………………………………（264）
　　（一）提升安全技术标准 ……………………………………………………（264）
　　（二）积极参与和配合国际海事组织工作 …………………………………（265）
　二、构建智慧航运管理体系 ……………………………………………………（266）
　　（一）推动航海技术发展 ……………………………………………………（266）
　　（二）促进海运便利 …………………………………………………………（267）
　　（三）应对船舶智能化发展的新问题 ………………………………………（269）
　三、强化绿色航运监管 …………………………………………………………（269）
　　（一）船舶污染防治 …………………………………………………………（270）
　　（二）温室气体减排 …………………………………………………………（271）
　　（三）新兴环境问题的积极应对 ……………………………………………（271）

附录：相关国际条约 ……………………………………………………………（274）
后　记 ……………………………………………………………………………（278）

前　言

　　东盟的新加坡、马来西亚、印度尼西亚、菲律宾、越南这五个国家，都是丝绸之路的重要节点和必经之地，都在海上贸易方面积累了丰富的经验。为了进一步提升与东盟五国海事管理国际合作的效能，本书课题组成员分别前往东盟五国实地考察，通过走访调研、专家访谈、学术论文检索、官网信息查询等途径获取了大量最新的一手研究资料；在此基础上分别对新加坡、马来西亚、印度尼西亚、菲律宾和越南五国的海事管理体制及法律，尤其是海事安全调查和海员服务管理体制及法律方面予以研究，并对比分析了东盟五国在海事管理体制与法律的异同和各自优势。

　　在海事管理体制方面，东盟五国各有特色。新加坡海事管理机构主要包括海事及港务管理局、交通安全调查局和海岸警卫队三大部分，海事及港务管理局、交通安全调查局隶属于交通部，海岸警卫队隶属于警察部队。马来西亚海事局是由马来西亚政府管辖的部门，负责管理包括海事在内的有关航运和港口的事项，马来西亚海事执法局作为执法机构直属于首相府。印度尼西亚采用相对集中与高层协调的综合管理模式，交通部海运总局负责航运、港口、船舶管理等海事事务，但海事执法相对比较分散；印度尼西亚每个省市均设有海事机构，在法律框架下独立管理有限海域。菲律宾采用由海事局集中管理、海岸警卫队协助联合执法的海事管理体制，海事局和海岸警卫队均隶属于交通运输部。越南海事局负责监管越南沿海海事事务，实行垂直管理体制，直属于交通部。

　　海事安全调查是海事管理中一项比较重要的职责。东盟五国的海事调查均属于"独立调查"，即独立于其他民事、行政和刑事类型的调查，而且调查报告只是就事故发生原因做分析，不会确定责任比例。这种独立调查模式更有利于查明事故发生的真正原因。越南港口水域外的事故调查由海事局负责，港口水域内的事故调查则由港务局负责。新加坡和菲律宾的海事安全调查分别由独立于海事局之外的交通安全调查局、海岸警卫队及其海事调查委员会负责。

　　海员是特殊的职业种类，常年在海上漂泊，工作艰辛、枯燥、风险高。东盟五国中以菲律宾的海员服务管理工作最为突出，其拥有较为先进合理的航海教育和培训制度、健全的法律监管体制，而且设有海外就业管理局这一专门服务管理机构以保障船员权益，海员享有免征所得税和专属医院诊治等待遇。

　　依法行政是海事治理现代化的重要基石。东盟五国的海事法源主要包括法律、总统令、行政命令、条例、细则、规则、办法、规程、准则与要点等附属法规，以及备忘录通告、海事管理咨询等非正式法源。在海事国际条约的国内化实施方面，菲律宾、越南和印度尼西亚加入的海事国际条约原则上具有直接效力，无须转化即可实施，但由于新加坡、马来西亚受英国影响，其加入的国际条约则通常需要转化为国内法律才能加以实施。

　　经过对比研究，课题组发现，东盟五国形成了各自不同的海事管理制度和法律；但东盟五国某些海事管理机制又有相同之处。例如，东盟五国海事部门都隶属于交通部，海事行政与海警事务相分离、海事行政与企业经营相分离。部分东盟国家存在海事和港口行政一体化、海事行政职责较为分散的特点。

在海事管理体制方面，以新加坡为代表的海事公共服务理念和电子政务，是一个很大的亮点。

在海事安全调查方面，各国可以通过修订海事安全调查法律法规，加强海事调查队伍建设，推动海事安全调查独立实施。

在船员服务管理和权益维护方面，可借鉴菲律宾的海员服务管理和权益维护体制，改变对海员重管理、轻服务的局面，进一步重视海员教育培训，强化相关机构人员力量，提升保护海员合法权益的能力，推动减免海员应缴个人所得税。

本课题由广东海事局、广东省律师协会、广东恒福律师事务所、广州市航运法学研究会等单位共同完成。研究报告由李华文、林翠珠、刘锋、杨运福、徐锦堂、张敏、林俏媛、沈燕咪、邝力飞、毕亚男、宋家艳、温望望、杨耀龙、梁子亮、黄竞博、苏晓军等人撰写。由于笔者水平所限，书中若有不当之处，敬请读者斧正。

第一章　新加坡海事管理法律研究

新加坡，旧称为星岛，别称为狮城，国土面积为724.4平方千米，海岸线长达200余千米，国土由64个岛屿组成，其中面积最大的岛屿是新加坡岛，约占国土面积的88%。新加坡北隔柔佛海峡与马来西亚为邻，南隔新加坡海峡与印度尼西亚相望，毗邻马六甲海峡南口。新加坡商贸服务业、交通与通信行业、金融服务业这三大服务业的蓬勃发展，为新加坡赢得亚洲金融中心、航运中心、贸易中心的地位奠定了坚实的基础。

新加坡先进的海事管理制度是现代海事管理的典范，它推动新加坡海事形成了蓬勃不息的生态系统，不断地提升新加坡全球枢纽港口的地位。尤其是新加坡海事与港务局（Maritime and Port Authority of Singapore，MPA），它坚持为航运及海事提供优质的服务、注重提升海事科技水平、依法处理海事工作、积极寻求制度上的完善与突破，最终使得新加坡海事管理在国际上处于相对领先的地位。

一、海事管理体制与机构设置

新加坡采用相对集中、政企分离的海事管理体制，由新加坡海事与港务局统一领导国家海事工作并履行各项海事职能。新加坡海事与港务局和民航局、陆路交通管理局、信息与通信发展管理局一同隶属于交通部。

（一）海事与港务局

海事与港务局是新加坡港口和海事发展的推动力量，承担港务局、港口监管机构、港口规划师和国家海事代表的角色。同时，新加坡海事与港务局注重跟其他机构的沟通与协作，注重加强港口水域的安全、推进环境保护、促进港口运营和增长、扩大海事辅助服务群、推进海事研发和发展人才。

1. 概况

新加坡在1996年以前实行海事与港口管理分离、港口政企合一的体制。1996年2月，新加坡进行海事与港口体制改革，将原新加坡海事处、国家海事局以及港务局合并，组建新加坡海事与港务局，实行海港合一、政企分离的管理体制，旨在将新加坡建成世界上首屈一指的港口和国际海事中心（International Maritime Centre，IMC）。新加坡海事与港务局作为交通部下设的独立机构，行使海事管理职能，成为新加坡管理海事与港口的唯一行政主管机构。原新加坡港务局的经营职能由新成立的新加坡港务集团公司替代，实现由行政主管部门到营利性企业的转型，致力于港口经营。

新加坡执行自由港政策并采取各种优惠措施，如对中转货物减免仓储费、装卸搬运费和货物管理费，以吸引世界各国船舶公司，进一步巩固其国际航运中心地位。新加坡海事与港务局（MPA）作为新加坡政府海上运输界的代表，捍卫新加坡航运和港口业在国际上的利益。其使命主要有三项：一是巩固新加坡全球枢纽港地位，二是保持新加坡的国际海事中心地位，三是维护并拓展新加坡海运及港口战略利益。新加坡海事与港务局负责管理新加坡水域的港口和海事服务、设施及活动，主要包括制定港口经济运营规则，建立强大的船舶运输队伍，监管在新加坡海域内运作的船只和全球范围内的新加坡注册船只，监管航行安全和海洋环境等；负责调查在新加坡海域发生的意外和事故，以及提供服务大众的海事服务。

2. 基本职能

一是作为港口主管部门，主要管理港口事务。例如，观测船舶航行动态、保障航海安全、提供海事服务与软硬件设施、防治海洋污染、促进环境保护等，并对港务服务和港口经贸业务进行管理。新加坡海事与港务局为应对日益繁忙的水路交通，将信息技术与港口实际情况相结合，成功研发出港口信息应用平台和贸易信息应用平台，整合来自政府部门、航运企业、物流中心等服务机构的数据信息，建设电子数据交换中心，提供"一站式"国际航运服务，积极打造全球综合海运信息平台，为海事从业者和全球客户提供全面而优质的海事及港口服务。新加坡海事与港务局在电子政务建设方面起步早，在海事监管领域广泛采用前沿科技成果，如信息网络技术，重视与国际技术力量协作，促进航运业可持续性发展。

二是作为港口规划部门，主要是有效控制船舶数量，发挥港口资源最大价值。对港口基础设施建设进行设计和规划，如常用航道、通道、锚地以及公共码头等。

三是作为海事管理机构，主要负责海事方面国际标准的制定、船员社会保障与救济、船员管理、船员职业发展与培训。

四是作为新加坡全国的海路运输代表，主要在水路运输安全和海洋污染防治方面做出贡献。例如，积极参与国际海事组织、航道测量组织等的活动，与行业翘楚切磋交流，为新加坡航运发展建言献策，等等。

五是作为"国际海事中心"，其任务是吸引更多大船公司在新加坡"落户"。新加坡海事与港务局为此制定了大量优惠政策，提供优质海事服务，如简化企业注册程序，就近安排办公地点，解决外籍工作人员医疗、教育等问题。截至目前，全球众多船东选择在新加坡注册船舶，总吨位已逾5000万吨。船舶悬挂新加坡旗好处颇多，如船东能享受到一系列税收优惠和金融激励政策，新加坡船舶注册处还拥有一大批经验丰富且极富责任心的人才，能够高效处理船舶登记事项和满足注册船舶需求。

3. 部门架构

新加坡海事与港务局下设8个部门，各部门下设专业性业务管理部门，分管海事及港口具体业务。例如，政策部放眼全球，立足于马六甲海峡，负责规划新加坡港口建设蓝图并制定相应策略、政策等，政策制定主要涵盖码头布局、港口业务布局，以及不断拓展业务范围，推动学术交流，开展业务培训并付诸实践。港埠发展处致力于港口规划和基础设施建设，旨在了解并把握全球港航局势，精心规划并制定策略，发挥新加坡港的优势，确保在全球航运业竞争中立于不败之地。新加坡海事与港务局的港埠管制处集中处理新加坡海事与港务局的许可管制业务①,旨在达成以下管制目标:第一,确保提供优质而丰富的港口服务并通过科学合理的制度来控制服务提供商的准入;第二,确保港口许可管制费用合理以及为公共许可证持有人提供高水准服务;第三,确保良性和公平的市场竞争环境。

4. 人员情况

新加坡海事与港务局现有雇员约 700 人,最高层为理事会,由理事长和其他 11 位理事会成员组成。② 理事会成员分别来自新加坡海事与港务局、贸易工业部、新加坡海运协会、新加坡海军部队、新加坡海员联合会及新加坡海运公司等。理事会下辖理事长办公室以及各功能部门。各部门分工协作,管理层权力相互制衡,既能提高效率,又能防止腐败专权,有助于新加坡海事与港务局发展壮大以及新加坡完善海事管理体制、巩固其国际航运中心的地位。

5. 执法船舶和其他装备

新加坡执法船舶装备主要为新加坡警察海岸警卫队所有。新加坡海事与港务局主要设有 VTS(交通服务)、AIS(船舶自动识别系统)基站及监控油污的设备。2018 年,新加坡升级了船舶交通信息系统(VTIS),同时,为促进岸上和船舶之间的实时数据传输,新加坡海事与港务局(MPA)将在未来三年投资 50 万美元用于 VHF(甚高频)数据交换系统(VDES)的开发。③ 新加坡海事与港务局还承诺将提供高达 80 万美元的资金,用于区域性客运渡轮的新型扣式救生衣和定制救生衣容器的供应、安装、交付和试运行服务。值得注意的是,对新型救生衣的规范和标准将更加严格,新型救生衣必须符合国际标准,如救生设备(LSA)规范。④ 海上安全一直是新加坡作为重要枢纽港和繁忙的国际航道关注的关键领域。⑤

(二)交通安全调查局

交通安全调查局(Transport Safety Investigation Bureau, TSIB)是新加坡空中和海上事故的调查机构。新加坡交通安全调查局的使命是根据国际通行做法,通过对空中和海上事故进行独立和客观的调查来促进航空和海上安全。

---

① 管制种类主要有三种:一是港口服务及设施的许可,主要是面向经营集装箱、常规货物及客运码头的服务提供商,目前共有 3 家,即 PSA(新加坡国际港务集团)、裕廊码头和客轮服务中心;二是引航服务许可,目前只有 1 家,由 PSA 承担;三是拖轮服务许可,目前已全部开放,共有 5 家经营公司。

② 新加坡海事与港务局理事会人员详情可参见官网,网址:http://www.mpa.gov.sg/web/portalhomeabout-mpa/list-of-board-members,2018 年 6 月 30 日访问。各部门负责人详情可参见网址:http://www.mpa.gov.sg/web/portalhomeabout-mpa/organisation-chart,2018 年 6 月 30 日访问。

③ 《新加坡海上安全新举措》,参见新加坡海事与港务局官网,网址:https://www.mpa.gov.sg/web/portal-homemedia-centre/news-releases/detail/131c9f9b-46a5-44c2-b219-315e41bf7763,2018 年 6 月 20 日访问。

④ 《重启海上安全运动,以促进海上安全第一的文化》,参见新加坡海事与港务局官网,网址:https://www.mpa.gov.sg/web/portal/home/media-centre/news-releases/detail/70462398-66d5-46e3-ba95-1f624216c35f,2018 年 6 月 18 日访问。

⑤ 参见新加坡海事与港务局官网,网址:https://www.mpa.gov.sg/web/portalhomemedia-centre/news-releases/detail/25574a0d-0e77-4f8d-9d03-a45f85de283b,2018 年 6 月 18 日访问。

1. 概况

2016年8月1日,新加坡交通部重组航空事故调查局,成立新的交通安全调查局,使其隶属于交通部。交通安全调查局是新加坡空中和海上意外事故的调查机构,它从新加坡海事与港务局接过调查海事意外和事故的任务,就这些事故展开独立安全调查,并提出加强海事交通安全的建议。交通安全调查局针对航空及海事意外和事故进行独立调查在国际上是通行的做法,其他国家如澳大利亚、日本、英国和美国也设有类似的调查机构。

2. 基本职责

交通安全调查局调查事故或事件的唯一目的是预防事故而非分摊责任。在进行调查时,交通安全调查局将收集、记录和分析关于事故的所有可用信息,确定原因和影响因素,确定可能的安全问题,提出建议来解决安全问题,制作调查报告。① 交通安全调查局海事安全调查处负责调查涉及新加坡注册船舶的非常严重的海难事故以及新加坡领海内涉及非新加坡注册船舶的事故。海事安全调查处根据《国际海事组织海上事故或事故安全调查国际标准和建议措施规则》开展调查。

3. 部门架构

新加坡交通部(MOT)是新加坡管理交通运输的政府部门,负责航空、海事、陆路部门的发展及监管,负责调控5个独立的政府法定机构:新加坡民航局(CAA)、新加坡陆路交通管理局(LTA)、新加坡海事与港务局(MPA)、新加坡公共交通理事会(PTC)和交通安全调查局。交通安全调查局由航空事故调查处(Air Accident Investigation Bureau,AAIB)和海事安全调查处(Marine Safety Investigation Branch,MSIB)组成。

(三)海岸警卫队

海岸警卫队(PCG)隶属于新加坡警察部队(Singapore Police Force,SPF)②,担负着海岸警卫任务。一般情况下,他国海上执法任务往往由独立军事力量或单独的职能部门承担。自1819年新加坡贸易港成立以来,海警部门便开始水上执法,防止海盗等不法力量的侵袭。1965年,新加坡独立后设立海事部。1993年2月13日,新加坡政府重组海事部,成立海岸警卫队,在原有权能的基础上,赋予其更大的海上执法权限,包括阻止非法移民入境和外国非法船舶入境等。依职能的不同,海岸警卫队被分为拦截中队、港口中队和海岸中队三大中队。1997年1月22日,海岸警卫队新设特殊任务中队(STS),负责对走私船舶和恐怖分子执行强行登船、截停、强击等特殊任务。

1. 基本职责

新加坡海岸警卫队对新加坡超过700平方千米的领海进行全天候的巡逻并负责海上

---

① 参见新加坡交通部官网,网址:https://www.mot.gov.sg/,2018年6月20日访问。
② 新加坡警察部队机构设置为:参谋部、行动局、人事局、后勤局、计划和组织局、行政管理和财政局、刑侦局、商业调查局、交通局、公共事务局、志愿人员管理局、培训局、国民服役警察局、电子计算机和通讯局、情报局、机场警察局、海岸警卫队、地区警署、安全警卫部队、特别行动部队、警察学院。详见于新加坡警察部队官网,网址:https://www.police.gov.sg/about-us/organisational-structure,2018年7月12日访问。

执法、维护新加坡绝大部分岛屿的秩序和安全，以及和新加坡海事与港务局、移民检查局共同肩负海上搜救重任。新加坡海岸警卫队（PCG）的任务是维护新加坡海岸的秩序与安全，具体而言有三类：一是防止非法移民进入新加坡海域；二是"9·11"事件后，新加坡为应对日益严峻的恐怖袭击威胁，提高了安全警戒等级，2004年以后，新加坡海岸警卫队在船舶上添加了检测爆炸物、毒品等违禁品的设备；三是新加坡海岸警卫队自1990年起便与其他机构展开联合执法协作。

2. 人员情况

新加坡海岸警卫队是目前新加坡最大的执法力量之一，拥有1000多名警员，这些警员由国家公务员和志愿警察构成，二者具有相同的执法权能。新加坡海岸警卫队的警员来源主要有三大途径：一是接受专业警察训练的学员；二是从其他警察部门调来的警员，因为新加坡海岸警卫队的工作极具职业特殊性，其警员一般不会调往其他警察部门；三是绕开海上专业训练，只接受内政群英学院（HTA）基础教育的学员。

3. 执法船舶和其他装备

目前，在马六甲海峡沿线国家中，新加坡海岸警卫队实力最强。新加坡海岸警卫队目前配备执法船舶的情况如下：普通船2艘，新型海岸巡逻艇10艘，第一代巡逻艇11艘、第二代巡逻艇8艘、第三代巡逻艇25艘、第四代新巡逻截阻艇11艘，新型巡逻艇32艘。其中，新型海岸巡逻艇在性能上远超普通船，更能满足海上安全与秩序维护的需要，并能自如地应对潜在的海上危险与挑战。巡逻艇共有四代，每一代巡逻艇都是在前一代的基础上升级与革新而来的，前三代巡逻艇配备通用机枪，第四代新巡逻截阻艇配备1 mm×0.5 mm机枪、STK ADDER遥控武器站，相较而言，后者更具实力，更能胜任巡逻、警戒任务。新型巡逻艇吨位小、航速高、机动灵活，非常适合日常勤务。另有第一代快艇和第二代快艇共17艘，虽然小，但航速高、机动灵活且威力大、隐蔽能力强，能够有效地突然袭击敌方。新加坡海岸警卫队还拥有复合艇共4艘，是所有船舶中最小的，在海上执法上发挥作用较小。

二、海事法律

新加坡海事管理法律以国会通过的法律为主，以海事与港务局制定的附属法规为辅。国会通过的法律适用于管理新加坡港口和全球挂新加坡船旗的船舶。附属法规灵活度高，针对技术性问题且便于修改。新加坡加入的海事国际条约通过转化为国内法在国内适用，新加坡的大部分海事立法都是从其加入的国际海事公约转化而来的，以更符合国际海事标准。新加坡海事与港务局可根据《海事与港务局法》，为加入的海事国际条约及其修正案制定国内化法规以供执法使用。新加坡独立的法律系统承继英国法，具国际性。

（一）国内法

1. 国会通过的法律

目前，新加坡国会通过并由新加坡海事与港务局（MPA）执行的法律有《海事与港务局法》《商船法》《防止海洋污染法》以及《商船（民事责任和油污赔偿）法》。《海事与港务局法》是新加坡议会颁布的一项法律，涵盖海事与港务局的职能、职责和权力，海员就业，港口管理和颁发许可证等。《商船法》是新加坡议会的立法成果，涵盖新加坡船舶注册、船员事宜以及安全问题。《防止海洋污染法》是新加坡议会颁布的一项法律，该法旨在防止源自陆地或船舶的海洋污染，该法还赋予新加坡海事与港务局采取预防措施以防止污染的权力，包括拒绝入境或扣留船舶。《商船（民事责任和油污赔偿）法》则涵盖石油污染的民事责任、石油污染强制保险、国际油类污染赔偿基金等内容。

2. 附属法规

为弥补国会立法的不足，新加坡在国会通过的法律之外，又制定了各种实施细则、规则、办法、规程、准则与要点等附属法规。目前，海事与港务局执行的附属法规包括新加坡《海事与港务局法》下的22种附属法规，新加坡《商船航运法》下的41种附属法规，《防止海洋污染法》下的13种附属法规，《商船法》下的2种附属法规。

新加坡的国内法梳理如下：

（1）商船法令
MERCHANT SHIPPING ACT
https://sso.agc.gov.sg/Act/MSA1995

（2）防止海洋污染法令
PREVENTION OF POLLUTION OF THE SEA ACT
https://sso.agc.gov.sg/Act/PPSA1990

（3）商船（油类污染民事责任和赔偿）法令
MERCHANT SHIPPING（CIVIL LIABILITY AND COMPENSATION FOR OIL POLLUTION）ACT
https://sso.agc.gov.sg/Act/MSCLCOPA1998

（4）商船（燃油污染民事责任和赔偿）法令
MERCHANT SHIPPING（CIVIL LIABILITY AND COMPENSATION FOR BUNKER OIL POLLUTION）ACT 2008
https://sso.agc.gov.sg/Act/MSCLCBOPA2008

（5）1911年海事公约法令
Maritime Conventions Act 1911, Cap. IA3
https://sso.agc.gov.sg/Act/MCA1911

（6）海上犯罪法令
Maritime Offences Act, Cap. 170B

https://sso.agc.gov.sg/Act/MOA2003

(7) 商船（油类污染民事责任和赔偿）法令
Merchant Shipping (Civil Liability and Compensation for Oil Pollution) Act, Cap. 180
https://sso.agc.gov.sg/Act/MSCLCOPA1998

(8) 防止海洋污染法令
Prevention of Pollution of the Sea Act, Cap. 243
https://sso.agc.gov.sg/Act/PPSA1990

(9) 防止海洋污染法令
Prevention of Pollution of the Sea Act, Cap. 243, s 34 (1) (b)
https://sso.agc.gov.sg/Act/PPSA1990

(10) 商船法令，2004 年商船（修正）法令
Merchant Shipping Act, Cap. 179 Merchant Shipping (Amendment) Act 2004 (No. 56 of 2004)
https://sso.agc.gov.sg/Act/MSA1995

(11) 商船（燃油污染民事责任和赔偿）法令
Merchant Shipping (Civil Liability and Compensation for Bunker Oil Pollution) Act, Cap. 179A
https://sso.agc.gov.sg/Act/MSCLCBOPA2008

(12) 2014 年商船（海事劳工公约）法令
Merchant Shipping (Maritime Labour Convention) Act 2014 (No. 6 of 2014)
https://sso.agc.gov.sg/Act/MSMLCA2014

(13) 新加坡电信局法令
Telecommunication Authority of Singapore Act Cap. 323
https://sso.agc.gov.sg/SL/323-OR1? DocDate = 19920401

(14) 1985 年商船（吨位）规例
Merchant Shipping (Tonnage) Regulations, S 241/1985
https://sso.agc.gov.sg/SL/179-RG12? DocDate = 19920325

(15) 商船（海上避碰）规例
Merchant Shipping (Prevention of Collisions at Sea) Regulations
https://sso.agc.gov.sg/SL/PPSA1990-S198-2010? DocDate = 20100331

（16）1984年商船（安全公约）规例
Merchant Shipping (Safety Convention) Regulations, S219/1984
https://sso.agc.gov.sg/SL/179-RG11? DocDate=20121217

（17）2010年商船（地效翼艇）规例
Merchant Shipping (Wing-in-ground Craft) Regulations 2010, S 200/2010
https://sso.agc.gov.sg/SL/MSA1995-S200-2010? DocDate=20100401

（18）1998年商船（培训、发证和配员）规例
Merchant Shipping (Training, Certification and Manning) Regulations, S 89/1998
https://sso.agc.gov.sg/SL/179-RG1? DocDate=20111227

（19）2000年商船（载重线）规例
Merchant Shipping (Load Line) Regulations, S 39/2000
https://sso.agc.gov.sg/SL/179-RG5? DocDate=20010131

（20）2014年商船（海事劳工公约）（厨师和餐饮人员培训与认证）规例
Merchant Shipping (Maritime Labour Convention) (Training and Certification of Cooks and Catering Staff) Regulations 2014
https://sso.agc.gov.sg/SL/MSMLCA2014-S179-2014? DocDate=20140311

（21）2010年防止海洋污染（防污底系统）规例
Prevention of Pollution of the Sea (Harmful Anti-Fouling Systems) Regulations 2010, S 198/2010
https://sso.agc.gov.sg/SL/PPSA1990-S198-2010? DocDate=20100331

（22）新加坡海事及港务管理局法
MARITIME AND PORT AUTHORITY OF SINGAPORE ACT
https://sso.agc.gov.sg/Act/MPASA1996

（23）海上货物运输法
Carriage of Goods by Sea Act, Cap. 33
https://sso.agc.gov.sg/Act/CGSA1972

（二）国际条约

新加坡曾是英属殖民地，法律制度大体继承英国普通法传统；新加坡参加的国际条约一般要转化为国内法才能适用。新加坡加入的国际条约较多，包括 1974 年《国际海上生命安全公约》（SOLAS）、1966 年《国际载重线公约》（LL）、1969 年《国际船舶吨位丈量公约》（ICM）、1973 年《国际防止船舶造成污染公约》（MARPOL）、1978 年《国际海员培训、发证和值班标准公约》（STCW）、1972 年《国际海上避碰规则公约》（COLREGS）和 2006 年《海事劳工公约》（ML）。新加坡于 2011 年 6 月 15 日加入《海事劳工公约》，2014 年完成公约国内化，制定了《商船（海事劳工公约）法》。

三、小　　结

通过对新加坡海事管理体制及机构设置的梳理和剖析，我们发现新加坡采用"相对集中"的海事管理体制，由新加坡海事与港务局（MPA）主管新加坡海事及港口的一切行政事项。新加坡自 1996 年开始进行港口管理体制改革，实行政企分离的管理模式，将港口经营权和管理权分离，设立新加坡海事与港务局（MPA）负责港口管理事项，设立新加坡港务集团负责港口生产、经营管理，对新加坡港务集团进行股份制改革和私有化。目前，新加坡港务集团已成为世界上第二大港口经营管理公司。新加坡在电子政务和海事服务建设方面效果卓著。新加坡海事服务能充分利用通信信息技术来改造其业务流程，在海事治理过程中大量使用云计算、大数据、物联网等最新技术，最大限度地实现了业务处理的自动化，面对公众的单一平台几乎整合了必需的所有系统和数据，并在后台利用大数据和云计算进行智能比对校验，自动识别各种差异或风险。

近年来，新加坡在海事调查方面迎来了新突破。2016 年，新加坡交通部成立新的交通安全调查局，交通安全调查局将专门对航空及海事事件进行独立调查。新加坡高效的海事管理体制、齐备的港航服务体系和科学的企业运作有效推动了新加坡跻身于世界航运中心行列。

四、附录：新加坡海事法律（国内法）文件

（一）附录1：新加坡海事及港务管理局法

THE STATUTES OF THE REPUBLIC OF SINGAPORE

MARITIME AND PORT AUTHORITY OF SINGAPORE ACT

(CHAPTER 170A)

(Original Enactment: Act 7 of 1996)

REVISED EDITION 1997

(30th May 1997)

Prepared and Published by

THE LAW REVISION COMMISSION
UNDER THE AUTHORITY OF
THE REVISED EDITION OF THE LAWS ACT (CHAPTER 275)

Informal Consolidation – version in force from 1/4/2018

CHAPTER 170A 1997 Ed.

Maritime and Port Authority of Singapore Act[①]

ARRANGEMENT OF SECTIONS

PART I

PRELIMINARY

Section
1. Short title
2. Interpretation
3. Declaration of ports by Minister

PART II

ESTABLISHMENT, INCORPORATION AND CONSTITUTION OF AUTHORITY

4. Establishment and incorporation of Maritime and Port Authority of Singapore
5. Common seal
6. Constitution of Authority

PART III

FUNCTIONS, DUTIES AND POWERS OF AUTHORITY

7. Functions and duties of Authority
8. Powers of Authority
9. Directions by Minister
10. Furnishing of information
11. [*Repealed*]
12. Appointment of committees and delegation of powers
13. Symbol, design or representation of Authority

PART IV

PROVISIONS RELATING TO STAFF

14. Chief Executive
15. Appointment of Port Master

Informal Consolidation – version in force from 1/4/2018

---

① 本法条引用自 https://sso.agc.gov.sg/Act/MPASA1996。

Section

16. Execution of orders, etc., of Port Master
17. Appointment of employees and agents
18. Protection from personal liability
19. [*Repealed*]

PART V

FINANCIAL PROVISIONS

20. Power to borrow
20A. Issue of shares, etc.
21. Duty of Authority in financial matters
22. Application of revenue
23. Annual estimates
24. Bank accounts and application of revenue
25. Power of investment
26. Financial year
27. Rates, charges, dues, etc., payable to Authority
28. Power of entry into vessels
29. Power to distrain for non-payment of dues, rates, etc.

PART VI

TRANSFER OF ASSETS, LIABILITIES AND EMPLOYEES

30. Transfer to Authority of property, assets and liabilities
31. Transfer of employees
32. Pension rights, etc., of employees to be preserved
33. No benefits in respect of abolition or reorganisation of office
34. Continuation and completion of disciplinary proceedings
35. Misconduct or neglect of duty by employee before transfer
36. Penalty to be served by employee
37. Existing agreements and pending proceedings

PART VII

EMPLOYMENT OF SEAMEN

38. Employment of seamen
39. Penalty for employment of seamen in contravention of section 38 or of regulations made under section 40
40. Regulations relating to seamen

PART VIII

REGULATION OF PORT

Section
41. Port regulations
42. Insurance policy
43. Power of Port Master in relation to vessel
44. Owner, agent or master of vessel to report arrival or departure
45. Port Master may require vessel in transit in the port or approaches thereto to provide information
46. No vessel to leave port without port clearance
47. Owner, agent or master of vessel not leaving within 48 hours after port clearance to return port clearance to Port Master
48. Power to prohibit vessel from entering territorial waters
49. Power to direct vessel to leave territorial waters
50. Penalty for disobedience of direction
51. Removal of certain obstructions and compensation therefor
52. Fire on board vessel
53. Power to board vessel
54. Execution of order, etc.
55. Exemption of vessels belonging to Singapore Armed Forces
56. Indemnity to Authority for act of Port Master

PART IX

REMOVAL OF VESSEL AND AIRCRAFT SUNK AND OTHER OBSTRUCTION

57. Power to require owner to raise, remove or destroy vessel, aircraft or other obstruction
58. Power to raise and remove vessel, aircraft or other obstruction

PART X

PILOTAGE

59. Declaration of pilotage districts
60. Authority may require vessel to be under pilotage
61. Failure to employ pilot under certain circumstances
62. Authorised pilot and berthing master
63. Vessel to be piloted by authorised pilots
64. Penalties as to employment of pilot
65. Employment of pilot
66. Appointment and functions of Pilotage Committee

Section
- 67. Constitution of Pilotage Committee
- 68. Examination for licence
- 69. Inquiries by Pilotage Committee
- 70. Submission of Pilotage Committee's finding and recommendation to Authority
- 71. Liability of master or owner in case of vessel under pilotage
- 72. Limitation of pilot's liability when bond is given
- 73. Offences of pilot
- 74. Pilotage Committee and Authority not liable for loss or damage caused by pilot
- 75. Members of Pilotage Committee to act as assessors in proceedings
- 76. Regulations relating to pilotage and conduct of pilot

PART XI

REGULATION AND CONTROL OF SEAWARD ACTIVITIES

- 77. Dredging limits
- 78. Hydrographic survey, etc., not to be carried out without approval of Authority
- 79. Restriction of certain works and operations
- 80. Salvage business not to be carried on without licence

PART XII

LICENSING OF MARINE AND PORT SERVICES AND FACILITIES

- 81. Licences authorising provision of marine or port services and facilities
- 82. Restriction on transfer of public licence
- 83. Modification of conditions of public licence
- 84. Suspension or cancellation of public licence, etc.
- 85. Direction affecting public licensee
- 86. General duties of public licensee

PART XIIA

CONTROL OF DESIGNATED PUBLIC LICENSEES, DESIGNATED BUSINESS TRUSTS AND DESIGNATED EQUITY INTEREST HOLDERS

- 86A. Interpretation of this Part
- 86B. What holding an equity interest means
- 86C. Meanings of "associate", "subsidiary" and "holding company"

Section

- 86D. Designation of public licensees, business trusts and equity interest holders
- 86E. Notice to Authority by 5% controller
- 86F. Approvals of Authority in relation to equity interests and control of voting power in certain cases
- 86G. Remedial directions
- 86H. Effect of remedial directions, etc.
- 86I. Penalties under this Part

PART XIII

CONTROL OF RELEVANT PUBLIC LICENSEES

- 87. Meaning and effect of special administration order
- 88. Special administration order made on application by Authority
- 89. Remuneration and expenses of Authority and others

PART XIV

LIABILITY OF AUTHORITY

- 90. Exclusion of liability of Authority
- 91. Limitation of Authority's liability for loss or damage to or on board any vessel

PART XV

OFFENCES

- 92. Damage to property of Authority
- 93. Unlawful operation of marine or port services or facilities
- 94. Evasion of dues
- 95. Penalty for giving false information as to draught of vessel, etc.
- 96. Offences in connection with safety of vessels, etc.
- 97. Penalty for obstructing Authority in performance of duties
- 98. Preservation of secrecy
- 99. General penalties
- 100. Offences by bodies of persons
- 101. Jurisdiction of Courts
- 102. Composition of offences
- 103. Fines to be paid to Authority
- 104. Presumption of jurisdiction
- 105. Service of documents
- 106. Saving of prosecutions under other laws

Informal Consolidation – version in force from 1/4/2018

PART XVI
MISCELLANEOUS PROVISIONS

Section
- 107. Master, owner or person in charge of vessel answerable for damage
- 108. Exemption from distress and attachment of property of Authority
- 109. Authority to provide free landing places
- 110. Restrictions on erection of wharves, docks, etc.
- 111. Notices, orders, receipts, etc., may be given by authorised officer
- 112. Vessel guidance, assistance or direction
- 113. Power to enter upon lands
- 114. Power to enter upon lands adjacent to works
- 115. Employee of Authority may require evidence of identity in certain cases
- 116. Compensation, damages and costs to be determined by District Court
- 117. Disposal of matters and things removed by Authority
- 118. Exemption by Authority
- 119. Regulations
- 120. Transitional provisions

First Schedule — Constitution and Proceedings of Authority
Second Schedule — Powers of Authority
Third Schedule — [Repealed]

An Act to establish and incorporate the Maritime and Port Authority of Singapore, to provide for its functions and powers, and for matters connected therewith.

[2nd February 1996]

PART I
PRELIMINARY

Short title

1. This Act may be cited as the Maritime and Port Authority of Singapore Act.

Interpretation

2. In this Act, unless the context otherwise requires —

"authorised pilot" means any person employed or authorised by the Authority to pilot vessels under section 62;

"Authority" means the Maritime and Port Authority of Singapore established under section 4;

"beacon" means a prominent specially constructed object forming a conspicuous mark as a fixed aid to navigation;

"berthing master" means any person authorised under section 62(2)(*b*) to act as a berthing master;

"buoy" includes a floating object of any size, shape and colour which is moored to the seabed and serves as an aid to navigation or for other specific purposes;

"Chairman" means the Chairman of the Authority and includes any acting Chairman of the Authority;

"Chief Executive" means the Chief Executive of the Authority, and includes any individual acting in that capacity;

[Act 5 of 2018 wef 01/04/2018]

"container" means a receptacle 6.1 metres or more in length equipped with corner castings to facilitate handling by mechanical equipment;

"dangerous cargoes" means such cargoes, whether packaged, carried in bulk packagings or in bulk, as may be prescribed;

"Deputy Chairman" means the Deputy Chairman of the Authority and includes any acting Deputy Chairman of the Authority;

"Director of Marine" means the Director of Marine appointed under section 4 of the Merchant Shipping Act (Cap. 179);

"dock" means an artificial excavation or construction in which vessels can be placed for loading, unloading, fitting out or repairing and includes gridirons, slips, keel blocks, inclined planes and all machinery, works, fixtures and things whatsoever attached or pertaining thereto;

"dues" includes port dues, goods dues and pilotage dues levied under this Act but does not include rates;

"equipment" includes any appliance, apparatus, machinery, system or accessory used or intended to be used for the purposes of providing marine or port services and facilities;

"goods" includes dangerous cargoes, animals, carcases, baggage, containers and any other movable property of any kind whatsoever and whether in a refrigerated form or otherwise;

"harbour craft" means any vessel which is used in the port for any purpose;

"lighthouse" means a distinctive structure on or off a coast exhibiting a major light designed to serve as an aid to navigation;

"marine services and facilities" means the towage and pilotage of vessels and the supply of water to vessels;

"master" includes every person, except a pilot, having command or charge of any vessel;

"member" means a member of the Authority;

"National Maritime Board" means the National Maritime Board established under the repealed National Maritime Board Act (Cap. 198, 1985 Ed.) in force immediately before 2nd February 1996;

"owner", in relation to any vessel, includes any part-owner, charterer, operator, consignee or mortgagee in possession of the vessel or any duly authorised agent of any such person;

"passenger" has the same meaning as in the Merchant Shipping Act (Cap. 179);

"pilot" means any person not belonging to a vessel who has the conduct thereof;

"Pilotage Committee" means the Pilotage Committee appointed under section 66;

"pilotage district" means any area in the port declared under section 59 to be a pilotage district;

"port" means any place in Singapore and any navigable river or channel leading into such place declared to be a port under section 3;

"port dues" means dues levied in respect of a vessel for entering, using, leaving or plying in the port;

"Port Master" means the Port Master appointed under section 15 and includes any Deputy Port Master appointed under that section;

"Port of Singapore Authority" means the Port of Singapore Authority established under the Port of Singapore Authority Act (Cap. 236);

"port services and facilities" means port terminal services and facilities for the handling, storage and transportation of goods on land adjoining the foreshore of Singapore and for the handling of passengers carried by vessels;

"premises" includes messuages, houses, buildings, structures, lands, tenements, easements and hereditaments of any tenure, whether open or enclosed, whether built on or not, whether public or private, and whether maintained or not under statutory authority;

"public licence" means a licence granted under section 81 and "public licensee" shall be construed accordingly;

"rates" means any rates or charges leviable by the Authority under this Act and includes any toll or rent but does not include dues;

"regulations" means regulations made under this Act;

"seaman" means any person normally engaged on ship's articles on any vessel going beyond the limits of the port, but does not include —

  (*a*) masters, mates, engineers, radio officers, pursers, cadets, laundrymen and stevedores;

(b) probationer deckhands, probationer engineroom hands and probationer catering hands under any training scheme approved by the Authority; and

(c) any other person employed on board the vessel who is engaged in duties which are not normally the duties of seamen;

"vehicle" has the same meaning as in the Road Traffic Act (Cap. 276);

"vessel" includes any ship or boat or air-cushioned vehicle or floating rig or platform used in any form of operations at sea or any other description of vessel;

"wharf" includes a quay, pier, jetty, ramp or other landing place.

Declaration of ports by Minister

3.—(1) The Minister may, after consultation with the Authority and by notification in the *Gazette*, declare any place in Singapore and any navigable river or waters leading into such place to be a port for the purposes of this Act.

(2) Every declaration under subsection (1) shall define the limits of the port.

PART II

ESTABLISHMENT, INCORPORATION AND CONSTITUTION OF AUTHORITY

Establishment and incorporation of Maritime and Port Authority of Singapore

4. There is hereby established a body to be known as the Maritime and Port Authority of Singapore which shall be a body corporate with perpetual succession and a common seal and shall, by that name, be capable of —

(a) suing and being sued;

(b) acquiring, owning, holding and developing or disposing of property, both movable and immovable; and

(c) doing and suffering such other acts or things as bodies corporate may lawfully do and suffer.

Common seal

5.—(1) All deeds and other documents requiring the seal of the Authority shall be sealed with the common seal of the Authority and such instruments to which the common seal is affixed shall be signed by any 2 officers generally or specially authorised by the Chief Executive for the purpose or by one officer and the Chief Executive.

(2) All courts, judges and persons acting judicially shall take judicial notice of the common seal of the Authority affixed to any document and shall presume that it was duly affixed.

Constitution of Authority

6.—(1) The Authority shall consist of —

(a) a Chairman; and

(b) not fewer than 3 other members as the Minister may from time to time determine.

[Act 16 of 2016 wef 10/06/2016]

[Act 40 of 2017 wef 15/01/2018]

(2) The First Schedule shall have effect with respect to the Authority, its members and proceedings.

PART III

FUNCTIONS, DUTIES AND POWERS OF AUTHORITY

Functions and duties of Authority

7.—(1) Subject to the provisions of this Act, it shall be the function and duty of the Authority —

(a) to promote the use, improvement and development of the port;

(b) to regulate and control navigation within the limits of the port and the approaches to the port;

(*c*) to provide and maintain adequate and efficient lighthouses, beacons, buoys and other aids to navigation in the territorial waters of Singapore and the approaches thereto, at Pedra Branca (Horsburgh), at Pulau Pisang and at such other places as the Authority may think fit;

(*d*) to disseminate navigational information;

(*e*) to exercise licensing and regulatory functions in respect of marine and port services and facilities;

(*f*) to secure that there are provided in the port (whether by itself or by any public licensee), adequate and efficient marine and port services and facilities on such terms as the Authority may think expedient;

(*g*) to secure that any person by whom any marine or port services and facilities fall to be provided in the port is able to provide the services and facilities efficiently whilst maintaining independent financial viability;

(*h*) to promote efficiency, reliability and economy on the part of public licensees in accordance with, as far as practicable, recognised international standards and public demand;

(*i*) to create an economic regulatory framework in respect of the provision of marine and port services and facilities which promotes and safeguards competition and fair and efficient market conduct or, in the absence of a competitive market, which prevents the misuse of monopoly or market power;

(*j*) to promote, provide and administer training schemes for members of the mercantile marine and the shipping and port industries;

(*k*) to develop, promote and regulate employment among members of the mercantile marine;

(*l*) to exercise regulatory functions in respect of merchant shipping and particularly in respect of safety at sea, the manning of vessels and the prevention of pollution at sea;

(*m*) to promote the development of merchant shipping;

(*n*) to advise the Government on all matters relating to sea transport and the provision of marine and port services and facilities;

(*o*) to act internationally as the national body representative of Singapore in respect of sea transport, marine and port matters;

(*p*) to discharge or facilitate the discharge of international obligations of the Government in respect of sea transport; and

(*q*) to perform such other functions as are conferred on the Authority by this Act or any other written law.

(2) In discharging the functions and duties imposed on it by subsection (1), the Authority shall have regard to —

(*a*) satisfying all reasonable demands for marine and port services and facilities;

(*b*) fostering the development and expansion of marine and port services and facilities in the world in collaboration with other countries and international organisations;

(*c*) enabling persons providing marine and port services and facilities in Singapore to compete effectively in the provision of such services and facilities outside Singapore;

(*d*) the promotion of measures for the safety of life in the port;

(*e*) the promotion of research and development in the fields of marine and port services and facilities;

[Act 11 of 2012 wef 01/07/2012]

(*f*) collaboration with educational institutions for the promotion of technical education in the fields of marine and port services and facilities;

[Act 11 of 2012 wef 01/07/2012]

(*g*) the promotion of energy efficiency within the port services and facilities sector; and

[Act 11 of 2012 wef 01/07/2012]

Informal Consolidation – version in force from 1/4/2018

(h) environmental protection and the sustainable development of sea transport.

[Act 11 of 2012 wef 01/07/2012]

(3) Nothing in this section shall be construed as imposing on the Authority, directly or indirectly, any form of duty or liability enforceable by proceedings before any court.

(4) In addition to the functions and duties imposed by this section, the Authority may undertake such other functions as the Minister may assign to the Authority and the Authority shall be deemed to be fulfilling the purposes of this Act and the provisions of this Act shall apply to the Authority in respect of such functions.

(5) Notwithstanding the provisions of this Act, the Authority may, until such time as the licences granted under Part XII come into effect, continue to provide any marine or port services and facilities that the Port of Singapore Authority was providing immediately before 2nd February 1996.

(6) Without prejudice to the provisions of Part XII, the Authority may provide any marine or port services and facilities in any of the following circumstances notwithstanding that it has granted a public licence to any person:

(a) if the Authority is of the opinion that the person has failed to discharge or is not discharging to the Authority's satisfaction the obligations imposed by the Authority on the person in the public licence; or

(b) to give effect to any direction of the Minister under section 9.

(7) The Authority shall furnish the Minister with information with respect to its property and activities in such manner and at such times as the Minister may require.

Powers of Authority

8.—(1) Subject to this Act, the Authority may carry on such activities as appear to the Authority to be advantageous, necessary or convenient for it to carry on for or in connection with the discharge of its functions and duties under this Act or any other written law, and in particular, may exercise any of the powers specified in the Second Schedule.

(2). This section shall not be construed as limiting any power of the Authority conferred by or under any other written law.

Directions by Minister

9.—(1) The Minister may, after consultation with a person to whom this section applies, give —

(a) if the person is the Authority, to the Authority any direction under section 5 of the Public Sector (Governance) Act 2018; or

(b) if the person is a public licensee, any directions as the Minister thinks fit as to the exercise by that licensee of his functions under this Act.

[Act 5 of 2018 wef 01/04/2018]

(2) In addition to the power mentioned in subsection (1), if it appears to the Minister to be requisite or expedient to do so —

(a) on the occurrence of any public emergency, in the public interest or in the interests of public security, national defence, or relations with the government of another country; or

(b) in order —

(i) to discharge or facilitate the discharge of an obligation binding on the Government by virtue of its being a member of an international organisation or a party to an international agreement;

(ii) to attain or facilitate the attainment of any other object the attainment of which is in the opinion of the Minister requisite or expedient in view of the Government being a member of such an organisation or a party to such an agreement; or

(iii) to enable the Government to become a member of such an organisation or a party to such an agreement, he may, after consultation with a person to whom this section applies, give such directions to that person as are necessary in the circumstances of the case.

[Act 5 of 2018 wef 01/04/2018]

(3) Any direction given under subsection (1) or (2) may include provisions for —

(a) the prohibition or regulation of any marine or port services and facilities;

(b) the taking of, the control of or the usage of any marine or port services and facilities for official purposes of all or any system and equipment relating thereto; and

(c) the carrying out of any other purposes which the Minister thinks necessary.

(4) A person to whom this section applies shall give effect to any direction given to that person under subsection (1) or (2) notwithstanding any other duty imposed on that person by or under this Act or any other written law.

(5) A person to whom this section applies shall not disclose any direction given to that person under subsection (1) or (2) if the Minister notifies that person that the Minister is of the opinion that the disclosure of the direction is against the public interest.

(6) The Minister may —

(a) pay compensation for any damage caused to a public licensee by reason of its compliance with the directions of the Minister under subsection (3)(b);

(b) make grants to public licensees for defraying or contributing towards any losses which they may sustain by reason of their compliance with the directions of the Minister under any other provision of this section.

(7) Any sum required by the Minister for paying compensation or making grants under subsection (6) shall be paid out of the Consolidated Fund.

(8) This section shall apply to the Authority and to every public licensee.

(9) If any doubt arises as to the existence of a public emergency or as to whether any act done under this section was in the public interest or in the interests of public security, national defence or relations with the government of another country, a certificate signed by the Minister shall be conclusive evidence of the matters stated therein.

Furnishing of information

10.—(1) The Authority or any person authorised by the Authority in that behalf may by notice require any person to furnish to the Authority or the person so authorised, within such period as shall be specified in the notice, all such documents or information relating to such matters as may be required by the Authority for the purposes of this Act and as are within the knowledge of that person or in his custody or under his control.

(2) Any person who, on being required by notice under subsection (1) to furnish any document or information, fails to comply with any requirement of the notice shall be guilty of an offence.

(3) A person who —

    (*a*) intentionally alters, suppresses or destroys any document which he has been required by any notice under subsection (1) to furnish; or

    (*b*) in furnishing any estimate, return or other information required of him under any notice under subsection (1), makes any statement which he knows to be false in any material particular,

shall be guilty of an offence.

11. [*Repealed by Act 5 of 2018 wef 01/04/2018*]

Appointment of committees and delegation of powers

12.—(1) The Authority may appoint from among its own members or other persons who are not members such number of committees as it thinks fit consisting of members or other persons or members and other persons for purposes which, in the opinion of the Authority, would be better regulated and managed by means of such committees.

(2) The Authority may, subject to such conditions or restrictions as it thinks fit, delegate to any such committee all or any of the powers, functions and duties vested in the Authority by this Act or any other written law, except the powers to prescribe or levy dues and rates and borrow money, and any power, function or duty so delegated may be exercised or performed by the committee in the name and on behalf of the Authority.

[Act 5 of 2018 wef 01/04/2018]

(3) The Authority may, subject to such conditions or restrictions as it thinks fit, delegate to any member or employee of the Authority or any person all or any of its powers, functions and duties vested in the Authority by this Act or any other written law, except the powers to prescribe or levy dues and rates and borrow money; and any power, function or duty so delegated may be exercised or performed by the member, employee or person in the name and on behalf of the Authority.

[Act 5 of 2018 wef 01/04/2018]

(4) *[Repealed by Act 5 of 2018 wef 01/04/2018]*

Symbol, design or representation of Authority

13.—(1) The Authority shall have the exclusive right to the use of such symbol, design or representation as it may select or devise and thereafter display or exhibit it in connection with its activities or affairs.

(2) Any person who uses a symbol, design or representation identical with that of the Authority or which so resembles the symbol, design or representation thereof as to deceive or cause confusion or to be likely to deceive or cause confusion shall be guilty of an offence and shall be liable on conviction to a fine not exceeding $2,000 or to imprisonment for a term not exceeding 6 months or to both.

Maritime and Port Authority of Singapore

PART IV

PROVISIONS RELATING TO STAFF

Chief Executive

14.—(1) There must be a Chief Executive of the Authority, whose appointment, removal, discipline and promotion must be in accordance with the Public Sector (Governance) Act 2018.

(2) The Authority may, subject to the Public Sector (Governance) Act 2018, appoint an individual to act temporarily as the Chief Executive during any period, or during all periods, when the Chief Executive —

(*a*) is absent from duty or Singapore; or

(*b*) is, for any reason, unable to perform the duties of the office.

[Act 5 of 2018 wef 01/04/2018]

Appointment of Port Master

15. The Authority shall appoint a Port Master and may appoint such number of Deputy Port Masters as it may think fit for the purposes of carrying out all or any of the functions and duties vested in the Authority by or under this Act or any other written law.

Execution of orders, etc., of Port Master

16. All acts, orders or directions authorised to be done or given by the Port Master may be done or given by any employee of the Authority subject to the control and authorisation of the Port Master.

Appointment of employees and agents

17. The Authority may, subject to the Public Sector (Governance) Act 2018, appoint and employ on such terms and conditions as the Authority may determine such other employees and agents as may be necessary for the effective performance of its functions.

[Act 5 of 2018 wef 01/04/2018]

Protection from personal liability

18. No suit or other legal proceedings shall lie personally against any member, officer or employee of the Authority or other person acting under the direction of the Authority for anything which is in good faith done or intended to be done in the execution or purported execution of this Act or any other written law.

19. [*Repealed by Act 5 of 2018 wef 01/04/2018*]

PART V
FINANCIAL PROVISIONS

Power to borrow

20. The Authority may, with the approval of the Minister, raise capital from banks and other financial institutions whether in Singapore or elsewhere by way of mortgage, overdraft or otherwise, with or without security, as it may require for the discharge of its functions under this Act.

Issue of shares, etc.

20A. As a consequence of the vesting of any property, rights or liabilities of the Government in the Authority under this Act, or of any capital injection or other investment by the Government in the Authority in accordance with any written law, the Authority shall issue such shares or other securities to the Minister for Finance as that Minister may from time to time direct.

[*5/2002 wef 15/07/2002*]

Duty of Authority in financial matters

21. It shall be the duty of the Authority so to exercise and perform its functions under this Act as to secure that the total revenues of the Authority are sufficient, taking one financial year with another, to meet its total outgoings properly chargeable to revenue account, including depreciation and interest on capital and to meet a reasonable proportion of the cost of the development of the services of the Authority.

Application of revenue

22.—(1) The revenue of the Authority for any financial year shall be applied in defraying the following charges:

 (*a*) the remuneration, fees and allowances of the members of the Authority;

 (*b*) the salaries, fees, remuneration, pensions, superannuation allowances and gratuities of the officers, agents, employees, advisers and former employees of the Authority;

 (*c*) working and establishment expenses and expenditure on, or provision for, the maintenance of any of the property of the Authority, and the discharge of the functions of the Authority properly chargeable to revenue account;

 (*d*) interest on any loan raised by the Authority;

 (*e*) sums required to be paid to the Government towards repayment of any loan made by the Government to the Authority;

 (*f*) sums required to be transferred to a sinking fund or otherwise set aside for the purpose of making provision for the repayment of borrowed money;

 (*g*) such sums as may be deemed appropriate to be set aside in respect of depreciation or renewal of the property of the Authority, having regard to the amounts set aside out of revenue under paragraphs (*c*) and (*f*);

 (*h*) the cost, or any portion thereof, of any new works, plants, vessels, vehicles, machinery, equipment or appliances not being a renewal of the property of the Authority, which the Authority may determine to charge to revenue;

 (*i*) such sums by way of contribution, for the purposes associated with the objects of this Act as the Authority may determine, to the public or for charities; and

 (*j*) any other expenditure authorised by the Authority and properly chargeable to revenue account.

(2) The balance of the revenue of the Authority shall be applied to the creation of a general reserve and such other reserves as the Authority may think fit.

Annual estimates

23.—(1) [*Repealed by Act 5 of 2018 wef 01/04/2018*]

(2) [*Repealed by Act 5 of 2018 wef 01/04/2018*]

(3) [*Repealed by Act 5 of 2018 wef 01/04/2018*]

(4) A summary of the annual estimates and supplementary estimates adopted by the Authority shall be published in the *Gazette*.

Bank accounts and application of revenue

24. The Authority shall open and maintain an account or accounts with such bank or banks as the Authority thinks fit; and every such account shall be operated upon as far as practicable by cheque signed by such person or persons as may, from time to time, be authorised in that behalf by the Authority.

Power of investment

25. The Authority may invest its moneys in accordance with the standard investment power of statutory bodies as defined in section 33A of the Interpretation Act (Cap. 1).

[45/2004 wef 15/12/2004]

Financial year

26. The financial year of the Authority begins on 1 January of each year and ends on 31 December of the same year.

[Act 5 of 2018 wef 01/04/2018]

Rates, charges, dues, etc., payable to Authority

27.—(1) Subject to the provisions of this Act, the Authority may levy such rates, charges and fees as the Authority may, with the approval of the Minister and by notification in the *Gazette*, from time to time, prescribe for the use of services and facilities provided by the Authority.

(2) The Authority may make such charges as it thinks fit for services or facilities provided or goods supplied by it in pursuance of the power conferred by this Act or any other written law in respect of which no rates, charges or fees have been prescribed under subsection (1).

(3) The Authority may require any person to furnish such security as the Authority may think fit for the payment of any rates, charges, dues and fees payable under this Act or for any other purpose of this Act.

(4) The Authority may determine the fees to be paid in respect of the issue or renewal of any licence or permit issued under this Act or the regulations.

(5) The Authority may, if it thinks fit, remit or waive the whole or any part of any rates, charges, dues and fees paid or payable under this Act.

(6) The owner, agent or master of every vessel which calls at the port of Singapore shall pay to the Authority or any person authorised by the Authority such maritime welfare fee as the Authority may, with the approval of the Minister and by notification in the *Gazette*, from time to time prescribe.

(7) The owner, agent or master of every vessel which enters, leaves, uses or plies within the port or calls at Singapore shall pay to the Authority such port dues and pilotage dues as the Authority may, with the approval of the Minister and by notification in the *Gazette*, from time to time prescribe.

(8) The Authority may, with the approval of the Minister and by notification in the *Gazette*, levy such goods dues as are prescribed on goods brought into or taken out of such private wharf or premises (by any means of transportation) as may be specified in the notification.

(9) Goods dues shall be paid by —

    (*a*) the owner or occupier of such wharf or premises;

    (*b*) the owner of the vehicle or vessel used in the carriage of the goods into or out of the wharf or premises or otherwise; or

Informal Consolidation – version in force from 1/4/2018

(c) any other person authorised to act as agent for the owner of such vehicle or vessel in the carriage of such goods into or out of the wharf or premises or otherwise.

(10) The Authority may recover such goods dues from any of the persons mentioned in subsection (9).

(11) A due, charge, fee or rate exigible by virtue of this section may be recovered by the Authority in any court of competent jurisdiction as if it were a simple contract debt.

(12) Maritime welfare fees under this section shall not be payable in respect of —

(a) any ship of war;

(b) any vessel belonging to or for the time being in the service or employment of the Government unless such vessel is carrying or habitually carries goods or passengers for freight or fares; and

(c) any vessel or class of vessels which has or have been exempted from the operation of this section by the Minister.

(13) The rates, charges, dues and fees applied by the Marine Department, the National Maritime Board or the Port of Singapore Authority immediately before 2nd February 1996 shall continue to be valid as though determined by the Authority under this section until rescinded, varied or otherwise determined by the Authority.

Power of entry into vessels

28.—(1) Any duly authorised officer of the Authority may enter into any vessel within the limits of the port or the approaches to the port in order to ascertain the amount of the rates, charges, dues and fees payable in respect of the vessel or on or in respect of any goods carried therein and to obtain any other information required for, or in connection with, the assessment and collection of the rates, charges, dues and fees.

(2) A master of a vessel who fails to comply with a reasonable request made by an authorised officer who has entered the vessel pursuant to subsection (1) for information or for the production of a

document shall be guilty of an offence and shall be liable on conviction to a fine not exceeding $5,000 and, in the case of a continuing offence, to a further fine not exceeding $500 for every day or part thereof during which the master continues to fail to comply with the request.

Power to distrain for non-payment of dues, rates, etc.

29.—(1) If the master or owner of any vessel in respect of which any rates, charges, dues, fees, damages or penalties or other sums are payable under this Act or the regulations refuses or neglects to pay the same or any part thereof on demand, the Authority may, in addition to any other remedy which it may be entitled to use, distrain or arrest of its own authority the vessel and the bunkers, tackle, apparel or furniture belonging thereto or any part thereof, and detain the same until the amount so due is paid.

(2) If any part of such rates, charges, dues, fees, damages or penalties or other sums, or of the costs of the distraint or arrest, or of the keeping of the vessel, bunkers, tackle, apparel or furniture belonging thereto remains unpaid for 14 days, the Authority may cause the vessel and the bunkers, tackle, apparel or furniture so distrained or arrested to be sold or disposed of in such manner as it thinks fit and may recover, as a debt in any court of competent jurisdiction from the master or owner of the vessel, the expenses of such distraint, arrest, sale or disposal or attempted sale or disposal of the vessel and the bunkers, tackle, apparel or furniture so distrained or arrested.

(3) The proceeds of sale of the vessel and bunkers, tackle, apparel or furniture so distrained or arrested may be used by the Authority to satisfy those rates, charges, dues, fees, damages or penalties or other sums and costs, including costs of sale remaining unpaid, rendering the surplus, if any, to the master or owner of the vessel on demand and, in case no such demand is made within one year from the date of the disposal of the vessel and bunkers, tackle, apparel or furniture, by paying the surplus to the account of the Authority, whereupon all rights to the same by such person shall be extinguished.

(4) If the Authority gives to the Port Master a notice stating that an amount therein specified is due in respect of rates, charges, dues, fees,

damages or penalties or other sums payable under this Act or the regulations against the vessel or the owner, agent or master of the vessel, the Port Master shall not grant port clearance until the amount so chargeable has been paid or security has been given to the satisfaction of the Authority for the amount thereof.

PART VI

TRANSFER OF ASSETS, LIABILITIES AND EMPLOYEES

Transfer to Authority of property, assets and liabilities

30.—(1) As from 2nd February 1996, such property, rights and liabilities vested in the National Maritime Board, the Port of Singapore Authority and the Government relating to the Marine Department as may be determined by the Minister for Finance shall become, by virtue of this section and without further assurance, the property, rights and liabilities of the Authority.

(2) If any question arises as to whether any particular property, right or liability has been transferred to or vested in the Authority under subsection (1), a certificate under the hand of the Minister for Finance shall be conclusive evidence that the property, right or liability was or was not so transferred or vested.

(3) Any immovable property to be transferred to and vested in the Authority under subsection (1) shall be held by the Authority upon such tenure and subject to such terms and conditions as the President may determine.

Transfer of employees

31.—(1) As from 2nd February 1996, such persons employed immediately before that date in the Marine Department, the National Maritime Board and the Port of Singapore Authority as the Minister may determine shall be transferred to the service of the Authority on terms no less favourable than those enjoyed by them immediately prior to their transfer.

(2) Until such time as terms and conditions of service are drawn up by the Authority, the scheme and terms and conditions of service in the Government, the National Maritime Board or the Port of

Singapore Authority, as the case may be, shall continue to apply to every person transferred to the service of the Authority under subsection (1) as if he were still in the service of the Government, the National Maritime Board or the Port of Singapore Authority, as the case may be.

Pension rights, etc., of employees to be preserved

32.—(1) The terms and conditions to be drawn up by the Authority shall take into account the salaries and terms and conditions of service, including any accrued rights to leave, enjoyed by the persons transferred to the service of the Authority under section 31 while in the employment of the Government, the National Maritime Board or the Port of Singapore Authority, as the case may be, and any such term or condition relating to the length of service with the Authority shall provide for the recognition of service under the Government, the National Maritime Board or the Port of Singapore Authority, as the case may be, by the persons so transferred to be service by them under the Authority.

(2) Nothing in the terms and conditions to be drawn up by the Authority shall adversely affect the conditions that would have been applicable to persons transferred to the service of the Authority as regards any pension, gratuity or allowance payable under the Pensions Act (Cap. 225) or the Port of Singapore Authority Act (Cap. 236), as the case may be.

(3) In every case where a person has been transferred to the service of the Authority under section 31, his employer immediately before the date of such transfer shall be liable to pay to the Authority such portion of any gratuity, pension or allowance payable to such person on his retirement as the same shall bear to the proportion which the aggregate amount of his pensionable emoluments during his service with such employer bears to the aggregate amount of his pensionable emoluments during his service under both the Authority and such employer.

(4) Where any person in the service of the Authority whose case does not fall within the scope of any pension or other schemes established under this section retires or dies in the service of the Authority or is discharged from such service, the Authority may grant

to him or to such person or persons wholly or partly dependent on him, as the Authority thinks fit, such allowance or gratuity as the Authority may determine.

No benefits in respect of abolition or reorganisation of office

33. Notwithstanding the provisions of the Pensions Act (Cap. 225), no person who is transferred to the service of the Authority under section 31 shall be entitled to claim any benefit under the Pensions Act on the ground that he has been retired from the service of the Government, the National Maritime Board or the Port of Singapore Authority, as the case may be, on account of abolition or reorganisation of office in consequence of the establishment and incorporation of the Authority.

Continuation and completion of disciplinary proceedings

34.—(1) Where on 2nd February 1996 any disciplinary proceedings were pending against any employee of the Government, the National Maritime Board or the Port of Singapore Authority transferred to the service of the Authority under section 31, the proceedings shall be carried on and completed by the Authority; but where on 2nd February 1996 any matter was in the course of being heard or investigated or had been heard or investigated by a committee acting under due authority but no order or decision had been rendered thereon, the committee shall complete the hearing or investigation and make such order, ruling or direction as it could have made under the authority vested in it before that date.

(2) Any order, ruling or direction made or given by a committee pursuant to this section shall be treated as an order, a ruling or a direction of the Authority and have the same force or effect as if it had been made or given by the Authority pursuant to the authority vested in the Authority under this Act.

Misconduct or neglect of duty by employee before transfer

35. The Authority may reprimand, reduce in rank, retire, dismiss or punish in some other manner a person who had, whilst he was in the employment of the Government, the National Maritime Board or the Port of Singapore Authority, as the case may be, been guilty of any misconduct or neglect of duty which would have rendered him liable to be reprimanded, reduced in rank, retired, dismissed or punished in some other manner if he had continued to be in the employment of the Government, the National Maritime Board or the Port of Singapore Authority, as the case may be, and if this Act had not been enacted.

Penalty to be served by employee

36. Where an employee of the Government, the National Maritime Board or the Port of Singapore Authority has been transferred to the service of the Authority under section 31, and on 2nd February 1996 any penalty (other than dismissal) has been imposed on the employee pursuant to disciplinary proceedings against him and the penalty has not been, or remains to be, served by the employee, he shall on his transfer to the service of the Authority, serve or continue to serve such penalty to its full term as if it had been imposed by the Authority and the penalty shall remain valid against the employee on his transfer and shall continue in full force and effect until he has served the penalty in full.

Existing agreements and pending proceedings

37.—(1) All deeds, bonds, agreements, instruments and working arrangements subsisting immediately before 2nd February 1996 affecting the portion of the property, rights and liabilities transferred to the Authority under section 30(1) or affecting any employee transferred to the service of the Authority under section 31 shall continue in full force and effect on and after that date and shall be enforceable by or against the Authority as if instead of the Government, the National Maritime Board or the Port of Singapore Authority, as the case may be, or any person acting on its behalf, the Authority had been named therein or had been a party thereto.

(2) Any proceedings or cause of action relating to the portion of the property, rights and liabilities transferred to the Authority under section 30(1) or to any employee transferred to the service of the Authority under section 31 pending or existing immediately before 2nd February 1996 by or against the Government, the National Maritime Board or the Port of Singapore Authority, as the case may

PART VII
EMPLOYMENT OF SEAMEN

Employment of seamen

38.—(1) No person other than an employer shall engage a seaman.

(2) No employer shall engage a seaman and no seaman shall accept employment on board any vessel except in accordance with regulations made under section 40.

(3) No employer shall enter into arrangements with any seaman to transport him outside Singapore for the purpose of engagement in contravention of regulations made under section 40.

(4) For the purpose of this Part, "employer" includes the shipowner, charterer or operator, the agent of the shipowner, charterer or operator and the master of the vessel.

Penalty for employment of seamen in contravention of section 38 or of regulations made under section 40

39.—(1) Any person or employer who —

  (*a*) contravenes section 38; or

  (*b*) selects or engages a seaman otherwise than in accordance with regulations made under section 40,

shall be guilty of an offence and shall be liable on conviction to a fine not exceeding $2,000 or to imprisonment for a term not exceeding 6 months or to both.

(2) Any person or seaman who accepts employment or works in a vessel as a seaman otherwise than in accordance with regulations made under section 40 shall be guilty of an offence and shall be liable on conviction to a fine not exceeding $2,000 or to imprisonment for a term not exceeding 6 months or to both.

Regulations relating to seamen

40. The Authority may, with the approval of the Minister, make regulations for the purposes of this Part and, in particular, may make regulations for the following purposes:

(*a*) to prescribe the age and other qualifications of applicants for registration as seamen;

(*b*) to prescribe the manner in which seamen may apply or be required to register;

(*c*) to make provisions for the medical examination of applicants for registration as seamen;

(*d*) to prescribe the procedures for dealing with the discipline of seamen;

(*e*) to prescribe the fee to be paid upon the issue of registration cards, and the fee for replacement of such cards when lost, destroyed or otherwise rendered unserviceable;

(*f*) to prescribe the conditions under which the Authority may cancel, suspend or alter the registration of seamen; and

(*g*) to prescribe the fee to be paid on selection in respect of seamen selected in accordance with the provisions of this Part.

PART VIII

REGULATION OF PORT

Port regulations

41.—(1) The Authority may, with the approval of the Minister, make regulations for the control and management of the port and the approaches thereto and for the maintenance of good order therein and generally for the purposes of this Act and any other written law and, in particular, may make regulations for or in respect of all or any of the following matters:

(*a*) regulating traffic and preventing and removing obstruction or impediment to navigation within the limits of the port and the approaches thereto;

Informal Consolidation – version in force from 1/4/2018

(b) the conduct of inquiries into any case where damage has been caused to or by a vessel;

(c) regulating the keeping or placing of private moorings or buoys;

(d) regulating the use of lights and the signals to be used in the port and the steps to be taken for avoiding collision by vessels navigating in the port;

(e) the information to be supplied by the masters, owners, agents and other persons in respect of vessels arriving and departing and the time and manner in which such information shall be supplied;

(f) regulating, directing and controlling the use of vessels within the territorial waters of Singapore and all activities carried on in the waters of the port in respect of vessels, including but not limited to prescribing the conditions for towage and sale and supply of water and fuel to vessels and prohibiting such towage, sale and supply except through the Authority or by agreement with the Authority, and providing for the licensing thereof;

(g) permitting, regulating and controlling the landing of personnel belonging to an armed service of any foreign country and the movement of such personnel in the port;

(h) keeping clean the basins, works and premises of the Authority and the waters of the port and the approaches thereto and preventing oil, filth, rubbish or any other thing from being thrown or entering therein or thereon;

(i) regulating and controlling the use and manning of harbour craft and providing for the licensing thereof;

(j) supervising, regulating and controlling all activities carried on in the waters of the port and providing for the licensing thereof;

(k) regulating the provision and maintenance of adequate and efficient pontoons for the landing of persons, mooring buoys, gangways, landing stages, moorings and berthing facilities and providing for the licensing thereof;

(*l*) regulating the provision and maintenance of beacons, lighthouses, buoys and other aids to navigation not owned or erected by the Authority and providing for the licensing thereof;

(*m*) prescribing the standards of competence to be attained by officers and crew of harbour craft in order to be qualified for the purposes of manning harbour craft and providing for, for such purposes, the conduct of any examinations, the conditions for admission to them and the issue, form and recording of licences or certificates and other documents;

(*n*) providing for and in respect of the construction and machinery, equipment, fittings, installations, appliances and apparatus of harbour craft, and the tests to be carried out and the maintenance in respect thereof, including the provision, maintenance and stowage of life-saving and fire-fighting appliances and apparatus and providing for and in respect of the survey of harbour craft, the issue, suspension, cancellation or extension and period of validity of certificates or exemption certificates, and the types and forms of the certificates;

(*o*) regulating the navigation and place of anchoring or mooring of vessels carrying dangerous cargoes;

(*p*) regulating the mode of utilizing, stowing and keeping dangerous cargoes on board vessels and the conveyance within the port of any kind of dangerous cargoes with any other kind of goods, articles or substances;

(*q*) regulating, declaring and defining the wharves and docks and on and from which goods shall be landed from and shipped in vessels;

(*r*) keeping free passages of such width as is deemed necessary in the port and along or near to the wharves, docks, moorings and other similar works in or adjoining the same and for marking out the spaces so to be kept free;

(s) the information to be supplied by the masters, owners or agents and other persons in respect of goods loaded or discharged at the wharves in the port, and the time and manner in which such information shall be supplied;

(t) prohibiting the embarkation and disembarkation of persons except at such places as may be authorised by the Authority for such purpose;

(u) prohibiting the loading and discharging of goods other than, in the case of dutiable goods, at wharves, docks and places authorised in the Customs Act (Cap. 70) or the regulations made thereunder and, in the case of non-dutiable goods, at wharves, docks and places named in the Regulation of Imports and Exports Act (Cap. 272A) or any regulations made thereunder and at such other wharves, docks and places approved by the Authority;

(v) prohibiting the loading, handling or discharging of dangerous cargoes at wharves or docks where such loading, handling or discharging appears specially dangerous to the public.

(2) The Authority may, in making any regulations under this section, provide that any contravention of or failure to comply with any regulation shall be an offence and may prescribe as a penalty in respect of any one offence a fine not exceeding $20,000 or imprisonment for a term not exceeding 6 months or both and, in the case of a continuing offence, a further fine not exceeding $2,000 for every day or part thereof during which such offence continues after conviction.

Insurance policy

42.—(1) Where by virtue of this Act or the regulations any person is required to take out and maintain a policy of insurance against liability for any risks or costs, such policy of insurance shall be —

(*a*) a policy of insurance that is issued by an insurer who at the time the policy is issued and during the period of insurance is lawfully carrying on insurance business in Singapore; and

(*b*) in accordance with such terms and conditions, including any minimum limit of indemnity, as may be prescribed.

(2) A policy shall be of no effect for the purposes of this Act or the regulations unless there is issued by the insurer to the person by whom the policy is effected, a certificate of insurance in the prescribed form and containing such particulars of any conditions subject to which the policy is issued and of any other matters as may be prescribed.

(3) Any condition in a policy of insurance issued or given for the purposes of this Act or the regulations which —

(*a*) provides that no liability shall arise under the policy or that any liability so arising shall cease; and

(*b*) purports to negate or restrict the liability of the insurer under the policy or to impose any condition with respect to the enforcement of any such liability of the insurer,

in the event of some specified thing being done or omitted to be done after the happening of the event giving rise to a claim under the policy shall be of no effect in connection with any claim in respect of any risk against which the policy of insurance was required to be taken out or maintained.

(4) Nothing in this section shall be taken to render void any provision in a policy of insurance requiring the person insured to repay to the insurer any sum which the insurer may have become liable to pay under the policy and which have been applied to the satisfaction of any claim in respect of any risk against which the policy of insurance was required to be taken out or maintained.

(5) The Authority may, by order published in the *Gazette*, prescribe the conditions, including a minimum limit of indemnity, of any policy of insurance which is required to be taken out or maintained under this Act or the regulations and the form and particulars to be stated in any certificate of insurance and different conditions, forms and

particulars may be prescribed in relation to different cases or circumstances.

Power of Port Master in relation to vessel

43. Notwithstanding the provisions of any regulations made under section 41, the Port Master may, subject to such conditions as the Port Master may think fit to impose —

   (*a*) direct where any vessel shall be berthed, moored or anchored and the method of anchoring in the territorial waters of Singapore;

   (*b*) direct the removal of any vessel from any place in the territorial waters of Singapore to any other place in the territorial waters of Singapore and the time within which such removal is to be effected in the territorial waters of Singapore;

   (*c*) regulate, restrict or prohibit the movement of vessels in the port and the approaches to the port; and

   (*d*) by notification in the *Gazette*, declare the berths, locations, anchorages and fairways which may be used by vessels and the areas which are prohibited or restricted areas.

Owner, agent or master of vessel to report arrival or departure

44.—(1) The Port Master may direct the owner, agent or master of any vessel intending to enter or leave the port to furnish, before entering or leaving the port, such information as the Port Master may require relating to the vessel, its cargo and the estimated time of entering or leaving the port.

(2) The owner, agent or master of any vessel arriving in the port shall —

   (*a*) on arrival, report or cause to be reported by such means as the Port Master may from time to time direct, the arrival of the vessel;

   (*b*) provide within such time and by such means to the Port Master —

(i) a general declaration of arrival in such form as the Port Master may determine;

(ii) the clearance from the last port;

(iii) a list of passengers on board;

(iv) a list of crew;

(v) a copy of the manifest of goods to be discharged or transhipped in the port; and

(vi) such other documents as may be required by the Port Master from time to time; and

(c) in the case of vessels belonging to a country not having a consular officer in Singapore, produce to the Director of Marine the certificate of registry and shall deposit with him the ship's articles.

(3) The owner, agent or master of any vessel who fails to comply with this section shall be guilty of an offence and shall be liable on conviction to a fine not exceeding $10,000.

Port Master may require vessel in transit in the port or approaches thereto to provide information

45.—(1) The Port Master may at any time require the owner or master of any vessel which is in transit in the port or the approaches thereto to provide him with such particulars of the vessel, its cargo and equipment as the Port Master may determine.

(2) Any owner or master of a vessel who fails to comply with subsection (1) shall be guilty of an offence and shall be liable on conviction to a fine not exceeding $10,000.

No vessel to leave port without port clearance

46.—(1) No vessel, other than a vessel referred to in subsection (3), shall leave the port without the owner, agent or master obtaining port clearance from the Port Master.

(2) The owner, agent or master of the vessel applying for port clearance under subsection (1) shall —

(a) provide to the Port Master within such time and by such means as the Port Master may determine —

    (i) a general declaration of departure in such form as the Port Master may determine;

    (ii) a list of crew;

    (iii) a list of passengers on board;

    (iv) a copy of the manifest of goods on board and cargo loaded on or discharged at the port; and

    (v) such other documents as may be required by the Port Master from time to time; and

(b) if so required by the Port Master, produce for inspection the certificate of registry and other documents relating to the vessel.

(3) This section shall not apply to —

(a) any ship of war;

(b) any vessel belonging to or for the time being in the service or employment of the Government unless such vessel is carrying or habitually carries cargo or passengers for freight or fares; and

(c) vessels which have been exempted from complying with this section by the Minister.

(4) If any vessel, not being exempted from complying with this section, leaves or attempts to leave the port without port clearance, the owner, agent or master of the vessel or any person who sends or attempts to send the vessel to sea shall, if that owner, agent, master or person is party or privy to the offence, be guilty of an offence and shall be liable on conviction for every offence to a fine not exceeding $10,000, and the vessel, if she has not left Singapore waters, may be detained.

(5) No port clearance shall be granted to any vessel —

(a) whose owner, agent or master has not complied with the Regulation of Imports and Exports Act (Cap. 272A), or any other written law relating to the import or export of goods into or from Singapore; or

(b) until the owner, agent or master of such vessel has declared to the Port Master the name of the country to which he claims that the vessel belongs, and if so required by the Port Master, has produced the certificate of registry of the vessel; and the Port Master shall thereupon inscribe that name on the port clearance.

(6) Where under this Act or any other written law a vessel is to be detained, the Port Master shall, and where under this Act or any other written law a vessel may be detained the Port Master may, refuse to grant port clearance to that vessel.

(7) The Port Master may refuse to grant port clearance to any vessel whose owner or master has not complied with, or has been charged with an offence under, any of the provisions of this Act or any other written law.

(8) The Port Master may refuse to grant port clearance to any vessel which has anchored in the submarine cable corridor unless the owner, agent or master of the vessel has deposited such sum of money or furnished such security as may be required by a public telecommunication licensee in order to meet the costs of making good the damage, whether actual or estimated by a public telecommunication licensee, to the submarine cable and its associated plant (referred to in this section as the submersible plant).

(9) Where a public telecommunication licensee has reason to believe that the submersible plant has been damaged by a vessel, the public telecommunication licensee may require the owner, agent or master of that vessel to carry out an inspection or survey of the submersible plant in such manner as it considers necessary.

(10) The expenses of any inspection or survey of the submersible plant carried out under subsection (9) shall be paid by the owner, agent or master of the vessel.

(11) For the purposes of this section, "submarine cable corridor" means the area designated by the Port Master as the submarine cable corridor.

Informal Consolidation – version in force from 1/4/2018

Owner, agent or master of vessel not leaving within 48 hours after port clearance to return port clearance to Port Master

47.—(1) The owner, agent or master of any vessel which fails to leave the port within 48 hours, or such shorter period as may be specified by the Port Master, after obtaining port clearance shall, within 6 hours after the expiry of the 48 hours or such shorter period, return to the Port Master the port clearance certificate and, if so required, obtain fresh port clearance.

(2) Any owner, agent or master of a vessel who fails to comply with subsection (1) shall be guilty of an offence and shall be liable on conviction for every offence to a fine not exceeding $5,000 and the vessel may be detained.

Power to prohibit vessel from entering territorial waters

48. The Port Master may prohibit any vessel from entering the territorial waters of Singapore if he is of the opinion that it would not be in the public interest for the vessel to enter Singapore.

Power to direct vessel to leave territorial waters

49.—(1) The Port Master may direct any vessel to leave the territorial waters of Singapore if he is of the opinion that it would not be in the public interest for the vessel to remain within the territorial waters of Singapore.

(2) Any person aggrieved by the direction of the Port Master under subsection (1) may, within 7 days of the receipt of such direction, appeal to the Minister whose decision shall be final.

(3) If any vessel fails to leave the territorial waters of Singapore within the time specified by the Port Master, or where an appeal has been made to the Minister under subsection (2), after the appeal has been refused, the Authority may take possession of and dispose of the vessel in any manner the Authority thinks fit.

Penalty for disobedience of direction

50.—(1) Any person who, without lawful excuse, refuses, neglects or fails to obey any direction lawfully given under this Part or any regulations made thereunder shall be guilty of an offence and shall be liable on conviction to a fine not exceeding $5,000 and, in the case of a continuing offence, to a further fine not exceeding $500 for every day or part thereof during which he wilfully continues to disobey such direction.

(2) In case of any refusal or neglect or failure to comply with this Part or any regulations made thereunder, the Authority may, whether any proceedings have been instituted against any person for such offence or not, do or cause to be done all such acts as are in its opinion reasonable or necessary for the purpose of carrying out such direction or complying with such direction, and may hire and employ such person as it considers proper and necessary for such purpose.

(3) All expenses incurred in doing such acts shall be paid and borne by the person or persons so offending.

Removal of certain obstructions and compensation therefor

51.—(1) Notwithstanding that any obstruction or impediment to the navigation of the port has been lawfully made or has become lawful by reason of the long continuance of such obstruction or impediment or otherwise, the Authority may, with the approval of the Minister, cause the same to be removed or altered, making to the persons who suffer damage by such removal or alteration reasonable compensation for the damage done.

(2) If any dispute arises concerning such compensation, the amount and, if necessary, any question of liability shall be summarily ascertained and determined by a court of competent jurisdiction.

(3) An appeal shall lie to the High Court from any decision of a Magistrate's Court or a District Court under this section, and the provisions of the Criminal Procedure Code (Cap. 68) shall apply, with the necessary modifications, to all such appeals.

Fire on board vessel

52.—(1) In the event of fire breaking out on board any vessel in the port, the Port Master or his authorised representative may proceed on board the vessel with such assistance and persons as he thinks fit, and may give such orders as seems to him necessary for scuttling the vessel, or for removing the vessel or any other vessel to such place as he thinks proper to prevent in either case danger to other vessels and for the taking of any other measures that appear to him expedient for the protection of life or property.

(2) If such orders are not forthwith carried out by the master of such vessel, the Port Master or his authorised representative may proceed to carry them into effect.

(3) Any expenses incurred in the exercise of the powers conferred by subsections (1) and (2) shall be recoverable from the master or owner of the vessel concerned as a civil debt.

Power to board vessel

53.—(1) The Port Master or his authorised representative or any officer of the Authority authorised by the Authority or any police officer may go on board any vessel in the port whenever he suspects that any offence against this Part has been or is about to be committed in any vessel, or whenever he considers it is necessary for him to do so in the discharge of any duty imposed upon him by this Part or otherwise by law.

(2) Any master of such vessel who, without lawful excuse, refuses to allow the Port Master or his authorised representative or any officer of the Authority authorised by the Authority or any police officer so to enter such vessel shall be guilty of an offence and shall be liable on conviction for each offence to a fine not exceeding $1,000.

Execution of order, etc.

54.—(1) All acts, orders or directions by this Part or any regulations made thereunder authorised to be done or given by a particular employee of the Authority may be done or given by any other employee of the Authority authorised in writing in that behalf by the Authority.

(2) Any person authorised to do any such act may call to his aid such assistance as is necessary.

Exemption of vessels belonging to Singapore Armed Forces

55. Except where expressly provided otherwise, this Part and any regulations made thereunder shall not apply to any vessel belonging to the Singapore Armed Forces.

Indemnity to Authority for act of Port Master

56. The Authority shall not be liable for any act, omission or default of the Port Master.

PART IX

REMOVAL OF VESSEL AND AIRCRAFT SUNK AND OTHER OBSTRUCTION

Power to require owner to raise, remove or destroy vessel, aircraft or other obstruction

57.—(1) If in the opinion of the Authority any vessel, aircraft or other object sunk, stranded or abandoned within the port or the approaches thereto is, or is likely to become, an obstruction, impediment or danger to navigation or to the safe and convenient use or operation of the port, the Authority may by notice in writing require the owner or agent of the vessel, aircraft or object to raise, remove or destroy the whole or any part of such vessel, aircraft or object within such time as may be specified in the notice.

(2) Any notice to be served by the Authority under subsection (1) shall be deemed to be sufficiently served if addressed to "the owner" of the vessel, aircraft or object, as the case may be, and —

    (*a*) sent by telex or registered post to the last known place of residence or business or registered office of the owner of the vessel, aircraft or object; or

    (*b*) affixed to some conspicuous part of the vessel, aircraft or object.

(3) Any person who fails to comply with a notice under subsection (1) shall be guilty of an offence and shall be liable on conviction to a fine not exceeding $10,000 and, in the case of a

continuing offence, to a further fine not exceeding $2,000 for every day or part thereof during which the notice is not complied with.

Power to raise and remove vessel, aircraft or other obstruction

58.—(1) Notwithstanding section 57, if the vessel, aircraft or other object is not raised, removed or destroyed within such time as may be given in the notice under that section, the Authority may —

  (*a*) take possession of and raise, remove or destroy the whole or any part of such vessel, aircraft or object;

  (*b*) light, mark or buoy such vessel, aircraft or object until the raising, removal or destruction thereof; and

  (*c*) sell, in such manner as it thinks fit, any such vessel, aircraft or object.

(2) The Authority may use the proceeds of the sale under subsection (1)(*c*) to reimburse itself for the whole of the expenses incurred by it in the exercise of its powers under this section.

(3) The Authority shall on demand pay the surplus, if any, of the proceeds of the sale under subsection (1)(*c*) to the owner or any person entitled to it and if no demand is made by the owner or any person entitled to the surplus within 12 months from the date of such sale, the surplus shall be paid into the funds of the Authority.

(4) If the proceeds of the sale under subsection (1)(*c*) are insufficient to reimburse the Authority for the whole expenses incurred by it, the Authority may recover the balance from the owner of the vessel, aircraft or object as a debt in any court of competent jurisdiction.

(5) If any vessel, aircraft or object or any part thereof is destroyed by the Authority under subsection (1)(*a*), the owner of such vessel, aircraft or object shall reimburse the Authority for the expenses incurred by the Authority in such destruction.

(6) For the purposes of this section, "vessel" or "aircraft" includes every article or thing or collection of things being or forming part of the tackle, equipment, cargo, stores or ballast of a vessel or an aircraft, as the case may be.

PART X

PILOTAGE

Declaration of pilotage districts

59.—(1) The Authority may, from time to time, by notification in the *Gazette*, declare any area in the port to be a pilotage district.

(2) Every such declaration shall define the limits of the pilotage district.

Authority may require vessel to be under pilotage

60.—(1) Every vessel while navigating in any pilotage district or part thereof shall be under pilotage and the owner, agent or master of the vessel shall comply with that requirement.

(2) A vessel while being moved within any area of the port which is or forms part of a pilotage district shall be deemed to be a vessel navigating in a pilotage district.

(3) The Authority may, if it appears to the Authority to be necessary, exempt any vessel or class of vessels while navigating in any pilotage district from being under pilotage subject to such conditions as it may think fit to impose.

Failure to employ pilot under certain circumstances

61. The owner, agent or master of a vessel navigating in circumstances in which the vessel is required by the Authority under section 60 to be under pilotage who does not employ an authorised pilot for such purpose shall be guilty of an offence and shall be liable on conviction to a fine not exceeding $5,000 and shall in addition be liable to pay to the Authority as penalty double the amount of pilotage dues and rates which would have been payable if the vessel had been under pilotage as required under that section.

Authorised pilot and berthing master

62.—(1) Subject to the provisions of this Act, the Authority may employ such number of pilots as it considers necessary or expedient for the purpose of providing an adequate and efficient pilotage service.

(2) Notwithstanding subsection (1) —

(*a*) the Authority may, if it considers expedient, authorise any person to pilot vessels in a pilotage district subject to such conditions as it thinks fit; and

(*b*) the owner of a wharf or dock may, with the approval of the Authority and subject to such conditions as the Authority may impose, authorise any person to act as a berthing master for the purposes of berthing and unberthing, docking and undocking vessels at that wharf or dock.

Vessel to be piloted by authorised pilots

63. No vessel shall be piloted in a pilotage district by any person other than an authorised pilot.

Penalties as to employment of pilot

64.—(1) Any person who, not being an authorised pilot, engages in any pilotage act or attempts to obtain employment as a pilot of a vessel entering or within any pilotage district shall be guilty of an offence and shall be liable on conviction to a fine not exceeding $5,000.

(2) Any owner, agent or master of a vessel entering or within any pilotage district who knowingly employs —

(*a*) as a pilot any person who is not employed by the Authority to pilot vessels under section 62(1);

(*b*) as a pilot any person who is not authorised to pilot vessels under section 62(2)(*a*); or

(*c*) as a berthing master any person who is not authorised to act as a berthing master under section 62(2)(*b*),

shall be guilty of an offence and shall be liable on conviction to a fine not exceeding $5,000.

(3) For the purposes of this section, a person employed under section 62(1) or authorised under section 62(2)(*a*) or (*b*) acting beyond the limits for which he is licensed or authorised to act or acting in contravention of any of the conditions imposed under

section 62(2)(*a*) or (*b*) or 70 shall be deemed not to be an authorised pilot.

(4) Any person may, without subjecting himself or his employer to any penalty, act as the pilot of a vessel entering or leaving any pilotage district, when such vessel is in distress or under circumstances making it necessary for the master to avail himself of the best assistance that can be found at the time.

Employment of pilot

65. No person shall be employed as an authorised pilot in a pilotage district unless he is in possession of a valid licence issued under section 68 to act as a pilot in that district.

Appointment and functions of Pilotage Committee

66. The Authority shall appoint a Pilotage Committee for the purpose of —

(*a*) holding examinations and issuing, on behalf of the Authority, licences to act as an authorised pilot;

(*b*) holding inquiries into the conduct of authorised pilots in the discharge of their duties;

(*c*) making such arrangements as may be necessary for the training of persons selected for or in the pilotage service;

(*d*) investigating and advising on such matters as may be referred to the Committee by the Authority; and

(*e*) carrying out such other functions as are conferred on the Committee by this Act.

Constitution of Pilotage Committee

67.—(1) The Pilotage Committee shall consist of —

(*a*) the Port Master who shall be the chairman of the Committee; and

(*b*) not less than 4 other persons, 3 of whom must have, in the opinion of the Authority, knowledge of or experience in nautical matters.

(2) A member of the Pilotage Committee shall hold office for such term, not exceeding 3 years, as the Authority may specify in its appointment and shall be eligible for re-appointment.

(3) At any meeting of the Committee, 3 members of the Pilotage Committee shall form a quorum.

(4) The chairman of the Pilotage Committee shall preside at all meetings thereof.

(5) If the chairman is absent from a meeting or any part thereof, such member, as the members of the Pilotage Committee present shall elect, shall preside in his place.

(6) The chairman or member presiding at any meeting of the Pilotage Committee shall have a vote and, in the case of an equality of votes, a second or casting vote.

(7) Members of the Pilotage Committee may be paid, out of the funds of the Authority, such fees and allowances as the Authority may, from time to time, determine.

(8) Subject to the provisions of this Act, the Authority may, from time to time, make rules for the purpose of regulating the meetings and proceedings of the Pilotage Committee.

Examination for licence

68.—(1) The Pilotage Committee shall examine candidates for employment as authorised pilots and on being satisfied as to a candidate's general fitness and competency, including physical fitness, to act as an authorised pilot may, on behalf of the Authority, issue to him a licence to act as such, and such licence may contain such conditions as the Committee may think fit.

(2) Every authorised pilot shall, whenever the Pilotage Committee considers that owing to changed conditions or for any other sufficient reason the further testing of the knowledge, efficiency or physical fitness of any such pilot is necessary, present himself for further examination, and shall in every such case first deposit with the Committee his licence issued by the Committee on behalf of the Authority to be returned or cancelled by the Committee on behalf of the Authority as the result of such test or examination.

Inquiries by Pilotage Committee

69.—(1) The Pilotage Committee may, and when directed by the Authority shall, hold an inquiry into the conduct of an authorised pilot where it appears that he has been guilty of misconduct affecting his capability as a pilot or has failed in or neglected his duty as a pilot or has become incompetent to act as a pilot.

(2) For the purposes of such inquiry, the Pilotage Committee may summon any person to attend any meeting of the Committee to give evidence on oath or produce any document or other thing in his possession and to examine him as a witness or require him to produce any document or other thing in his possession relating to the matters which are the subject matter of such inquiry.

(3) Any person who —

(a) being summoned to attend any such inquiry, fails to do so;

(b) offers any act of disrespect or any insult or threat to the Pilotage Committee or any member thereof during an inquiry; or

(c) being required by the Pilotage Committee to give evidence on oath or affirmation or to produce a document or other thing, refuses to do so,

shall be guilty of an offence and shall be liable on conviction to a fine not exceeding $2,000.

Submission of Pilotage Committee's finding and recommendation to Authority

70.—(1) Where the Pilotage Committee, after due inquiry in accordance with the provisions of this Part and after hearing any statement that may be offered in defence, finds that an authorised pilot has been guilty of misconduct or indiscipline affecting his capability or duties as a pilot or has failed in or neglected his duty as a pilot or has become incompetent to act as a pilot, the Committee shall submit to the Authority a copy of the record of the inquiry and its findings and recommendations in respect of the inquiry.

(2) The Authority may, after considering the findings and recommendations of the Pilotage Committee, suspend or cancel the licence of such authorised pilot or impose such other punishment as the Authority may think fit.

(3) Any authorised pilot who is aggrieved by any decision of the Authority made under subsection (2) may, within 14 days from the date of the decision, appeal to the Minister whose decision shall be final.

(4) Where the Pilotage Committee, after due inquiry in accordance with the provisions of this Part, finds that any authorised pilot has been negligent in piloting any vessel or has become incompetent to act as a pilot, the Committee shall submit its findings to the Authority and the Authority shall thereupon suspend or revoke such authorisation as the Authority may consider fit.

Liability of master or owner in case of vessel under pilotage

71. The master or owner of a vessel navigating in circumstances in which pilotage is compulsory shall be answerable for any loss or damage caused by the vessel or by any fault of the navigation of the vessel in the same manner as he would if pilotage were not compulsory.

Limitation of pilot's liability when bond is given

72.—(1) An authorised pilot who has given a bond in accordance with subsection (2) shall not be liable for neglect, want of skill or incapacity in office beyond the penalty of such bond and the amount payable to the Authority on account of pilotage in respect of the voyage in which he was engaged when he became so liable.

(2) Every pilot shall give a bond in the sum of $1,000 in favour of the Authority for the proper performance of his duties under this Part and any regulations made thereunder.

(3) Any bond given by an authorised pilot in accordance with this section shall not be liable to stamp duty.

(4) Where any proceedings are taken against an authorised pilot for any neglect, want of skill or incapacity in office in respect of which his liability is limited as provided by this section, and other claims are made in respect of the same neglect, want of skill or incapacity in office, the court in which the proceedings are taken may —

(a) determine the amount of the pilot's liability and, upon payment by him of that amount into court, distribute the amount rateably among the several claimants;

(b) stay any proceedings pending in any other court in relation to the same matter; and

(c) proceed in such manner and subject to such directions as to making persons interested parties to the proceedings, and as to the exclusion of any claimant who has not submitted his claim within a certain time, and as to requiring security from the pilot, and as to payment of any costs as the court thinks fit.

Offences of pilot

73.—(1) Any authorised pilot who —

(a) is in any way, directly or indirectly, concerned in any corrupt practices relating to vessels, their tackle, furniture, cargoes, crew or passengers, or to persons in distress at sea or by shipwreck, or to their moneys, goods or chattels;

(b) lends his licence;

(c) acts as pilot while suspended;

(d) acts as pilot when in a state of intoxication;

(e) refuses or wilfully delays, when not prevented by illness or other reasonable cause, to pilot any vessel within the limits for which he is licensed by the Authority upon being required to do so by any employee of the Authority duly authorised in that behalf; or

(f) quits the vessel under his pilotage without the consent of the master, before the service for which he was engaged has been performed, shall be guilty of an offence and shall be liable on conviction to a fine not exceeding $2,000.

(2) Any person who procures, aids, abets or connives at the commission of any offence under this section shall be guilty of an offence and shall be liable on conviction to a fine not exceeding $2,000.

Pilotage Committee and Authority not liable for loss or damage caused by pilot

74.—(1) The issue of a licence to a pilot by the Pilotage Committee on behalf of the Authority under section 68 or the authorisation given by the Authority to any person to pilot vessels in the pilotage district pursuant to section 62(2)(*a*) shall not impose any liability on the Pilotage Committee or the Authority for any loss or damage caused by any act, omission or default of such pilot.

(2) Any authorised pilot while engaged in any pilotage act shall be deemed to be the employee only of the master or owner of the vessel under pilotage and the Authority shall not be liable for any loss or damage caused by any act, omission or default of such pilot.

Members of Pilotage Committee to act as assessors in proceedings

75. A Magistrate's Court or a District Court may, if it thinks fit, call upon 2 members of the Pilotage Committee to sit with it as assessors in any proceedings affecting authorised pilots under this Act or the regulations.

Regulations relating to pilotage and conduct of pilot

76.—(1) The Authority may, with the approval of the Minister, make regulations for regulating pilotage in any pilotage district and for the maintenance of good conduct and discipline of authorised pilots and for matters relating to their duties.

(2) The Authority may, in making regulations under this section, provide that any contravention of or failure to comply with any of the regulations shall be an offence and may prescribe as a penalty in respect of any one offence a fine not exceeding $5,000.

PART XI

REGULATION AND CONTROL OF SEAWARD ACTIVITIES

Dredging limits

77.—(1) The Authority may, with the approval of the Minister, by notification in the *Gazette*, prescribe the limits within which and the levels to which dredging may be carried out by the Authority in the port and the approaches thereto.

(2) The Authority shall not be liable for any loss or damage whatsoever to any sea or river wall, wharf, dock or other property arising out of any dredging by the Authority in the port.

Hydrographic survey, etc., not to be carried out without approval of Authority

78.—(1) No person shall carry out or cause to be carried out any hydrographic or hydrologic survey or other study of the waters and sea-bed within the territorial limits of Singapore except with the approval of the Authority.

(2) The Authority may grant the approval referred to in subsection (1) with or without conditions or may refuse to grant such approval.

(3) Any person who contravenes subsection (1) shall be guilty of an offence and shall be liable on conviction to a fine not exceeding $5,000 or to imprisonment for a term not exceeding 6 months or to both.

(4) This section shall not apply to any hydrographic or hydrologic survey or other study carried out for or on behalf of the Government.

Restriction of certain works and operations

79.—(1) Subject to this section, no person shall, without the consent in writing of the Authority, carry out any of the following operations:

    (*a*) construct, alter or improve any work on, under or over any part of a river, waterway or the seashore lying below the high-water mark of ordinary tides;

(*b*) deposit any object or any material on any part of a river, waterway or the seashore as aforesaid; or

(*c*) remove any object or any material from any part of a river, waterway or the seashore as aforesaid.

(2) The Authority may, as a condition of considering an application for consent under this section, require to be furnished with such plans and particulars of the proposed operations as the Authority may consider necessary; and on receipt of any such application the Authority may cause notice of the application, and of the time within which and the manner in which objections thereto may be made, to be published in such manner as the Authority may consider appropriate for informing persons affected thereby, and, before granting its consent may, if the Authority thinks fit, direct an inquiry to be held.

(3) If the Authority is of the opinion that any operation in respect of which an application is made under this section should not for any reason be carried out or should be carried out subject to such conditions as the Authority thinks necessary to impose, the Authority may either refuse its consent or give its consent subject to such conditions as the Authority thinks fit.

(4) A consent of the Authority under this section may be given so as to continue in force, unless renewed, only if the operation for which the consent is given has begun or is completed within such period as may be specified in the consent; and any renewal of such a consent may be limited in the like manner.

(5) The restriction imposed by subsection (1) shall not apply to the carrying out of any dredging operation or reclamation work authorised by the Government in accordance with the provisions of any written law.

(6) Nothing in this section shall be deemed to be in derogation of any of the powers or rights of the Government in respect of the foreshore or territorial waters of Singapore.

(7) Nothing in this section shall be deemed to confer upon the Authority any power or right in respect of the foreshore not vested in the Authority.

(8) Any person who —

 (*a*) carries out any operation in contravention of subsection (1); or

 (*b*) fails to comply with any condition subject to which any consent of the Authority has been given under this section,

shall be guilty of an offence and shall be liable on conviction to a fine not exceeding $5,000 or to imprisonment for a term not exceeding 6 months or to both.

(9) Without prejudice to any proceedings under subsection (8), where any person has constructed, altered or improved any work or deposited any object or material on a river, waterway or the seashore in contravention of subsection (1) or has failed to comply with any condition subject to which any consent of the Authority has been given under this section, the Authority may serve a notice on that person requiring him to remove, within such period (not being less than 30 days) as may be specified in the notice, the object or material, as the case may be, or, if it appears to the Authority necessary to do so, the Authority may itself remove or alter the work or remove the object or material.

(10) If within the period specified in any notice under subsection (9) the person upon whom the notice is served fails to comply therewith, the Authority may remove or alter the work or remove the object or material as specified in the notice.

(11) Where under subsection (9) or (10) the Authority removes or alters any work or removes any object or material, the Authority shall be entitled to recover the expense thereof as certified by the Authority, from the person by whom or for whom the work was constructed, altered or improved, or the object or material was deposited.

(12) For the purposes of this section —

 "seashore" includes the sea-bed under the territorial waters of Singapore;

 "work" includes any architectural or engineering operation.

Salvage business not to be carried on without licence

80.—(1) No person shall carry on the business of rendering salvage services in the territorial waters of Singapore without a valid licence granted by the Authority for that purpose.

(2) The Authority may grant the licence with or without conditions or may refuse to grant the licence.

(3) Any person who contravenes subsection (1) shall be guilty of an offence and shall be liable on conviction to a fine not exceeding $10,000 or to imprisonment for a term not exceeding 12 months or to both.

(4) Any person aggrieved by —

 (*a*) the refusal of the Authority to grant or renew a licence; or

 (*b*) the cancellation of a licence,

may, within 30 days after receiving the Authority's notification of its decision, appeal to the Minister whose decision shall be final.

PART XII

LICENSING OF MARINE AND PORT SERVICES AND FACILITIES

Licences authorising provision of marine or port services and facilities

81.—(1) No person shall provide —

 (*a*) any marine service or facility; or

 (*b*) any port service or facility,

unless he is authorised to do so by a public licence or an exemption granted by the Authority.

(2) Every public licence granted under this section shall be in such form and for such period and may contain such conditions as the Authority may determine.

(3) The Authority may, with the consent of, or in accordance with the terms of a general authority given by the Minister, grant a public

licence either unconditionally or subject to such conditions as the Authority may impose and specify in the licence and either irrevocably or subject to revocation as therein specified, authorising any person to provide any marine service or facility or any port service or facility.

(4) Without prejudice to the generality of subsection (3), a public licence may be granted either to any person, class of persons or a particular person, and may include conditions requiring the public licensee —

> (*a*) to enter into agreements or arrangements with any other person, class of persons or another public licensee for —
>
>> (i) the interconnection with, access to and use of any installation of the licensee (wherever situated and whether or not used for the purpose of carrying on the activities authorised by the licence); and
>>
>> (ii) such other purpose as may be specified in the licence,
>
> and on such conditions as may be agreed to by the licensee and such other persons or, in default of agreement, as may be determined by the Authority;
>
> (*b*) to prepare itself to deal with any public emergency;
>
> (*c*) to pay to the Authority a fee on the grant of the licence or pay to the Authority periodic fees during the currency of the licence or both, of such amount as may be determined by or under the licence;
>
> (*d*) to comply with any direction given by the Authority as to such matters as are specified in the licence or are of a description so specified; and
>
> (*e*) to do or not to do such things as are specified in the licence or are of a description so specified.

(5) Conditions in a public licence may contain —

> (*a*) control and restriction, directly or indirectly, on the creation, holding or disposal of shares in the public licensee or its shareholders or interests in the undertaking of the licensee or any part thereof;

Informal Consolidation – version in force from 1/4/2018

(b) restriction on the carrying on by the public licensee of any trade or business which is not related to the activity which the licensee is authorised by its public licence to carry on;

(c) provision for the conditions to cease to have effect or be modified at such times, in such manner and in such circumstances as may be specified in or determined by or under the conditions; and

(d) provision controlling or fixing the prices to be charged by the public licensee in respect of the handling and storage of goods other than such category of goods as the Minister may by notification in the *Gazette*, from time to time declare to be transhipment goods, including —

    (i) the setting of pricing policies or principles; and

    (ii) the setting of prices with reference to a general price index, the cost of production, a rate of return on assets employed or any other specified factors.

(6) Any provision included by virtue of subsection (5)(c) in a public licence shall have effect in addition to the provision made by this Part with respect to the modification of the conditions of a public licence.

(7) A payment required by subsection (4) to be rendered to the Authority may be recovered by it in any court of competent jurisdiction as if it were a simple contract debt.

(8) No person shall question whether the grant of a public licence under subsection (3) was, or was not, effected with the consent of or in accordance with the terms of a general authority given by the Minister, and the validity of a licence granted under that subsection shall not be impugned on the ground that it was granted neither with the consent of nor in accordance with the terms of a general authority given by the Minister.

(9) The grant and renewal of public licences under this section shall be at the discretion of the Authority.

(10) Nothing in this section shall prevent the Minister from directing the Authority to grant a public licence in any specific case or be construed as requiring the Authority to obtain a licence

where it undertakes any activity mentioned in subsection (1) and any person aggrieved by a refusal of the Authority to grant a licence may, within 14 days of the refusal, appeal to the Minister whose decision shall be final.

Restriction on transfer of public licence

82.—(1) No public licence shall be transferable to any other person without the prior consent in writing of the Authority to the transfer to that person.

(2) Any purported transfer of any public licence shall for all purposes be void and of no effect.

Modification of conditions of public licence

83.—(1) Subject to this section, the Authority may modify the conditions of a public licence granted.

(2) Before making modifications to the conditions of a public licence under this section, the Authority shall give notice to the licensee —

(a) stating that it proposes to make the modifications in the manner as specified in the notice and the compensation payable for any damage caused thereby; and

(b) specifying the time (not being less than 28 days from the date of service of notice on such licensee) within which written representations with respect to the proposed modifications may be made.

(3) Upon receipt of any written representation referred to in subsection (2), the Authority shall consider such representation and may —

(a) reject the representation; or

(b) amend the proposed modifications or compensation payable in accordance with the representation, or otherwise,

and, in either event, it shall thereupon issue a direction in writing to such public licensee requiring that effect be given to the proposed modifications specified in the notice or to such modifications as subsequently amended by the Authority within a reasonable time.

(4) Any public licensee aggrieved by the decision of the Authority under subsection (3) may, within 14 days of the receipt by it of the direction, appeal to the Minister whose decision shall be final.

(5) The Authority shall not enforce its direction —

(a) during the period referred to in subsection (4); and

(b) whilst the appeal of the public licensee is under consideration by the Minister.

(6) If no written representation is received by the Authority within the time specified in subsection (2) or if any written representation made under subsection (2) is subsequently withdrawn, the Authority may forthwith carry out the modifications as specified in the notice given under subsection (2).

Suspension or cancellation of public licence, etc.

84.—(1) If the Authority is satisfied that —

(a) a public licensee is contravening, or is likely to contravene or has contravened any of the conditions of its public licence or any of the provisions of this Act or any regulations or any direction issued by the Minister or the Authority to, or applicable to, that licensee;

(b) a public licensee has gone or is likely to go into compulsory or voluntary liquidation other than for the purpose of amalgamation or reconstruction;

[Act 40 of 2017 wef 15/01/2018]

(c) a public licensee has made any assignment to, or composition with, its creditors; or

(d) the public interest or security of Singapore requires,

the Authority may, by notice in writing and without any compensation, do either or both of the following:

(i) cancel its public licence or suspend its licence for such period as the Authority thinks fit;

(ii) require the payment of a fine in such amount as the Authority thinks fit.

(2) Any person who is aggrieved by any decision of the Authority under this section may, within 14 days after such person has been given the notice in writing referred to in subsection (1), appeal to the Minister whose decision shall be final.

Direction affecting public licensee

85.—(1) The Authority may give directions for or with respect to standards of performance and procedures to be observed by public licensees and other persons —

(*a*) to ensure the reliability of the supply of marine services and facilities or port services and facilities, as the case may be, to the public; or

(*b*) in the interests of public safety.

(2) Any person who fails to comply with any direction given under this section shall be guilty of an offence.

General duties of public licensee

86. It shall be the duty of a public licensee to provide reliable, efficient and economical marine services and facilities or port services and facilities, as the case may be, to the public in accordance with the conditions of the public licence granted to it and the directions of the Authority.

PART XIIA

CONTROL OF DESIGNATED PUBLIC LICENSEES, DESIGNATED BUSINESS TRUSTS AND DESIGNATED EQUITY INTEREST HOLDERS

[Act 40 of 2017 wef 15/01/2018]

Interpretation of this Part

86A.—(1) In this Part, unless the context otherwise requires —

"5% controller", in relation to a designated public licensee, designated business trust or designated equity interest holder, means a person who, alone or together with the person's associates —

(a) holds 5% or more, but less than 25%, of the total equity interests in; or

(b) is in a position to control 5% or more, but less than 25%, of the voting power in,

the designated public licensee, designated business trust or designated equity interest holder, as the case may be;

"25% controller", in relation to a designated public licensee, designated business trust or designated equity interest holder, means a person who, alone or together with the person's associates —

(a) holds 25% or more, but less than 50%, of the total equity interests in; or

(b) is in a position to control 25% or more, but less than 50%, of the voting power in,

the designated public licensee, designated business trust or designated equity interest holder, as the case may be;

"50% controller", in relation to a designated public licensee, designated business trust or designated equity interest holder, means a person who, alone or together with the person's associates —

(a) holds 50% or more, but less than 75%, of the total equity interests in; or

(b) is in a position to control 50% or more, but less than 75%, of the voting power in,

the designated public licensee, designated business trust or designated equity interest holder, as the case may be;

"75% controller", in relation to a designated public licensee, designated business trust or designated equity interest holder, means a person who, alone or together with the person's associates —

(a) holds 75% or more of the total equity interests in; or

(b) is in a position to control 75% or more of the voting power in,

the designated public licensee, designated business trust or designated equity interest holder, as the case may be;

"acquisition" includes an agreement to acquire, but does not include —

(a) an acquisition by will or by operation of law; or

(b) an acquisition by way of enforcement of a loan security;

"arrangement" includes any formal or informal scheme, arrangement or understanding, and any trust whether express or implied;

"business trust" has the same meaning as in section 2 of the Business Trusts Act (Cap. 31A);

"control" includes control as a result of, or by means of, any trust, agreement, arrangement, understanding or practice, whether or not having legal or equitable force and whether or not based on legal or equitable rights;

"corporation" has the same meaning as in section 4(1) of the Companies Act (Cap. 50);

"decrease", in relation to the holding of equity interest, includes a decrease to a point of nil;

"Depository" has the same meaning as in section 81SF of the Securities and Futures Act (Cap. 289);

"designated business trust" means a business trust that has been designated under section 86D to be a designated business trust;

"designated equity interest holder" means a person that has been designated under section 86D to be a designated equity interest holder;

"designated public licensee" means a public licensee that has been designated under section 86D to be a designated public licensee;

"director" has the same meaning as in section 4(1) of the Companies Act;

"entity" includes a corporation and a limited liability partnership;

"equity interest" means —

    (a) in relation to a body corporate, a voting share in that body corporate;

    (b) in relation to an entity other than a body corporate, any right or interest, whether legal or equitable, in that entity, by whatever name called, which gives the holder of that right or interest voting power in that entity; and

    (c) in relation to a business trust, a unit in that business trust;

"increase", in relation to the holding of equity interest, includes an increase from a starting point of nil;

"indirect controller", in relation to a designated public licensee, designated business trust or designated equity interest holder, means any person, whether acting alone or together with any other person, and whether with or without holding equity interests or controlling the voting power in the designated public licensee, designated business trust or designated equity interest holder, as the case may be —

    (a) whose directions, instructions or wishes the director or other officers of the designated public licensee, the trustee-manager of the designated business trust, or the designated equity interest holder, as the case may be, are accustomed or under an obligation, whether formal or informal, to act in accordance with; or

(b) who is in a position to determine the policy of the designated public licensee, designated business trust or designated equity interest holder, as the case may be,

but does not include —

(i) any person who is a director or other officer of the designated public licensee, the trustee-manager of the designated business trust, or the designated equity interest holder, as the case may be; or

(ii) any person whose directions, instructions or wishes the directors or other officers of the designated public licensee, the trustee-manager of the designated business trust, or the designated equity interest holder, as the case may be, are accustomed to act in accordance with by reason only that they act on advice given by the person in that person's professional capacity;

"limited liability partnership" has the same meaning as in section 2(1) of the Limited Liability Partnerships Act (Cap. 163A);

"liquidator" includes the Official Receiver when acting as the liquidator of a corporation;

"officer", in relation to a corporation, includes —

(a) a director or secretary of, or a person employed in an executive capacity by, the corporation;

(b) any receiver or manager, or any receiver and manager, of any part of the undertaking of the corporation, appointed under a power contained in any instrument or by the High Court or by the creditors;

(c) any liquidator of the corporation appointed in a voluntary winding up or by the High Court or by the creditors; and

(d) any judicial manager of the corporation appointed by the High Court under Part VIIIA of the Companies Act;

"Official Receiver" means the Official Assignee as defined in section 2(1) of the Bankruptcy Act (Cap. 20);

"related corporation", in relation to a corporation, means another corporation that is deemed under section 86C(2) to be related to that corporation;

"share", in relation to a corporation, means a share in the share capital of the corporation and includes stock into which all or any of the share capital of the corporation has been converted;

"treasury share" has the same meaning as in section 4(1) of the Companies Act;

"trustee-manager" has the same meaning as in section 2 of the Business Trusts Act;

"unit" has the same meaning as in section 2 of the Business Trusts Act;

"voting share" has the same meaning as in section 4(1) of the Companies Act but does not include a treasury share.

(2) A reference in this Part to the control of a percentage of the voting power in a designated public licensee, designated business trust or designated equity interest holder is a reference to the control, whether direct or indirect, of that percentage of the total number of votes that might be cast in a general meeting of the designated public licensee, designated business trust or designated equity interest holder, as the case may be.

(3) In ascertaining a person's control of the percentage of the total votes that might be cast at a general meeting mentioned in subsection (2), the number of votes that the person is entitled to

cast at the meeting by reason of having been appointed a proxy or representative to vote at the meeting is to be disregarded.

[Act 40 of 2017 wef 15/01/2018]

What holding an equity interest means

86B.—(1) In this Part, a person holds an equity interest if the person —

 (*a*) has or is deemed to have an equity interest in accordance with subsections (2) to (7); or

 (*b*) otherwise has a legal or equitable interest in that equity interest,

except for any interest prescribed under section 119 as an interest that is to be disregarded.

(2) Subject to subsection (3), a person has an equity interest if the person has authority (whether formal or informal, or express or implied) to dispose of, or to exercise control over the disposal of, that equity interest.

(3) It is immaterial that the authority of a person to dispose of, or to exercise control over the disposal of, the equity interest mentioned in subsection (2) is, or is capable of being made, subject to restraint or restriction.

(4) It is immaterial, for the purposes of determining whether a person has an equity interest that the interest cannot be related to a particular share, an interest or right that gives its holder voting power, or a unit of a business trust, as the case may be.

(5) A person is deemed to have an equity interest if —

 (*a*) any property held in trust consists of or includes the equity interest; and

 (*b*) that person knows, or has reasonable grounds for believing, that that person has an interest under that trust.

(6) A person is also deemed to have an equity interest if that person —

 (*a*) has entered into a contract to purchase the equity interest;

Maritime and Port Authority of Singapore

(b) has a right, otherwise than by reason of having an interest under a trust, to have the equity interest transferred to (or to the order of) that person, whether the right is exercisable presently or in the future and whether on the fulfilment of a condition or not;

(c) has the right to acquire the equity interest under an option, whether the right is exercisable presently or in the future and whether on the fulfilment of a condition or not; or

(d) is entitled (otherwise than by reason of having been appointed a proxy or representative to vote at a general meeting of the entity in question) to exercise or control the exercise of a right attached to the equity interest, not being an equity interest in which that person has a legal or equitable interest.

(7) A person is not to be deemed as not having an equity interest by reason only that the person has the equity interest jointly with another person.

[Act 40 of 2017 wef 15/01/2018]

Meanings of "associate", "subsidiary" and "holding company"

86C.—(1) In this Part, a person (A) is an associate of another person (B) if —

(a) A is the spouse, or a parent, step-parent or remoter lineal ancestor, or a son, stepson, daughter, stepdaughter or remoter issue, or a brother or sister, of B;

(b) A is a partner of B in a partnership or limited liability partnership;

(c) A is a corporation of which B is an officer;

(d) B is a corporation of which A is an officer;

(e) A and B are officers of the same corporation;

(f) A is an employee of B;

(g) B is an employee of A;

(h) A and B are employees of the same employer;

(*i*) *A* is the trustee of a discretionary trust where *B* (or another person who is an associate of *B* by virtue of any paragraph (except this paragraph and paragraphs (*j*) and (*r*)) of this subsection benefits, or is capable (whether by exercise of a power of appointment or otherwise) of benefitting, under the trust, either directly or through interposed entities or trusts;

(*j*) *B* is the trustee of a discretionary trust where *A* (or another person who is an associate of *A* by virtue of any paragraph (except this paragraph and paragraphs (*i*) and (*r*)) of this subsection benefits, or is capable (whether by exercise of a power of appointment or otherwise) of benefitting, under the trust, either directly or through interposed entities or trusts;

(*k*) *A* is a corporation whose directors are accustomed or under an obligation, whether formal or informal, to act in accordance with the directions, instructions or wishes of *B* or, where *B* is a corporation, of the directors of *B*;

(*l*) *B* is a corporation whose directors are accustomed or under an obligation, whether formal or informal, to act in accordance with the directions, instructions or wishes of *A* or, where *A* is a corporation, of the directors of *A*;

(*m*) *A* is a person who is accustomed or under an obligation, whether formal or informal, to act in accordance with the directions, instructions or wishes of *B* or, where *B* is a corporation, of the directors of *B*;

(*n*) *B* is a person who is accustomed or under an obligation, whether formal or informal, to act in accordance with the directions, instructions or wishes of *A* or, where *A* is a corporation, of the directors of *A*;

(*o*) *A* is a related corporation of *B*;

(*p*) *A* is a corporation in which *B*, alone or together with other associates of *B* as described in paragraphs (*b*) to (*o*), is in a position to control not less than 20% of the voting power in *A*;

Informal Consolidation – version in force from 1/4/2018

(q) *B* is a corporation in which *A*, alone or together with other associates of *A* as described in paragraphs (*b*) to (*o*), is in a position to control not less than 20% of the voting power in *B*; or

(r) *A* is a person with whom *B* enters, or proposes to enter, into an agreement or arrangement (whether oral or in writing and whether express or implied) that relates to any of the following matters:

   (i) *A* and *B* being in a position, by acting together, to control any of the voting power in a designated public licensee, designated business trust or designated equity interest holder;

   (ii) *A* and *B* acting together with respect to the acquisition, holding or disposal of equity interests or other interests in a designated public licensee, designated business trust or designated equity interest holder;

   (iii) the power of *A* and *B*, by acting together, to appoint or remove a director of a designated public licensee or designated equity interest holder, or a director of the trustee-manager of a designated business trust;

   (iv) the situation where one or more of the directors of —

   (A) a designated public licensee or designated equity interest holder; or

   (B) the trustee-manager of a designated business trust,

   are accustomed or under an obligation (whether formal or informal) to act in accordance with the directions, instructions or wishes of *A* and *B* acting together.

(2) A corporation (*A*) and another corporation (*B*) are deemed to be related to each other for the purposes of this section where *A* is —

   (a) the holding company of *B*;

   (b) a subsidiary of *B*; or

(c) a subsidiary of the holding company of B.

(3) For the purposes of subsection (2), a corporation (A) is, subject to subsection (5), deemed to be a subsidiary of another corporation (B) if —

    (a) B controls the composition of the board of directors of A;

    (b) B controls more than half of the voting power of A; or

    (c) A is a subsidiary of any corporation which is B's subsidiary.

(4) For the purposes of subsection (3), the composition of A's board of directors is deemed to be controlled by B if B, by the exercise of some power exercisable by it without the consent or concurrence of any other person, can appoint or remove all or a majority of the directors, and for the purposes of this provision, B is deemed to have power to make such an appointment if —

    (a) a person cannot be appointed as a director without the exercise in the person's favour by B of such a power; or

    (b) a person's appointment as a director follows necessarily from that person being a director or other officer of B.

(5) In determining whether one corporation (A) is the subsidiary of another corporation (B) —

    (a) any shares held or power exercisable by B in a fiduciary capacity is treated as not held or exercisable by B;

    (b) subject to paragraphs (c) and (d), any shares or power exercisable —

        (i) by any person as a nominee for B (except where B is concerned only in a fiduciary capacity); or

        (ii) by, or by a nominee for, a subsidiary of B, not being a subsidiary which is concerned only in a fiduciary capacity,

    is to be treated as being held or exercisable by B;

    (c) any shares held or exercisable by any person by virtue of the provisions of any debentures of A, or of a trust deed for securing any issue of such debentures, are to be disregarded; and

(d) any shares held or exercisable by, or by a nominee for, B or its subsidiary (not being held or exercisable as mentioned in paragraph (c)) is to be treated as not held or exercisable by B if the ordinary business of B or its subsidiary, as the case may be, includes the lending of money and the shares are so held or power is so exercisable by way of security only for the purposes of a transaction entered into in the ordinary course of that business.

(6) A reference in this section to the holding company of a corporation is to be read as a reference to a corporation of which the last mentioned corporation is a subsidiary.

(7) For the purposes of this section, the Depository is not to be regarded as a holding company of a corporation by reason only of the shares it holds in that corporation as a bare trustee.

(8) The Authority may, with the approval of the Minister, make regulations prescribing that any person or class of persons are not associates of another person for the purposes of any provision of this Part.

(9) In this section, "officer", in relation to a corporation, means a director or secretary of, or any person employed in an executive capacity by, the corporation.

[Act 40 of 2017 wef 15/01/2018]

Designation of public licensees, business trusts and equity interest holders

86D. The Authority may, after consultation with the Minister, by notification in the *Gazette* —

(a) designate a public licensee as a designated public licensee;

(b) designate, as a designated business trust, a business trust that is established wholly or partly in respect of a business operated or managed by a trustee-manager licensed under section 81 to provide any marine service or facility or any port service or facility in or through that business; or (*c*) designate a person who holds any equity interest in a designated public licensee or designated business trust as a designated equity interest holder,

if the Authority considers that such designation is necessary in the public interest.

[Act 40 of 2017 wef 15/01/2018]

Notice to Authority by 5% controller

86E.—(1) If a person becomes a 5% controller of a designated public licensee, designated business trust or designated equity interest holder as a result of an increase in the holding of equity interest, or in the voting power controlled, by that person or any associate of that person, that person must within 7 days after becoming the 5% controller give notice in writing to the Authority of that fact.

(2) Any person who contravenes subsection (1) shall be guilty of an offence.

(3) In any proceedings for an offence in relation to a contravention of subsection (1), it is a defence for the accused to prove that the accused —

(*a*) was not aware of the contravention when it occurred; and

(*b*) notified the Authority of the contravention within a period of 14 days after becoming aware of the contravention.

(4) In any proceedings for an offence in relation to a contravention of subsection (1), it is also a defence for the accused to prove that, though the accused was aware of the contravention —

(*a*) the contravention occurred as a result of an increase in the holding of equity interest, or in the voting power controlled, by any of the associates of the accused, in the designated public licensee, designated business trust or designated equity interest holder, as the case may be;

(*b*) the accused has no agreement or arrangement (whether oral or in writing and whether express or implied) with that associate with respect to the acquisition, holding or disposal of equity interests or other interests, or under which they act together in exercising their voting power, in relation to the designated public licensee, designated business trust or designated equity interest holder, as the case may be; and

(c) the accused notified the Authority of the contravention within a period of 7 days after the contravention of subsection (1).

(5) Except as provided in subsections (3) and (4), it is not a defence in any proceedings for an offence in relation to a contravention of subsection (1) to prove that the accused did not intend to or did not knowingly contravene subsection (1).

[Act 40 of 2017 wef 15/01/2018]

Approvals of Authority in relation to equity interests and control of voting power in certain cases

86F.—(1) Except with the prior written approval of the Authority, a person must not —

(a) as a result of an increase in the holding of equity interest, or in the voting power controlled, by that person or any associate of that person, become a 25% controller or 50% controller of a designated public licensee, designated business trust or designated equity interest holder; or

(b) as a result of a decrease in the holding of equity interest, or in the voting power controlled, by that person or any associate of that person, cease to be a 50% controller or 75% controller of a designated public licensee, designated business trust or designated equity interest holder.

(2) Subsection (1) does not apply where the transaction through which a person becomes a 25% controller or 50% controller, or ceases to be a 50% controller or 75% controller, is entered into before the relevant date.

(3) A person must not become an indirect controller of a designated public licensee, designated business trust or designated equity interest holder on or after the relevant date, unless the person has obtained the prior written approval of the Authority.

(4) The Authority may approve an application under subsection (1)(*a*) or (3) if the Authority is satisfied —

(*a*) that the person who is to become a 25% controller or 50% controller or an indirect controller of a designated public licensee, designated business trust or designated equity interest holder, as the case may be, and every associate of that person, is a fit and proper person;

(*b*) that having regard to the influence of —

(i) the person mentioned in paragraph (*a*); and

(ii) every associate of that person,

the designated public licensee, designated business trust or the designated equity interest holder, as the case may be, will continue to conduct its business prudently and comply with the provisions of this Act; and

(*c*) that it is in the public interest to do so.

(5) The Authority may approve an application under subsection (1)(*b*) if the Authority is satisfied that —

(*a*) the provision of any marine service or facility or any port service or facility by —

(i) the designated public licensee of which the applicant is a 50% controller or 75% controller;

(ii) the trustee-manager of the designated business trust of which the applicant is a 50% controller or 75% controller; or

(iii) in the case where the applicant is a 50% controller or 75% controller of a designated equity interest holder, the designated public licensee or the trustee-manager of the designated business trust, in relation to which the designated equity interest holder is so designated,

as the case may be, will continue to be reliable, efficient and economical with reference to recognised international standards and any codes or standards issued or set by the Authority;

(b) the designated public licensee mentioned in paragraph (*a*)(i) or (iii) will continue to conduct its business prudently and comply with the provisions of this Act, or the trustee-manager mentioned in paragraph (*a*)(ii) or (iii) will continue to conduct the business of the designated business trust prudently and comply with the provisions of this Act; and

(c) it is in the public interest to do so.

(6) An approval of the Authority under this section may be granted subject to such conditions as the Authority considers appropriate to impose.

(7) Any condition imposed by the Authority under subsection (6) has effect despite the provisions of any other written law or anything contained in the memorandum or articles of association, trust deed or other constitution of the designated public licensee, designated business trust or designated equity interest holder in relation to which the application for approval under subsection (1) or (3) is made.

(8) Any person who is aggrieved by the refusal of the Authority to grant an approval required under subsection (1) or (3), or by the imposition under subsection (6) of any condition, may within 14 days after being informed of the refusal or the imposition of the condition, as the case may be, appeal to the Minister whose decision is final.

(9) Any person who contravenes subsection (1) or (3) shall be guilty of an offence.

(10) In any proceedings for an offence in relation to a contravention of subsection (1), it is a defence for the accused to prove that —

(a) the accused was not aware of the contravention when it occurred;

(b) the accused notified the Authority of the contravention within a period of 14 days after becoming aware of the contravention; and

(c) where the Authority issued any direction under section 86G relating to the contravention and the holding of equity interests or the control of voting power by the accused in the designated public licensee, designated business trust or designated equity interest holder, as the case may be —

 (i) the accused complied with the direction within the period determined by the Authority under that section; or

 (ii) the period determined by the Authority under that section for the compliance of the direction has not expired.

(11) In any proceedings for an offence in relation to a contravention of subsection (1), it is also a defence for the accused to prove that even though the accused was aware of the contravention —

 (*a*) the contravention occurred as a result of an increase or decrease in the holding of equity interest, or in the voting power controlled, by any of the associates of the accused, in the designated public licensee, designated business trust or designated equity interest holder, as the case may be;

 (*b*) the accused has no agreement or arrangement (whether oral or in writing and whether express or implied) with that associate with respect to the acquisition, holding or disposal of equity interests or other interests, or under which they act together in exercising their voting power, in relation to the designated public licensee, designated business trust or designated equity interest holder, as the case may be;

 (*c*) the accused notified the Authority of the contravention within a period of 7 days after the contravention; and

 (*d*) where the Authority issued any direction under section 86G relating to the contravention and the holding of equity interests or the control of voting power by the accused in the designated public licensee, designated business trust or designated equity interest holder, as the case may be —

(i) the accused complied with the direction within the period determined by the Authority under that section; or

(ii) the period determined by the Authority under that section for the compliance of the direction has not expired.

(12) In any proceedings for an offence in relation to a contravention of subsection (3), it is a defence for the accused to prove that —

(*a*) the accused was not aware of the contravention when it occurred;

(*b*) the accused notified the Authority of the contravention within a period of 14 days after the contravention; and

(*c*) where the Authority issued any direction under section 86G relating to the contravention and the accused becoming an indirect controller of the designated public licensee, designated business trust or designated equity interest holder, as the case may be —

(i) the accused complied with the direction within the period determined by the Authority under that section; or

(ii) the period determined by the Authority under that section for the compliance of the direction has not expired.

(13) Except as provided in subsections (10), (11) and (12), it is not a defence in any proceedings for an offence in relation to a contravention of subsection (1) or (3) to prove that the accused did not intend to or did not knowingly contravene subsection (1) or (3), as the case may be.

(14) In subsections (2) and (3), "relevant date" means the 14th day after the date of commencement of section 8 of the Maritime and Port Authority of Singapore (Amendment) Act 2017.

[Act 40 of 2017 wef 15/01/2018]

Remedial directions

86G.—(1) Subsection (2), (3) or (4) applies if the Authority is satisfied that —

(*a*) the person mentioned in that subsection has contravened section 86F(1) or (3) (called in this section a defaulter);

(*b*) any condition of approval imposed on the defaulter under section 86F(6) has not been complied with; or

(*c*) the defaulter has furnished false or misleading information or documents in connection with an application for approval under section 86F(1) or (3).

(2) Where a defaulter is a 25% controller or 50% controller of a designated public licensee, designated business trust or designated equity interest holder, the Authority may do any one or more of the following:

(*a*) direct the defaulter to take such steps as are necessary, within such period as may be specified by the Authority, to cease to be a 25% controller or 50% controller, as the case may be, of the designated public licensee, designated business trust or designated equity interest holder, as the case may be;

(*b*) direct the transfer or disposal of all or any of the equity interest in the designated public licensee, designated business trust or designated equity interest holder, as the case may be, held by the defaulter or any of the defaulter's associates (called in this section and section 86H the specified equity interest), within such time and subject to such conditions as the Authority considers appropriate;

(*c*) restrict the transfer or disposal of all or any of the specified equity interest, subject to such conditions as the Authority considers appropriate;

(*d*) make such other direction as the Authority considers appropriate.

(3) Where, as a result of a person (called in this subsection the transferee) acquiring any equity interest from a defaulter who is a

50% controller or 75% controller of a designated public licensee, designated business trust or designated equity interest holder (called in this section and section 86H the specified acquired equity interest), the defaulter ceases to be a 50% controller or 75% controller, as the case may be, the Authority may do any one or more of the following:

(*a*) direct the transferee to take such steps as are necessary, within such period as may be specified by the Authority, to cease to hold all or any of the specified acquired equity interest;

(*b*) direct the defaulter to take such steps as are necessary within such period as may be specified by the Authority, to resume being a 50% controller or 75% controller, as the case may be;

(*c*) direct the acquisition, transfer or disposal of all or any of the specified acquired equity interest within such time and subject to such conditions as the Authority considers appropriate;

(*d*) restrict the transfer or disposal of all or any of the specified acquired equity interest, subject to such conditions as the Authority considers appropriate;

(*e*) make such other direction as the Authority considers appropriate.

(4) Where a defaulter is an indirect controller of a designated public licensee, designated business trust or designated equity interest holder, the Authority may do one or both of the following:

(*a*) direct the defaulter, or direct the designated public licensee, the trustee-manager of the designated business trust, or the designated equity interest holder, as the case may be, to take such steps as are necessary, within such period as may be specified by the Authority, to cease to be such an indirect controller or to cause the defaulter to cease to be such an indirect controller;

(*b*) make such other direction as the Authority considers appropriate.

(5) Before issuing any direction to a person under subsection (2), (3) or (4), the Authority must —

(a) unless the Authority decides that it is not practicable or desirable to do so, give the person written notice of the Authority's intention to issue the direction and to specify a date by which the person may make written representations with regard to the direction; and

(b) consider every written representation from the person received on or before the specified date mentioned in paragraph (a).

(6) The Authority may, at any time, revoke, vary or discharge any direction given by it under subsection (2), (3) or (4) or suspend the operation of any such direction.

(7) Any person who is aggrieved by the Authority's decision to issue a direction under subsection (2), (3) or (4) or to vary a direction under subsection (6) may, within 14 days after being informed of the decision, appeal to the Minister whose decision is final.

(8) Despite the fact that any appeal under subsection (7) is pending, any direction issued by the Authority under subsection (2), (3) or (4) and any variation of a direction under subsection (6), takes effect from the date specified by the Authority, unless the Minister otherwise directs.

(9) Any person who fails to comply with a direction issued by the Authority under subsection (2), (3) or (4) (including a direction that is varied under subsection (6)) within the period specified by the Authority, shall be guilty of an offence.

[Act 40 of 2017 wef 15/01/2018]

Effect of remedial directions, etc.

86H.—(1) Any direction issued to a person, and any condition imposed, under section 86G(2) or (3) takes effect, despite —

(a) the Business Trusts Act (Cap. 31A), the Companies Act (Cap. 50) and the Limited Liability Partnerships Act (Cap. 163A);

(b) anything in any listing rules as defined in section 2(1) of the Securities and Futures Act (Cap. 289); and

(c) the provisions of the memorandum or articles of association, trust deed or other constitution of the designated public licensee, designated business trust or designated equity interest holder in question.

(2) Without affecting subsection (1), where any direction is issued under section 86G(2) or (3), then, until the direction is carried out or is suspended or revoked —

(a) the voting rights in respect of the specified equity interest or specified acquired equity interest that is subject to the direction, are not exercisable unless the Authority expressly permits such rights to be exercised;

(b) the voting power that the person to whom the direction is issued controls, whether alone or together with that person's associates, in the designated public licensee, designated business trust or designated equity interest holder, as the case may be, is not exercisable unless the Authority expressly permits such power to be exercised;

(c) no equity interest in the designated public licensee, designated business trust or designated equity interest holder is to be issued or offered (whether by way of dividends or otherwise) in respect of the specified equity interest or specified acquired equity interest that is subject to the direction, unless the Authority expressly permits such issue or offer; and

(d) no amount may be paid (whether by way of profits, income or otherwise) in respect of the specified equity interest or specified acquired equity interest that is subject to the direction, unless the Authority expressly authorises such payment.

(3) Subsection (2)(d) does not apply in the event of a winding up of the designated public licensee, designated business trust or designated equity interest holder, as the case may be.

[Act 40 of 2017 wef 15/01/2018]

Penalties under this Part

86I. A person guilty of an offence under this Part shall be liable on conviction —

>   (*a*) in the case of an individual, to a fine not exceeding $500,000 or to imprisonment for a term not exceeding 3 years or to both and, in the case of a continuing offence, to a further fine not exceeding $50,000 for every day or part of a day during which the offence continues after conviction; or

>   (*b*) in any other case, to a fine not exceeding $1 million and, in the case of a continuing offence, to a further fine not exceeding $100,000 for every day or part of a day during which the offence continues after conviction.

[*Act 40 of 2017 wef 15/01/2018*]

PART XIII

CONTROL OF RELEVANT PUBLIC LICENSEES

Meaning and effect of special administration order

87.—(1) A special administration order is an order of the Minister made in accordance with section 88 in relation to a company which is a relevant public licensee and directing that, during the period for which the order is in force, the affairs, business and property of the company shall be managed by the Authority —

>   (*a*) for the achievement of all or any of the purposes of such an order; and

>   (*b*) in a manner which protects the respective interests of the members, creditors and customers of the company.

(2) The purposes of a special administration order made in relation to any company shall be —

>   (*a*) the security and reliability of the supply of port services and facilities relating to container terminal services and facilities to the public;

(b) the survival of the company, or the whole or part of its undertaking as a going concern;

(c) the transfer to another company, or (as respects different parts of the area to which the company's public licence relates, or different parts of its undertaking) to 2 or more different companies, as a going concern, of so much of the company's undertaking as it is necessary to transfer in order to ensure that the functions which have been vested in the company by virtue of its public licence may be properly carried out; and

(d) the carrying out of those functions pending the making of the transfer and the vesting of those functions in the other company or companies (whether by virtue of the transfer or of an authorisation or variation which replaces the former company as public licensee).

(3) The Minister may make regulations for giving effect to this Part, including making provision for applying, omitting or modifying provisions of Part VIIIA of the Companies Act (Cap. 50) where a special administration order is made.

(4) For the purposes of this Part, "relevant public licensee" means any public licensee authorised to provide any port service or facility relating to container terminal service or facility.

Special administration order made on application by Authority

88.—(1) If, on an application made to the Minister by the Authority, the Minister is satisfied in relation to any company which is a relevant public licensee that any one or more of the grounds specified in subsection (2) is satisfied in relation to that company, the Minister may make any one or more of the following orders:

(a) a special administration order in relation to that company;

(b) an order requiring the company forthwith to take any action or to do or not to do any act or thing in relation to its business as the Minister may consider necessary;

(c) an order appointing a person to advise the company in the proper conduct of its business.

(2) The grounds mentioned in subsection (1) are, in relation to any company —

(a) that the company is or is likely to be unable to pay its debts;

(b) that the Minister considers it in the interest of the security and reliability of the provision of port services and facilities relating to container terminal services and facilities to the public; or

(c) that the Minister otherwise considers it in the public interest.

(3) Notice of any application under subsection (1) shall be given forthwith by the Authority to such persons and in such manner as may be prescribed.

(4) Where a company is a relevant public licensee —

(a) the company shall not be wound up voluntarily without the consent of the Authority;

(b) no judicial management order under Part VIIIA of the Companies Act (Cap. 50) shall be made in relation to the company; and

(c) no step shall be taken by any person to enforce any security over the company's property except where that person has served 14 days' notice of his intention to take that step on the Authority.

(5) The Authority shall be a party to any proceedings under the Companies Act relating to the winding up of the affairs of a company which is a relevant public licensee.

(6) Any decision of the Minister under subsection (1) shall be final.

(7) For the purposes of this section, a company is unable to pay its debts if it is a company which is deemed to be so unable under section 254(2) of the Companies Act (Cap. 50).

Remuneration and expenses of Authority and others

89.—(1) The Authority may at any time (whether or not the appointment of the person has terminated) fix the remuneration and expenses to be paid by a company which is a public licensee to any person appointed by the Minister under section 88(1)(*c*) to advise the company in the proper conduct of its business.

(2) Where a special administration order has been made under section 88(1)(*a*) in relation to a company which is a relevant public licensee, the Authority may, at any time, whether or not the order is still in force, fix the remuneration and expenses to be paid by the company to the Authority.

PART XIV
LIABILITY OF AUTHORITY

Exclusion of liability of Authority

90. Notwithstanding the grant of any public licence, the Authority shall not be liable in any circumstances for any injury, loss, damage or cost sustained by any person as a result of any default, negligence, breach or other wrongful act or omission of any public licensee or any agent or employee of the licensee.

Limitation of Authority's liability for loss or damage to or on board any vessel

91.—(1) The Authority shall not, where, without its actual fault or privity, any loss, damage or destruction is caused to any vessel or to any goods or other thing whatsoever on board any vessel, be liable to damages beyond an aggregate amount not exceeding in the currency of Singapore the equivalent of 1,000 gold francs for each ton of the vessel's tonnage.

(2) For the purposes of this section —

(*a*) the amount to be taken in the currency of Singapore as equivalent to 1,000 gold francs shall be as published in the *Gazette* under section 136(3) of the Merchant Shipping Act (Cap. 179); and

(b) the tonnage of any vessel shall be ascertained as provided by section 136(2) of that Act, and the register of any vessel shall be sufficient evidence that the gross tonnage and the deduction therefrom and the registered tonnage are as therein stated.

(3) This section shall be without prejudice to any limitation of liability for loss or damage which may be available to the Authority under section 136 of the Merchant Shipping Act (Cap. 179).

PART XV

OFFENCES

Damage to property of Authority

92.—(1) If any person wilfully removes, destroys or damages any property belonging to or in the custody or possession of the Authority or hinders or prevents such property from being used or hinders or prevents such property from being used or operated in the manner in which it is intended to be used or operated, he shall be guilty of an offence and shall be liable on conviction to a fine not exceeding $10,000 and shall make good any loss, destruction or damage suffered by the Authority, including the expenses of any inspection or survey carried out by the Authority to ascertain such loss, destruction or damage.

(2) Any person may apprehend any other person if such other person within his view commits an offence against this section and shall on such apprehension, without unreasonable delay, hand the person so apprehended over to a police officer.

Unlawful operation of marine or port services or facilities

93. Any person who establishes, installs, maintains, provides or operates any marine service or facility or any port service or facility without a public licence shall be guilty of an offence and shall be liable on conviction to a fine not exceeding $10,000 or to imprisonment for a term not exceeding 3 years or to both and, in the case of a continuing offence, to a further fine not exceeding

$1,000 for every day or part thereof during which the offence continues after conviction.

Evasion of dues

94.—(1) Any owner, agent or master of any vessel who, by any means whatsoever, evades or attempts to evade any port dues, goods dues or pilotage dues payable under this Act shall be guilty of an offence and shall be liable on conviction to a fine not exceeding $10,000 or to imprisonment for a term not exceeding 6 months or to both, and shall in addition be liable to pay to the Authority as penalty double the amount of the dues he evaded or attempted to evade.

(2) The tender to or acceptance by the Authority or any of its officers of any dues, the payment of which has been previously evaded shall not release or discharge any person from any liability for any damages or penalty consequent upon such evasion.

Penalty for giving false information as to draught of vessel, etc.

95.—(1) Any owner, agent or master of a vessel entering or leaving or within the port or the approaches thereto who makes any negligent mis-statement or gives false information of the type of vessel, its draught, length, beam or height to the Authority shall be guilty of an offence and shall be liable on conviction to a fine not exceeding $20,000 or to imprisonment for a term not exceeding 6 months or to both.

(2) For the purposes of this section, "height of vessel" shall be the height of the vessel measured vertically from the waterline of the vessel to the highest point of the vessel including its cargo, structure or equipment on board.

Offences in connection with safety of vessels, etc.

96. Any person who —

  (*a*) wilfully and without lawful excuse loosens or removes from its moorings or from its fastenings alongside any wharf or dock, any vessel in the port without leave or authority from the master or owner of such vessel or person in charge of such wharf or dock;

(b) wilfully and without lawful excuse lifts, injures, makes a vessel fast to, loosens or sets adrift any moorings, buoys, beacons or sea or land marks;

(c) without any lawful excuse discharges any gun in the port except for the purpose of making a signal of distress or for such other purpose as is allowed under any written law;

(d) graves, breams or smokes any vessel in the port, or boils or heats any pitch, tar, resin, dammar, turpentine oil or other such combustible matter on board any vessel within the port, at any time or within any limits at or within which such act is prohibited by any order of the Minister, or contrary to the orders or directions of the Port Master or the master of such vessel;

(e) does or omits any act on board any vessel in the port which has caused or may cause fire on board such vessel; or

(f) uses a vessel or permits a vessel to be used in the port —

    (i) when such vessel is in such a state that by reason of the defective condition of its hull, equipment or machinery, or by reason of under-manning or otherwise, the life of any person is likely to be endangered;

    (ii) when such vessel is loaded with goods or passengers or with both goods and passengers as to —

        (A) exceed the number of passengers allowed by the vessel's safety certificate to be carried or received on the vessel; and

        (B) submerge the appropriate subdivision load line on each side of the vessel when the vessel has no list, that is to say, the subdivision load line appropriate to the space for the time being allotted to passengers on the vessel, is lower than the load line indicating the maximum depth to which the vessel is for the time being entitled under any written law to be loaded when the vessel has no list;

(iii) in contravention of the regulations thereby endangering the life of any person,

shall be guilty of an offence and shall be liable on conviction to a fine not exceeding $10,000 or to imprisonment for a term not exceeding 6 months or to both.

Penalty for obstructing Authority in performance of duties

97. Any person who at any time hinders, obstructs or molests the Authority or any of its employees, agents or contractors in the performance and execution of their duty or of anything which they are respectively empowered or required to do so by virtue or in consequence of this Act, or removes any mark set up for the purpose of indicating any level or direction necessary to the execution of works authorised by this Act, shall be guilty of an offence and shall be liable on conviction to a fine not exceeding $5,000 or to imprisonment for a term not exceeding 6 months or to both.

Preservation of secrecy

98.—(1) Except for the purpose of the performance of his duties or the exercise of his functions or when lawfully required to do so by any court or where required or allowed by the provisions of any written law, no person who is or has been a member, an officer, an employee, an adviser or an agent of the Authority or a member of a committee of the Authority shall disclose any information relating to the affairs of the Authority or of any other person which has been obtained by him in the performance of his duties or the exercise of his functions.

[Act 5 of 2018 wef 01/04/2018]

(2) Any person who contravenes subsection (1) shall be guilty of an offence and shall be liable on conviction to a fine not exceeding $2,000 or to imprisonment for a term not exceeding 6 months or to both.

General penalties

99. Any person guilty of an offence under this Act or the regulations for which no penalty is expressly provided shall, in addition to the forfeiture of any article seized, be liable on conviction to a fine not exceeding $5,000 or to imprisonment for a term not exceeding 6 months or to both.

Offences by bodies of persons

100. Where an offence under this Act or the regulations has been committed by a company, firm, society or other body of persons, any person who at the time of the commission of the offence was a director, manager, secretary or other similar officer or a partner of the company, firm, society or other body of persons or was purporting to act in such capacity shall be guilty of that offence and shall be liable to be proceeded against and punished accordingly unless he proves that the offence was committed without his consent, connivance or privity and that he exercised all such diligence to prevent the commission of the offence as he ought to have exercised, having regard to the nature of his functions in that capacity and to all the circumstances.

Jurisdiction of Courts

101. A Magistrate's Court or a District Court shall have jurisdiction to hear and determine all offences under this Act or the regulations and, notwithstanding anything to the contrary in the Criminal Procedure Code (Cap. 68), shall have power to impose the full penalty or punishment in respect of any offence under this Act or the regulations.

Composition of offences

102.—(1) Any police officer not below the rank of sergeant specially authorised by name in that behalf by the Minister, or any employee of the Authority specially authorised by name in that behalf by the Chief Executive, may in his discretion compound any such offence under this Act or the regulations as may be prescribed as being an offence which may be compounded by collecting from the person reasonably suspected of having committed the offence a sum not exceeding $500.

(2) The Authority may, with the approval of the Minister, make regulations prescribing the offences which may be compounded.

Fines to be paid to Authority

103. All fines imposed for any offence under this Act or the regulations and all sums collected under section 102 shall be paid into the Consolidated Fund.

[Act 40 of 2017 wef 15/01/2018]

Presumption of jurisdiction

104. If, in any legal proceedings under this Act or the regulations, a question arises as to whether or not any vessel or person is within the provisions of this Act or the regulations or some part thereof, the vessel or person shall be taken to be within those provisions unless the contrary is proved.

Service of documents

105.—(1) Unless otherwise expressly provided in this Act, any notice, order or document required or authorised by this Act or the regulations to be given or served on any person, and any summons issued by a court in connection with any offence under this Act or the regulations may be served on the person concerned —

  (*a*) by delivering it to the person or to some adult member or employee of his family at his last known place of residence;

  (*b*) by leaving it at his usual or last known place of residence or business in a cover addressed to him;

  (*c*) by affixing it to some conspicuous part of his last known place of residence;

  (*d*) by sending it by registered post addressed to the person at his usual or last known place of residence or business; or

  (*e*) where the person is a body corporate —

    (i) by delivering it to the secretary or other like officer of the body corporate at its registered or principal office; or

    (ii) by sending it by registered post addressed to the body corporate at its registered or principal office.

(2) Any notice, order, document or summons sent by registered post to any person in accordance with subsection (1) shall be deemed to be duly served on the person to whom the letter is addressed at the time when the letter would, in the ordinary course of post, be delivered and in proving service of the same it shall be sufficient to prove that the envelope containing the notice, order, document or summons was properly addressed, stamped and posted by registered post.

Saving of prosecutions under other laws

106. Nothing in this Act shall prevent any person from being prosecuted under any other written law for any act or omission which constitutes an offence under this Act or the regulations, or from being liable under that other written law to any punishment or penalty higher or other than that provided by this Act or the regulations, but no person shall be punished twice for the same offence.

PART XVI
MISCELLANEOUS PROVISIONS

Master, owner or person in charge of vessel answerable for damage

107.—(1) Where damage is done to any property of the Authority by any vessel or float of timber, the cost of making good the damage, including the expenses of any inspection or survey carried out by the Authority to ascertain such damage, may be recovered by the Authority as a debt from the master, owner or person in charge of the vessel or float of timber, as the case may be.

(2) The Authority may detain any such vessel or float of timber until the costs of making good such damage and the expenses described in subsection (1) have been paid to the Authority or may require the master, owner or person in charge of the vessel or float of timber to deposit such sum of money or furnish such security as may be required by the Authority in order to meet such costs and expenses.

Maritime and Port Authority of Singapore   CAP. 170A

Exemption from distress and attachment of property of Authority

108. When any apparatus, fixture or fitting belonging to the Authority is placed in or upon any premises not being in the possession of the Authority for the purposes of carrying out the functions of the Authority, such apparatus, fixture or fitting shall not be subject to distress nor be taken in execution under process of any court or any proceedings in bankruptcy against the person in whose possession it is.

Authority to provide free landing places

109. The Authority shall provide such number of public landing places as it may, from time to time, consider necessary or expedient for use by the public.

Restrictions on erection of wharves, docks, etc.

110.—(1) Notwithstanding the provisions of the Foreshores Act (Cap. 113), no plan and specification for —

(*a*) the erection, within the port or the approaches to the port, of a new wharf or dock or for the re-erection, extension or alteration of the same; or

(*b*) the erection of any sea-wall or any revetment along the bank of the port or for the re-erection, extension or alteration of the same,

shall be approved under that Act without previous reference to, and the concurrence of, the Authority.

(2) The Authority may determine the fee to be paid for the perusal of the plans and specifications.

(3) Where the Authority omits or refuses to give its concurrence to the plans and specifications referred to in subsection (1), the Building Authority appointed under section 3 of the Building Control Act (Cap. 29) may refer the matter to the Minister whose decision shall be final.

Notices, orders, receipts, etc., may be given by authorised officer

111.—(1) All notices, orders, receipts and other documents and all information of whatsoever nature which the Authority is empowered to give by this Act or the regulations or by any other written law may be given by any means including electronic and mechanical means and by any employee authorised thereunto by the Authority.

(2) Where any such notice, order, receipt, document or information requires authentication, the signature or a facsimile thereof of the Chief Executive or any employee authorised thereunto by the Authority affixed thereto shall be sufficient authentication.

Vessel guidance, assistance or direction

112. Where the Authority provides any service for the guidance, assistance or direction of any vessel, neither the Authority nor any of its employees or agents shall be liable for any loss or damage suffered by any person of whatsoever nature or howsoever caused —

   (*a*) by reason of any act or omission of the Authority, its employees or agents which is made in good faith and in the ordinary course of the discharge of the duties of those employees or agents; or

   (*b*) if the loss or damage occurred or arose as a result of any defect or breakdown in the service of any equipment used for the provision of such service or for the receipt or provision of such information and not as a result of any act or omission of the Authority.

Power to enter upon lands

113.—(1) The Authority may, for the purposes of this Act, by its employees, agents or contractors, enter at all reasonable hours in the daytime into and upon any building or land for the purpose of making any survey or inspection and for the purpose of executing any work authorised by this Act to be executed by them without being liable to any legal proceedings or molestation whatsoever on account of such entry or of anything done in any part of such building or land in pursuance of this Act.

(2) The Authority shall not enter into any dwelling-house in actual occupation, unless with the consent of the occupier thereof and with 6 hours' previous notice to such occupier.

Power to enter upon lands adjacent to works

114.—(1) The Authority may, by its employees, agents or contractors, enter upon any land adjoining to or being within the distance of 90 metres of any works by this Act authorised to be made, for the purpose of depositing upon such land any soil, gravel, sand, lime, brick, stone or other materials or for any other purposes connected with the formation of the works without making any previous payment, tender or deposit.

(2) In exercising the powers conferred under subsection (1) to enter upon any land, the Authority shall —

(*a*) do as little damage to the land as possible; and

(*b*) pay compensation for —

(i) the temporary occupation of, or the temporary damage to, the land as and when such temporary occupation or temporary damage occurs; and

(ii) any permanent injury to the land.

(3) If any dispute arises touching the amount or apportionment of such compensation, the same shall be determined in the manner provided by section 116.

(4) Before the Authority makes any such temporary use under subsection (1) of the land adjoining or lying near to the works, the Authority shall give 7 days' notice in writing of its intention to the owners and the occupiers of such land and shall set apart by sufficient fences so much of the land as is required to be so used from the other land adjoining thereto.

Employee of Authority may require evidence of identity in certain cases

115.—(1) Any police officer or any employee of the Authority who reasonably believes that any person has committed an offence under this Act or the regulations may require such person to furnish evidence of his identity and the person shall thereupon furnish such evidence of his identity as may be required by such police officer or employee of the Authority.

(2) Any person who refuses to furnish any information required of him by any police officer or any employee of the Authority under this section or wilfully mis-states such information shall be guilty of an offence and shall be liable on conviction to a fine not exceeding $1,000.

Compensation, damages and costs to be determined by District Court

116.—(1) Except as otherwise provided in this Act, in all cases where damages, expenses, the cost of making good or other costs are by this Act directed to be paid, the amount and, if necessary, the apportionment of the same and any question of liability shall, in case of dispute, be summarily ascertained and determined by a District Court.

(2) If the amount of damages, expenses, the cost of making good or other costs is not paid by the party liable to pay the same within 7 days after demand, that amount may be reported to the District Court and recovered in the same way as if it were a fine imposed by the District Court.

(3) An appeal shall lie to the High Court from any decision of a District Court under this section, and the provisions of the Criminal Procedure Code (Cap. 68) shall apply, with the necessary modifications, to such appeal.

Disposal of matters and things removed by Authority

117.—(1) Any matter or thing removed by the Authority in executing any work which it is entitled to execute under this Act or the regulations shall, except as otherwise provided, be the property of the Authority and may be sold by public auction or, if the Authority thinks the circumstances of the case require, may be sold otherwise or be disposed of without sale.

(2) The moneys arising from the sale may be retained by the Authority and applied in or towards the expenses incurred and the

surplus, if any, shall be paid on demand to the owner of that matter or thing.

(3) If the surplus is not claimed within one year of the sale, it shall be paid into the funds of the Authority.

(4) If any matters or things belonging to several persons are removed by the Authority in executing any such work, the Authority shall cause those matters or things, if so, to be sold separately.

Exemption by Authority

118.—(1) The Authority may, with the approval of the Minister, exempt any person, vessel, vehicle or premises or any class or description of persons, vessels, vehicles or premises from any of the provisions of this Act or the regulations.

(2) Any exemption granted by the Authority under subsection (1) shall not reduce or in any way affect the responsibility of the person to whom the exemption is granted or of the owner or master of a vessel or of the owner of a vehicle or the premises to whom the exemption is granted and the Authority shall not be liable for any death or injury of any person or for any loss, damage or destruction of any property arising from such exemption.

Regulations

119. The Authority may, with the approval of the Minister, make regulations for carrying out the purposes and provisions of this Act.

Transitional provisions

120.—(1) Any scheme, contract, document, licence, permission or resolution prepared, made, granted or approved under the repealed provisions of the Port of Singapore Authority Act (Cap. 236) or the repealed National Maritime Board Act (Cap. 198, 1985 Ed.) shall, so far as it is not inconsistent with the provisions of this Act and except as otherwise expressly provided in this Act or in any other written law, continue and be deemed to have been prepared, made, granted or approved by the Authority under the corresponding provisions of this Act.

(2) Any subsidiary legislation made under the repealed provisions of the Port of Singapore Authority Act or the repealed National Maritime Board Act and in force immediately before 2nd February 1996 shall, so far as it is not inconsistent with the provisions of this Act, continue in force as if made under this Act until it is revoked or repealed by subsidiary legislation made under this Act.

(3) Any seaman who immediately before 2nd February 1996 was registered under the provisions of the repealed National Maritime Board Act shall be deemed to be registered under this Act.

(4) The Minister may, by order published in the *Gazette*, repeal or amend any written law which appears to him to be unnecessary having regard to the provisions of this Act or to be inconsistent with any provision of this Act.

FIRST SCHEDULE

Section 6

CONSTITUTION AND PROCEEDINGS OF AUTHORITY

Appointment of Chairman and other members

1.—(1) The Chairman and other members of the Authority shall be appointed by the Minister.

(2) The Minister may appoint one of the members to be the Deputy Chairman; and the Deputy Chairman so appointed may, subject to such directions as may be given by the Chairman, exercise all or any of the powers exercisable by the Chairman under this Act.

(3) The Minister may appoint the Chief Executive to be a member of the Authority.

Tenure of office of members

2. A member shall hold office on such terms and conditions and for such period as the Minister may determine, and shall be eligible for reappointment.

Temporary members

3. The Minister may appoint any person to be a temporary member of the Authority during the temporary incapacity from illness or otherwise, or during the temporary absence from Singapore, of any member.

FIRST SCHEDULE — *continued*

Revocation of appointment

4. The Minister may, at any time, revoke the appointment of the Chairman or any member without assigning any reason.

Resignation

5. Any member may resign from his appointment at any time by giving notice in writing to the Minister.

Chairman may delegate functions

6. The Chairman may, by instrument in writing, authorise any member to exercise any power or perform any function conferred on the Chairman by or under this Act.

Vacation of office

7. The office of a member shall become vacant —

   (*a*) on the death of the member;

   (*b*) if the member, without sufficient cause (the sufficiency thereof to be decided by the Authority) fails to attend 3 consecutive meetings of the Authority; or

   (*c*) if the member becomes in any manner disqualified from membership of the Authority.

Filling of vacancies

8. If a member dies, resigns or has his appointment revoked or otherwise vacates his office before the expiry of the term for which he has been appointed, the Minister may appoint a person to fill the vacancy for the residue of the term for which the vacating member was appointed.

Disqualification from membership

9. No person shall be appointed or shall continue to hold office as a member if he —

   (*a*) is an undischarged bankrupt or has made any arrangement with his creditors; or

   (*b*) has been sentenced to imprisonment for a term of 6 months or more and has not received a free pardon.

10. [*Repealed by Act 5 of 2018 wef 01/04/2018*]

Salaries, etc., payable to members

11. There shall be paid to the members out of the funds of the Authority such salaries, fees and allowances as the Minister may from time to time determine.

Meetings

12.—(1) The Authority shall meet for the despatch of business at such times and places as the Chairman may from time to time appoint.

(2) The quorum at every meeting of the Authority shall be one-third of the total number of members or 3 members, whichever is the higher.

[Act 25 of 2009 wef 15/01/2010]

(3) A decision at a meeting of the Authority shall be adopted by a simple majority of the members present and voting except that in the case of an equality of votes the Chairman or member presiding shall have a casting vote in addition to his original vote.

(4) The Chairman or in his absence the Deputy Chairman shall preside at meetings of the Authority.

(5) Where both the Chairman and the Deputy Chairman are absent at a meeting, such member as the Chairman appoints as an acting Chairman shall preside at that meeting.

Vacancies

13. The Authority may act notwithstanding any vacancy in its membership.

Procedure at meetings

14. Subject to the provisions of this Act and the Public Sector (Governance) Act 2018, the Authority may make rules to regulate its own procedure generally and, in particular, regarding the holding and proceedings of meetings, the notice to be given of such meetings, the keeping of minutes and the custody, production and inspection of such minutes.

[Act 5 of 2018 wef 01/04/2018]

Validity of proceedings

15. The validity of any proceedings of the Authority shall not be affected by any defect in the appointment of any member.

[Act 5 of 2018 wef 01/04/2018]

SECOND SCHEDULE

Section 8

POWERS OF AUTHORITY

1. To give directions to any person granted a licence under this Act or the regulations.

2. To lay down standards and codes to be observed by all providers and users of marine and port services and facilities.

3. To levy such charges and fees for the granting of licences, permits, approvals, consents and concurrences and for services and facilities provided by the Authority as may in its opinion be appropriate.

4. To own and operate vessels for the purpose of providing any of the port services and facilities which the Authority is required or empowered to provide.

5. To supply water to vessels.

6. To regulate and control operations to clean up oil spills within the territorial waters of Singapore.

7. To reclaim, excavate, enclose or raise any part of the lands vested in the Authority.

8. To provide and use, within the territorial waters of Singapore or otherwise, vessels and appliances for the purpose of rendering assistance to any vessel, or recovering property lost, sunk or stranded.

9. To provide accommodation and recreational facilities for persons employed by the Authority and members of the mercantile marine as the Authority may consider necessary.

10. To promote the welfare of members of the mercantile marine.

11. To form or participate —

   (*a*) in the formation of any company for the purpose of carrying out all or any of the functions of the Authority;

   (*b*) with the approval of the Minister, in the formation of any company for such other purposes as may be approved by the Minister; and

   (*c*) in any joint venture or partnership.

12. To grant or guarantee loans to officers or employees of the Authority for such purposes specifically approved by the Authority as are likely to increase the efficiency of officers or employees or otherwise for the purpose of the functions of the Authority.

13. To make provision for gratuities, pensions, allowances or other benefits for employees or former employees of the Authority or its predecessors.

SECOND SCHEDULE — *continued*

14. To offer bursaries and scholarships for study at any school or institution of higher learning to members of the public and officers or employees of the Authority and members of their families.

15. To provide financial grant, aid or assistance to any person for all or any of the purposes of this Act.

16. To receive donations and contributions from any source and raise funds by all lawful means.

17. To do anything incidental to any of its functions.

THIRD SCHEDULE

[*Repealed by Act 5 of 2018 wef 01/04/2018*]

Informal Consolidation – version in force from 1/4/2018

LEGISLATIVE HISTORY
MARITIME AND PORT AUTHORITY OF SINGAPORE ACT
(CHAPTER 170A)

This Legislative History is provided for the convenience of users of the Maritime and Port Authority of Singapore Act. It is not part of the Act.

1. Act 7 of 1996 — Maritime and Port Authority of Singapore Act 1996

Date of First Reading	: 5 December 1995 (Bill No. 46/1995 published on 6 December 1995)
Date of Second and Third Readings	: 18 January 1996
Date of commencement	: 2 February 1996

2. 1997 Revised Edition — Maritime and Port Authority of Singapore Act

Date of operation	: 30 May 1997

3. Act 5 of 2002 — Statutory Corporations (Capital Contribution) Act 2002
(Consequential amendments made to Act by)

Date of First Reading	: 3 May 2002 (Bill No. 7/2002 published on 4 May 2002)
Date of Second and Third Readings	: 24 May 2002
Date of commencement	: 15 July 2002 (item (21) of the Schedule)

4. Act 45 of 2004 — Trustees (Amendment) Act 2004
(Consequential amendments made to Act by)

Date of First Reading	: 21 September 2004 (Bill No. 43/2004 published on 22 September 2004)
Date of Second and Third Readings	: 19 October 2004
Date of commencement	: 15 December 2004

5. Act 25 of 2009 — Quorums of Statutory Boards (Miscellaneous Amendments) Act 2009

Date of First Reading	: 14 September 2009 (Bill No. 19/2009 published on 14 September 2009)
Date of Second and Third Readings	: 19 October 2009

Informal Consolidation – version in force from 1/4/2018

ii

Date of commencement	:	15 January 2010

6. Act 11 of 2012 — Energy Conservation Act 2012

Date of First Reading	:	8 March 2012 (Bill No. 8/2012 published on 8 March 2012)
Date of Second and Third Readings	:	9 April 2012
Date of commencement	:	1 July 2012

7. Act 16 of 2016 — Statutes (Miscellaneous Amendments) Act 2016

Date of First Reading	:	14 April 2016 (Bill No. 15/2016 published on 14 April 2016)
Date of Second and Third Readings	:	9 May 2016
Date of commencement	:	10 June 2016

8. Act 40 of 2017 — Maritime and Port Authority of Singapore (Amendment) Act 2017

Date of First Reading	:	11 September 2017 (Bill No. 31/2017 published on 11 September 2017)
Date of Second and Third Readings	:	2 October 2017
Date of commencement	:	15 January 2018

9. Act 5 of 2018 — Public Sector (Governance) Act 2018

Date of First Reading	:	6 November 2017 (Bill No. 45/2017 published on 6 November 2017)
Date of Second and Third Readings	:	8 January 2018
Date of commencement	:	1 April 2018

Informal Consolidation – version in force from 1/4/2018

(二) 附录2：海上货物运输法

THE STATUTES OF THE REPUBLIC OF SINGAPORE

CARRIAGE OF GOODS BY SEA ACT

(CHAPTER 33)

(Original Enactment: Act 30 of 1972)

REVISED EDITION 1998

(30th May 1998)

Prepared and Published by

THE LAW REVISION COMMISSION
UNDER THE AUTHORITY OF
THE REVISED EDITION OF THE LAWS ACT (CHAPTER 275)

Informal Consolidation – version in force from 30/5/1998

CHAPTER 33

1998 Ed.

Carriage of Goods by Sea Act[①]

ARRANGEMENT OF SECTIONS

Section
1. Short title
2. Definition
3. Application of Rules
4. Absolute warranty of seaworthiness not to be implied in contracts to which Rules apply
5. Modification of paragraphs 4 and 5 of Article III of Rules in relation to bulk cargoes
6. Saving and operation of other written law

The Schedule — The Hague Rules as amended by the Brussels Protocol 1968

An Act to make further provision with respect to the carriage of goods by sea.

[16th January 1978]

Short title

1. This Act may be cited as the Carriage of Goods by Sea Act.

Definition

2. In this Act, "Rules" means the International Convention for the unification of certain rules of law relating to bills of lading made at Brussels on 25th August 1924, as amended by the Protocol made at Brussels on 23rd February 1968, and as set out in the Schedule.

Application of Rules

3.—(1) The provisions of the Rules, as set out in the Schedule to this Act, shall have the force of law.

[6/95]

(2) Without prejudice to subsection (1), the provisions of the Rules shall also have effect (and have the force of law) in relation to and in connection with the carriage of goods by sea in ships where the port

---

[①] 本法条引用自 https://sso.agc.gov.sg/Act/CGSA1972。

of shipment is a port in Singapore, whether or not the carriage is between ports in 2 different States within the meaning of Article X of the Rules.

[6/95]

(3) Subject to subsection (4), nothing in this section shall be construed as applying anything in the Rules to any contract for the carriage of goods by sea, unless the contract expressly or by implication provides for the issue of a bill of lading or any similar document of title.

[6/95]

(4) Without prejudice to paragraph (*c*) of Article X of the Rules, the Rules shall have the force of law in relation to —

   (*a*) any bill of lading if the contract contained in or evidenced by it expressly provides that the Rules shall govern the contract; and

   (*b*) any receipt which is a non-negotiable document marked as such if the contract contained in or evidenced by it is a contract for the carriage of goods by sea which expressly provides that the Rules are to govern the contract.

(5) Where subsection (4)(*b*) applies, the Rules shall apply —

   (*a*) as if the receipt referred to therein were a bill of lading; and

   (*b*) subject to any necessary modifications and in particular with the omission of the second sentence of paragraph 4 and of paragraph 7 in Article III of the Rules.

[6/95]

(6) If and so far as the contract contained in or evidenced by a bill of lading or receipt referred to in paragraph (*a*) or (*b*) of subsection (4) applies to deck cargo or live animals, the Rules as given the force of law by that subsection shall have effect as if Article I (*c*) did not exclude deck cargo and live animals.

[6/95]

(7) In subsection (6), "deck cargo" means cargo which by the contract of carriage is stated as being carried on deck and is so carried.

[6/95]

Informal Consolidation – version in force from 30/5/1998

(8) The Minister may, from time to time by order published in the *Gazette*, specify the respective amounts which, for the purposes of paragraph 5 of Article IV and of Article IV bis of the Rules, are to be taken as equivalent to the sums expressed in francs which are mentioned in paragraph 5(*a*) of Article IV.

[6/95]

Absolute warranty of seaworthiness not to be implied in contracts to which Rules apply

4. There shall not be implied in any contract for the carriage of goods by sea to which the Rules apply any absolute undertaking by the carrier of the goods to provide a seaworthy ship.

Modification of paragraphs 4 and 5 of Article III of Rules in relation to bulk cargoes

*5. Where under the custom of any trade the weight of any bulk cargo inserted in the bill of lading is a weight ascertained or accepted by a third party other than the carrier or the shipper and the fact that the weight is so ascertained or accepted is stated in the bill of lading, then, notwithstanding anything in the Rules, the bill of lading shall not be deemed to be prima facie evidence against the carrier of the receipt of goods of the weight so inserted in the bill of lading, and the accuracy thereof at the time of shipment shall not be deemed to have been guaranteed by the shipper.

Saving and operation of other written law

*6. Nothing in this Act shall affect the operation of sections 135 and 136 of the Merchant Shipping Act (Cap. 179) as amended by any subsequent Act, or the operation of any other enactment for the time being in force limiting the liability of the owners of sea-going vessels.

---

*The former sections 5 and 6 were repealed by Act 6/95.

Informal Consolidation – version in force from 30/5/1998

1998 Ed. *Carriage of Goods by Sea* Cap. 33 4

THE SCHEDULE

Sections 2 and 3(1)

THE HAGUE RULES AS AMENDED BY
THE BRUSSELS PROTOCOL 1968

ARTICLE I

In these Rules the following words are employed, with the meanings set out below:

(*a*) "Carrier" includes the owner or the charterer who enters into a contract of carriage with a shipper.

(*b*) "Contract of carriage" applies only to contracts of carriage covered by a bill of lading or any similar document of title, in so far as such document relates to the carriage of goods by sea, including any bill of lading or any similar document as aforesaid issued under or pursuant to a charter party from the moment at which such bill of lading or similar document of title regulates the relations between a carrier and a holder of the same.

(*c*) "Goods" includes goods, wares, merchandise, and articles of every kind whatsoever except live animals and cargo which by the contract of carriage is stated as being carried on deck and is so carried.

(*d*) "Ship" means any vessel used for the carriage of goods by sea.

(*e*) "Carriage of goods" covers the period from the time when the goods are loaded on to the time they are discharged from the ship.

ARTICLE II

Subject to the provisions of Article VI, under every contract of carriage of goods by sea the carrier, in relation to the loading, handling, stowage, carriage, custody, care and discharge of such goods, shall be subject to the responsibilities and liabilities, and entitled to the rights and immunities hereinafter set forth.

ARTICLE III

1. The carrier shall be bound before and at the beginning of the voyage to exercise due diligence to —

(*a*) Make the ship seaworthy.

(*b*) Properly man, equip and supply the ship.

(*c*) Make the holds, refrigerating and cool chambers, and all other parts of the ship in which goods are carried, fit and safe for their reception, carriage and preservation.

Informal Consolidation – version in force from 30/5/1998

THE SCHEDULE — *continued*

2. Subject to the provisions of Article IV, the carrier shall properly and carefully load, handle, stow, carry, keep, care for, and discharge the goods carried.

3. After receiving the goods into his charge the carrier or the master or agent of the carrier shall, on demand of the shipper, issue to the shipper a bill of lading showing among other things —

(*a*) The leading marks necessary for identification of the goods as the same are furnished in writing by the shipper before the loading of such goods starts, provided such marks are stamped or otherwise shown clearly upon the goods if uncovered, or on the cases or coverings in which such goods are contained, in such a manner as should ordinarily remain legible until the end of the voyage.

(*b*) Either the number of packages or pieces, or the quantity, or weight, as the case may be, as furnished in writing by the shipper.

(*c*) The apparent order and condition of the goods.

Provided that no carrier, master or agent of the carrier shall be bound to state or show in the bill of lading any marks, number, quantity, or weight which he has reasonable ground for suspecting not accurately to represent the goods actually received, or which he has had no reasonable means of checking.

4. Such a bill of lading shall be prima facie evidence of the receipt by the carrier of the goods as therein described in accordance with paragraph 3 (*a*), (*b*) and (*c*). However, proof to the contrary shall not be admissible when the bill of lading has been transferred to a third party acting in good faith.

5. The shipper shall be deemed to have guaranteed to the carrier the accuracy at the time of shipment of the marks, number, quantity and weight, as furnished by him, and the shipper shall indemnify the carrier against all loss, damages and expenses arising or resulting from inaccuracies in such particulars. The right of the carrier to such indemnity shall in no way limit his responsibility and liability under the contract of carriage to any person other than the shipper.

6. Unless notice of loss or damage and the general nature of such loss or damage be given in writing to the carrier or his agent at the port of discharge before or at the time of the removal of the goods into the custody of the person entitled to delivery thereof under the contract of carriage, or, if the loss or damage be not apparent, within 3 days, such removal shall be prima facie evidence of the delivery by the carrier of the goods as described in the bill of lading.

The notice in writing need not be given if the state of the goods has, at the time of their receipt, been the subject of joint survey or inspection.

Subject to paragraph 6*bis* the carrier and the ship shall in any event be discharged from all liability whatsoever in respect of the goods, unless suit is brought within

Informal Consolidation – version in force from 30/5/1998

1998 Ed. *Carriage of Goods by Sea* Cap. 33

THE SCHEDULE — *continued*

one year of their delivery or of the date when they should have been delivered. This period may, however, be extended if the parties so agree after the cause of action has risen.

In the case of any actual or apprehended loss or damage the carrier and the receiver shall give all reasonable facilities to each other for inspecting and tallying the goods.

6*bis*. An action for indemnity against a third person may be brought even after the expiration of the year provided for in the preceding paragraph if brought within the time allowed by the law of the Court seized of the case. However, the time allowed shall be not less than 3 months, commencing from the day when the person bringing such action for indemnity has settled the claim or has been served with process in the action against himself.

7. After the goods are loaded the bill of lading to be issued by the carrier, master, or agent of the carrier, to the shipper shall, if the shipper so demands, be a "shipped" bill of lading, provided that if the shipper shall have previously taken up any document of title to such goods, he shall surrender the same as against the issue of the "shipped" bill of lading, but at the option of the carrier such document of title may be noted at the port of shipment by the carrier, master, or agent with the name or names of the ship or ships upon which the goods have been shipped and the date or dates of shipment, and when so noted, if it shows the particulars mentioned in paragraph 3 of Article III, shall for the purpose of this article be deemed to constitute a "shipped" bill of lading.

8. Any clause, covenant, or agreement in a contract of carriage relieving the carrier or the ship from liability for loss or damage to, or in connection with, goods arising from negligence, fault, or failure in the duties and obligations provided in this article or lessening such liability otherwise than as provided in these Rules, shall be null and void and of no effect. A benefit of insurance in favour of the carrier or similar clause shall be deemed to be a clause relieving the carrier from liability.

ARTICLE IV

1. Neither the carrier nor the ship shall be liable for loss or damage arising or resulting from unseaworthiness unless caused by want of due diligence on the part of the carrier to make the ship seaworthy, and to secure that the ship is properly manned, equipped and supplied, and to make the holds, refrigerating and cool chambers and all other parts of the ship in which goods are carried fit and safe for their reception, carriage and preservation in accordance with the provisions of paragraph 1 of Article III. Whenever loss or damage has resulted from unseaworthiness the burden of proving the exercise of due diligence shall be on the carrier or other person claiming exemption under this Article.

Informal Consolidation – version in force from 30/5/1998

THE SCHEDULE — *continued*

2. Neither the carrier nor the ship shall be responsible for loss or damage arising or resulting from —

    (*a*) Act, neglect, or default of the master, mariner, pilot, or the servants of the carrier in the navigation or in the management of the ship.

    (*b*) Fire, unless caused by the actual fault or privity of the carrier.

    (*c*) Perils, dangers and accidents of the sea or other navigable waters.

    (*d*) Act of God.

    (*e*) Act of war.

    (*f*) Act of public enemies.

    (*g*) Arrest or restraint of princes, rulers or people, or seizure under legal process.

    (*h*) Quarantine restrictions.

    (*i*) Act or omission of the shipper or owner of the goods, his agent or representative.

    (*j*) Strikes or lockouts or stoppage or restraint of labour from whatever cause, whether partial or general.

    (*k*) Riots and civil commotions.

    (*l*) Saving or attempting to save life or property at sea.

    (*m*) Wastage in bulk or weight or any other loss or damage arising from inherent defect, quality or vice of the goods.

    (*n*) Insufficiency of packing.

    (*o*) Insufficiency or inadequacy of marks.

    (*p*) Latent defects not discoverable by due diligence.

    (*q*) Any other cause arising without the actual fault or privity of the carrier, or without the fault or neglect of the agents or servants of the carrier, but the burden of proof shall be on the person claiming the benefit of this exception to show that neither the actual fault or privity of the carrier nor the fault or neglect of the agents or servants of the carrier contributed to the loss or damage.

3. The shipper shall not be responsible for loss or damage sustained by the carrier or the ship arising or resulting from any cause without the act, fault or neglect of the shipper, his agents or his servants.

4. Any deviation in saving or attempting to save life or property at sea or any reasonable deviation shall not be deemed to be an infringement or breach of these

Informal Consolidation – version in force from 30/5/1998

THE SCHEDULE — *continued*

Rules or of the contract of carriage, and the carrier shall not be liable for any loss or damage resulting therefrom.

5.—(*a*) Unless the nature and value of such goods have been declared by the shipper before shipment and inserted in the bill of lading, neither the carrier nor the ship shall in any event be or become liable for any loss or damage to or in connection with the goods in an amount exceeding the equivalent of 10,000 francs per package or unit or 30 francs per kilo of gross weight of the goods lost or damaged, whichever is the higher.

(*b*) The total amount recoverable shall be calculated by reference to the value of such goods at the place and time at which the goods are discharged from the ship in accordance with the contract or should have been so discharged.

The value of the goods shall be fixed according to the commodity exchange price, or, if there be no such price, according to the current market price, or, if there be no commodity exchange price or current market price, by reference to the normal value of goods of the same kind and quality.

(*c*) Where a container, pallet or similar article of transport is used to consolidate goods, the number of packages or units enumerated in the bill of lading as packed in such article of transport shall be deemed the number of packages or units for the purpose of this paragraph as far as these packages or units are concerned. Except as aforesaid such article of transport shall be considered the package or unit.

(*d*) A franc means a unit consisting of 65.5 milligrammes of gold of millesimal fineness 900. The date of conversion of the sum awarded into national currencies shall be governed by the law of the Court seized of the case.

(*e*) Neither the carrier nor the ship shall be entitled to the benefit of the limitation of liability provided for in this paragraph if it is proved that the damage resulted from an act or omission of the carrier done with intent to cause damage, or recklessly and with knowledge that damage would probably result.

(*f*) The declaration mentioned in sub-paragraph (*a*) of this paragraph, if embodied in the bill of lading, shall be prima facie evidence, but shall not be binding or conclusive on the carrier.

(*g*) By agreement between the carrier, master or agent of the carrier and the shipper other maximum amounts than those mentioned in sub-paragraph (*a*) of this paragraph may be fixed, provided that no maximum amount so fixed shall be less than the appropriate maximum mentioned in that sub-paragraph.

(*h*) Neither the carrier nor the ship shall be responsible in any event for loss or damage to, or in connection with, goods if the nature or value thereof has been knowingly mis-stated by the shipper in the bill of lading.

Informal Consolidation – version in force from 30/5/1998

THE SCHEDULE — *continued*

6. Goods of an inflammable, explosive or dangerous nature to the shipment whereof the carrier, master or agent of the carrier has not consented with knowledge of their nature and character, may at any time before discharge be landed at any place, or destroyed or rendered innocuous by the carrier without compensation and the shipper of such goods shall be liable for all damages and expenses directly or indirectly arising out of or resulting from such shipment. If any such goods shipped with such knowledge and consent shall become a danger to the ship or cargo, they may in like manner be landed at any place, or destroyed or rendered innocuous by the carrier without liability on the part of the carrier except to general average, if any.

ARTICLE IV BIS

1. The defences and limits of liability provided for in these Rules shall apply in any action against the carrier in respect of loss or damage to goods covered by a contract of carriage whether the action be founded in contract or in tort.

2. If such an action is brought against a servant or agent of the carrier (such servant or agent not being an independent contractor), such servant or agent shall be entitled to avail himself of the defences and limits of liability which the carrier is entitled to invoke under these Rules.

3. The aggregate of the amounts recoverable from the carrier, and such servants and agents, shall in no case exceed the limit provided for in these Rules.

4. Nevertheless, a servant or agent of the carrier shall not be entitled to avail himself of the provisions of this article, if it is proved that the damage resulted from an act or omission of the servant or agent done with intent to cause damage or recklessly and with knowledge that damage would probably result.

ARTICLE V

A carrier shall be at liberty to surrender in whole or in part all or any of his rights and immunities or to increase any of his responsibilities and obligations under these Rules, provided such surrender or increase shall be embodied in the bill of lading issued to the shipper. The provisions of these Rules shall not be applicable to charter parties, but if bills of lading are issued in the case of a ship under a charter party they shall comply with the terms of these Rules. Nothing in these Rules shall be held to prevent the insertion in a bill of lading of any lawful provision regarding general average.

ARTICLE VI

Notwithstanding the provisions of the preceding Articles, a carrier, master or agent of the carrier and a shipper shall in regard to any particular goods be at liberty to enter into any agreement in any terms as to the responsibility and

THE SCHEDULE — *continued*

liability of the carrier for such goods, and as to the rights and immunities of the carrier in respect of such goods, or his obligation as to seaworthiness, so far as this stipulation is not contrary to public policy, or the care or diligence of his servants or agents in regard to the loading, handling, stowage, carriage, custody, care and discharge of the goods carried by sea, provided that in this case no bill of lading has been or shall be issued and that the terms agreed shall be embodied in a receipt which shall be a non-negotiable document and shall be marked as such.

Any agreement so entered into shall have full legal effect.

Provided that this Article shall not apply to ordinary commercial shipments made in the ordinary course of trade, but only to other shipments where the character or condition of the property to be carried or the circumstances, terms and conditions under which the carriage is to be performed are such as reasonably to justify a special agreement.

ARTICLE VII

Nothing herein contained shall prevent a carrier or a shipper from entering into any agreement, stipulation, condition, reservation or exemption as to the responsibility and liability of the carrier or the ship for the loss or damage to, or in connection with, the custody and care and handling of goods prior to the loading on, and subsequent to the discharge from, the ship on which the goods are carried by sea.

ARTICLE VIII

The provisions of these Rules shall not affect the rights and obligations of the carrier under any statute for the time being in force relating to the limitation of the liability of owners of sea-going vessels.

ARTICLE IX

These Rules shall not affect the provisions of any international Convention or national law governing liability for nuclear damage.

ARTICLE X

The provisions of these Rules shall apply to every bill of lading relating to the carriage of goods between ports in 2 different States if:

  (*a*) the bill of lading is issued in a contracting State, or

  (*b*) the carriage is from a port in a contracting State, or

  (*c*) the contract contained in or evidenced by the bill of lading provides that these Rules or legislation of any State giving effect to them are to govern the contract, whatever may be the nationality of the ship, the carrier, the shipper, the consignee, or any other interested person.

LEGISLATIVE HISTORY
CARRIAGE OF GOODS BY SEA ACT
(CHAPTER 33)

This Legislative History is provided for the convenience of users of the Carriage of Goods by Sea Act. It is not part of the Act.

1. Ordinance 4 of 1927 — Carriage of Goods by Sea Ordinance, 1927

    Date of First Reading : 11 October 1927
(Bill No. 1680/1926)

    Date of Second Reading : 1 November 1926

    Date of commencement : 20 April 1927

2. 1936 Revised Edition — Carriage of Goods by Sea Ordinance (Chapter 156)

    Date of operation : 1 September 1936

3. 1955 Revised Edition — Carriage of Goods by Sea Ordinance (Chapter 173)

    Date of operation : 1 July 1956

4. 1970 Revised Edition — Carriage of Goods by Sea Act (Chapter 184)

    Date of operation : 1 July 1971

5. Act 30 of 1972 — Carriage of Goods by Sea Act 1972

    Date of First Reading : 24 October 1972
(Bill No. 34/1972)

    Date of Second and Third Readings : 3 November 1972

    Date of commencement : 16 January 1978

6. Act 13 of 1982 — Carriage of Goods by Sea (Amendment) Act 1982

    Date of First Reading : 3 March 1982
(Bill No. 2/1982)

    Date of Second and Third Readings : 26 March 1982

    Date of commencement : 11 June 1982

7. 1985 Revised Edition — Carriage of Goods by Sea Act (Chapter 33)

    Date of operation : 30 March 1987

Informal Consolidation – version in force from 30/5/1998

ii

8. Act 6 of 1995 — Carriage of Goods by Sea (Amendment) Act 1995

Date of First Reading	: 23 January 1995 (Bill No. 4/1995)
Date of Second and Third Readings	: 1 March 1995
Date of commencement	: 31 March 1995

9. 1998 Revised Edition — Carriage of Goods by Sea Act

Date of operation	: 30 May 1998

Informal Consolidation – version in force from 30/5/1998

第二章　马来西亚海事管理法律研究

马来西亚国土面积为 330345 平方千米，位于太平洋和印度洋之间，全境被南中国海分成马来西亚半岛（简称"半岛"）和沙巴砂拉越（简称"沙砂"）。半岛位于马来西亚半岛南部，北与泰国接壤，西濒马六甲海峡，东临南中国海，南濒柔佛海峡与新加坡毗邻，半岛上共有 11 州属；沙砂即沙巴州和砂拉越州，位于婆罗洲北部。全境处于北纬 1°—7°、东经 97°—120°，海岸线长 4192 千米。马来西亚内河运输欠发达，对外航依赖程度高。马来西亚大力推进港口建设、完善港口设施，港口总数达 19 个，主要国际港口包括巴生港、马六甲港和柔佛港。

一、海事管理体制与机构设置

马来西亚采用"分散型"海事管理体制，多个部门共同承担国家海事管理职能，并由专门协调机制处理中央与各个部门的分工协作问题，其中最为重要的两大部门分别是交通部所属的马来西亚海事局（MD）和直属于首相署的马来西亚海事执法局（MMEA）。

（一）海事局

海事局是马来西亚交通部辖下的部门，由马来半岛海事处、沙捞越海事处以及沙巴海事处合并而来。马来西亚海事局负责马来西亚航运及港口行政管理事项，其中包括马来西亚水域的海事事务。

1. 基本职能

马来西亚海事局致力于实施船舶、海员、港口设施安保、海上训练管理以及海上事故调查。具体而言，该部门的主要职责包括船舶的登记和颁发许可证、检查船舶安全和确认船舶国籍、执行航运相关的法律、进行海上事故调查、管理海洋污染等。

需要指出的是，马来西亚对海事调查重视程度较高，其遵循 2010 年 1 月 1 日生效的《国际海事调查规则》，特别强调安全调查的独立性①和调查报告不得用于安全以外的其他目的。调查报告不直接指出责任比例，只分析事故原因，责任比例由法庭决定；并且提出海事安全调查的目的不在于确定过错、分摊责任、赔偿损失，而在于防范风险，避免日后海上事故的再次发生。

2. 部门架构

马来西亚海事局（MD）下属部门包括管理服务处、行业管控处、航行安全处、海

---

① 《国际海事调查规则》总则第 1 条、第 2 条规定："海上安全调查应和任何其他形式的调查分开，并独立于任何其他形式的调查。但是规则并不是要排除任何其他形式的调查，包括对民事、刑事和行政管理行为的调查。"

运培训处。部门架构如图 2-1 所示。

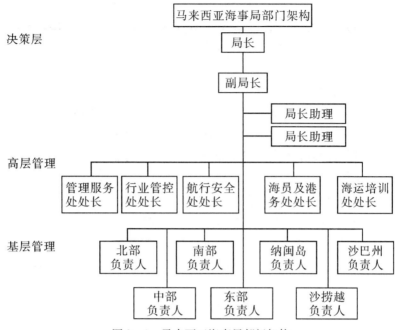

图 2-1 马来西亚海事局部门架构

（1）管理服务处。马来西亚海事局中的管理服务处包括人事管理部门、信息技术与电子政务部门、财政及信托基金管理机构、资产管理机构。

（2）行业管控处。马来西亚海事局中的行业管控处包括船舶登记机构、船舶安全审核机构（ISM）、船舶检验机构。

船舶安全审核机构（ISM）根据 ISM 规则对船运公司和船舶进行审核、对海事部门机构进行审核、对海上事故进行调查。船舶登记机构根据 1952 年的《商船条例》协调和监督该地区的船舶登记活动，以确保船舶登记工作有效运行。船舶检验机构主要职能包括：第一，规范港口监督、检查工作；第二，对在马来西亚注册的船只进行检验和检查管理，以确保船舶符合国家规定、国际条约和规定指南中规定的环境标准。

（3）航行安全处。马来西亚海事局中的航行安全处包括：航标机构、海上交通服务（VTS）机构、海上安全（水文）机构、海洋环境保护机构。

航标机构旨在保证马来西亚水域内的船舶安全和提供安全的导航系统，实施针对船舶溢油的行动以避免环境污染。

海上交通服务机构旨在确保有序、高效、经济的海上交通系统和确保航行安全以及减少海上事故，并在马来西亚水域建立有效的搜救协调系统。该部门的主要职责有以下三个：第一，提供有效的巡航信息和发出警报；第二，控制和监测海上交通路线；第三，指导航运和提供运输建议。

海上安全（水文）机构旨在确保海事安全系统的高效运行和建立一个安全的导航网络。该机构主要职能是：第一，规划和实施水文测量；第二，疏浚活动管理部门要制订定期疏浚计划，为每个疏浚项目准备需求说明，确保疏浚工作符合规范要求；第三，负责沉船的打捞、搜救及管理。

海洋环境保护机构打造了一个高效的海上应急系统,以维护马来西亚海域的安全、防治污染和清除巡航障碍。该机构的主要职责在于:第一,处理石油泄漏事故;第二,管理所有的溢油应急设备资产;第三,召开国家溢油委员会会议等。

(4)海运培训处。海运培训处(ILPL)于2009年6月22日正式成立,下设培训发展机构、研发机构、管理服务机构,主要进行海上运输管理培训活动。该机构的目标是到2020年成为卓越的海上运输研究中心。海运培训处的主要职能在于:人力资源管理、文件管理、资产和财务管理、通信管理、设施的管理和维护、图书馆管理、提供职业发展培训、研究和开发课程和培训、进行有关海上运输安全的研究。在职业技能培训方面,旨在通过提供优质课程和培训,如航运安全课程、信息技术培训等,以满足马来西亚所有海事行政部门对高绩效服务的需求。比较特殊的是,海运培训处的课程仅提供给行政部门员工,与国际海事公约适用有关的课程只会提供给相关政府或私人机构,海运培训处的讲师也来自部门员工。但是,该部门也可能会邀请相关政府或私人机构的教员。海运培训处为海运行政部门和行业提供完整、舒适、设备齐全的培训基础设施,为工业界和其他政府机构提供公共设施、培训空间,分享海运业的专业知识,开展海上运输领域的研究和开发,在海运业的培训和研究方面与本地、外国机构合作,以期为海运业提供高性能部门服务并符合国家和国际安全标准。

海员及港务部门和海运培训处将在海员教育培训和服务管理体制的相应部分进行介绍。

3. 人员情况

马来西亚海事局(MD)下设26个部门,工作人员共193人,其中最高权力机构名为总干事办公室,由总干事、首席信息官和两名助理组成。海上交通服务单位人员最为充裕,共33名,多为海事军官或海事军官助理。

4. 执法船舶和设备

马来西亚海事执法船舶由海事执法局管理,海事局并无自有执法船舶,只有用于浮标维护(4艘)、灯塔维护和污染防治的船舶,以及4艘巡逻船。马来西亚海事局配备有VTS、AIS基站及监控油污的设备。

(二)海事执法局

2004年5月,马来西亚议会颁布了《海事执法机构法》(第633号法律)。2005年该法律正式生效,马来西亚海事执法局自此成立。马来西亚海事执法局又称马来西亚海岸警卫队,刚建立时隶属于交通部,后来直属于首相署,马来西亚海事执法局直接向首相署报告工作,并不隶属于马来西亚武装部队。

1. 基本职能

马来西亚海事执法局的主要任务是负责维护马来西亚海洋区域和公海的法律秩序,协调搜救行动,确保马来西亚海洋区域的和平、安保和维护国家主权,以及落实国内法及国际法。马来西亚海事执法局可以在紧急情况、特殊危机或战时期间,由马来西亚武装部队指挥和管理。马来西亚海事执法局与美国海岸警卫队(USCG)和日本海岸警卫队（JCG）保持密切联系。

马来西亚海事执法局自2005年成立以来具有较大实权，拥有与内陆警察同样的管辖权等权力。马来西亚执法局成立之前，海事执法由马来西亚海事局（MD）、皇家海军等多个政府机构进行，当时的马来西亚法律规定，马来西亚海事局需向警察报告之后才能拘捕嫌疑人、收集证据及申请开庭审判。执法局成立之后，对于犯罪行为在海上发生而嫌疑人窜逃内陆的情况，马来西亚海事执法局有权追查到底，直至将嫌疑人缉拿归案。如果在过程中遇到困难，马来西亚海事执法局有权请求内陆警察的帮助。另外，马来西亚海事执法局目前拥有自己的特种部队，称为STAR，负责特殊任务和救援。它由马来西亚皇家空军（RMAF）和马来西亚皇家海军（RMN）的成员组成，该特种部队的任务是在浅水区域进行人质救援工作和在马来西亚海域进行反恐行动。

马来西亚海事执法局权限涵盖执法管辖权、运营管辖权、法律管辖权三大板块，具体权能包括：执行马来西亚海事法律和维护海事法律秩序，在马来西亚海域和公海上执行海上搜救任务，预防和制止在马来西亚海域的犯罪行为；根据2002年《刑事事项互助法》（第621号法律）的规定，应外国的请求提供任何刑事事项方面的援助、进行空中和海岸监测，建立和管理海事培训机构，履行职责来确保海上商贸的繁荣和安全，在公海执行海上搜救任务，控制和防止公海海上污染，防止和打击盗版，防止和制止非法分销麻醉药品；在紧急状态、特殊危机或战争期间，该机构以及该机构的任何部分都受到马来西亚武装部队总司令的管控。从马来西亚海事执法局的职权可见，该局权力之大、涵盖内容之广、分工之精细，无不透露出马来西亚海事执法局的地位及权威。

2. 人员情况

马来西亚海事执法局现共有7000名官员，马来西亚政府提出适时增加海事执法局人员编制的方针政策，以提升海事执法局在马来西亚海域主权和安全方面的实力和效率。目前，马亚西亚政府已经批准在2020年之前再给海事执法局增加10000～20000个岗位。届时，马来西亚海事执法局将拥有足够的执法人员来实行国家水域执法和巡逻任务。

马来西亚海事执法局局长由首相署任命，负责马来西亚海事执法局的行动、指挥、控制和监督，是该局的主要负责人。局长由3名副局长协助，副局长们主要负责管理业务和后勤。马来西亚海事执法局局长是一个开放的职位，可以由民事、军事或警务人员来担任该职位。

3. 执法船舶

马来西亚海事执法局拥有足够的现代化武器装备用于国家水域执法和巡逻任务。到目前为止，该局拥有多艘巡逻船、不同类别的快艇、3架直升机和1架飞机，能够随时用于检测或搜索救援行动。马来西亚海上搜救中心隶属于马来西亚海事执法局，统一负责组织指挥海上搜救行动，可以依法调动、指挥海事空巡队、巡逻艇、海军以及其他海上力量。

（三）海员教育培训与服务管理体制

海员是海运业的基石，马来西亚注重优质海员的孵化和培养。马来西亚海员教育培训与服务管理体制呈现出海事培训体制与海事教育行政体制相结合的特点。在行政管理层面，马来西亚海事局（MD）下辖的海员和港务处（HEPP）宏观管理海员事项，如资格认证、福利保障、海员培训机构认证等，尤其重视对海员能力证书的验证和颁发。换言之，海员和港务处并不直接参与海员的培训，海员教育和培训的重任交由专门性的海事院校承担。在海事教育层面，现代化的海事培训机构以培训优质海事人才为己任，为马来西亚海事及港口产业提供源源不断的人才。

1. 海员服务管理体制

马来西亚海事局下辖的海员和港务处是主管马来西亚海员事务的行政机关，马来西亚海员和港务处由评估及培训机构、港口货物交易管理机构和海员发展机构构成。海员和港务处的主要目标和宗旨是使马来西亚的海事管辖权在国际上得到广泛承认、保障海员权益、监管港口及码头、遵守《海员培训、发证和值班标准公约》（STCW）和1952年的《商船条例》。海员和港务处参与如下海员管理事项：①在海员证书管理方面，海员和港务处组织并开展海员考试、颁发海员证书、评估和确认海员能力证书、为海员相关的能力考试提供建议并制定标准。②在海事培训机构认证管理方面，海员和港务处主要负责海员培训机构的申请、对海事培训机构进行审核、对海员能力证书进行验证、认证马来西亚海员资格。③在海员福利保障方面，海员和港务处主要负责监督海员福利的保障和发放、提供海员必要的设施。马来西亚完备的海员服务管理体制有效加强海员管理、维护海员合法权益并保障马来西亚海上交通安全。

2. 海员教育与培训体制

马来西亚海员教育与培训体制较为完备。马来西亚海事培训学校共7所，3所由政府组建，4所由私人发起、成立、运营。在马来西亚海事培训学校走向市场化的进程中，私立海事培训学校大量出现，通过公平竞争，激励一般公立海事培训学校提升教育水平和办学质量。其中，马来西亚海事学院（ALAM）最具代表性，截至目前，它已为马来西亚培养了10000多名船舶驾驶和轮机管理高级人才。

马来西亚海事学院是马来西亚国家最高航海学府和马来西亚国内第一家正式的高级海员教育与培训类院校，被指定为瑞典世界海事大学的分校，并与美国、澳大利亚、挪威、荷兰、新加坡、英国等国家的航海院校建立了联合培训关系。学院拥有雄厚的师资力量，具有航海专业的博士、硕士学位和船长、轮机长职务的教师共65人，学院拥有目前世界最先进的、规模最大的航海和轮机模拟器、油货操作模拟器、天然气船舶模拟器以及学院自己的实习船。学院开设130余种不同的由国际海事机构认可的专业培训课程，是亚洲目前单项专业培训课程最多的海事学院，其颁发的培训证书得到美国、挪威等世界著名船级社的认可。目前，在校全日制本专学历的学生除来自本国以外，还有来自中国大陆、印度、菲律宾、孟加拉国、巴基斯坦、印度尼西亚、也门等国的学员。

马来西亚海事学院注重教学实战化，通过实战演练，培养学生们的动手能力、适任能力和社会适应能力。例如，在自给式呼吸器穿戴训练中，老师在亲自讲授和示范之后，监督并指导学生实训，直到每位学员都掌握为止。但是，培训费用也比较昂贵，比如GMDSS通用操作员证（GOC）的培训时间只有短短2周，但培训费用高达3000马币，约为人民币5000元。

马来西亚海事学院注重学员综合素质的提升：一是重视学生身体锻炼，如下午下课后要统一进行跑步训练；二是重视服从意识的培养，如学生对老师、低年级学生对高年级学生尊重和服从的做法已蔚然成风；三是重视养成学生良好的生活习惯，如要求学生生活要有规律、讲究个人卫生等。马来西亚海事学院强调教师的实践能力，实行教师终身进修制度，教师要定期参与航海实践工作。马来西亚海事学院还重视教学方法和手段的多样性，在教学场所方面，除了传统的教室，还有码头、教学船、大海等"新型教室"；在教学方式上，在传统讲授式教学方式的基础上，创新出案例分析、角色扮演、分组讨论、模拟操作、拓展训练等多种形式，在交流讨论中互相启迪，形成"互通、互助、互联、互促"的交流氛围，从而在潜移默化之中，增进学员的自信，培养沟通与思辨能力，优化学习效果。马来西亚海事学院十分重视人才供给定向化，学员费用由公司承担，学员学成之后为公司服务一定期限，较好地解决了学员在就业和学费方面的困难，从而实现了学校、学员、企业三方的多赢格局。

二、海事法律

马来西亚海事法律旨在处理船舶碰撞、海难救助、船舶残骸清除、船舶污染海洋环境、共同海损、海上人身伤亡损害赔偿和海事索赔等问题。

（一）国内法

马来西亚海事局（MD）执法相关的法律文件较多，涉及对引航管理、港口管理、打捞救助、港口设施建设、船舶登记、船舶配员和发证、船员管理、船舶检验、货物运输、法律援助等内容和海事案件的管辖、取证、审判和救济等诉讼程序的规范和调整。实务操作中，高频使用到的法律有1952年的《商船条例》（MSO）。

马来西亚海事执法局执法法律文件中最核心也是最重要的一部是2004年的《海事执法机构法》（第633号法律），该法律于2005年2月15日生效，赋予马来西亚海事执法局执法职能，以维护马来西亚的海洋区域安全、秩序稳定和国家利益。

马来西亚的国内法梳理如下：

ACT

1. 1952年商船条例
Merchant Shipping Ordinance 1952
http：//www.marine.gov.my/jlmeng/pic/article/law/Ordinan_Perkapalan_Saudagar_1952_BI.pdf

2. 1960年商船条例
Merchant Shipping Ordinance 1960
http：//www.marine.gov.my/jlmeng/pic/article/law/MSO1960-SARAWAK.pdf

3. 1953年联邦灯标税法令（250号法案）
Federation Light Dues Act 1953（Act 250）
http://www. marine. gov. my/jlmeng/pic/article/law/Federation_Light_Dues_ACT_1953. pdf

4. 302号法案-1984年石油（安全措施）条例
Act 302-Petroleum（Safety Measures）Act 1984
http://www. marine. gov. my/jlm/pic/article/law/act%20302-petroleum%20（safety%20measures）%20act%201984. pdf

5. A807号法案-1991年石油（安全措施）（修正）条例
Petroleum（Safety Measures）（Amendment）Act 1991
http://www. marine. gov. my/jlmeng/pic/article/law/petroleum%20（safety%20measures）%20（amendment）act%201991. pdf

SUBSIDIARY LAWS

1. 1393号法案-2011年商船（修正及扩展）条例
Act 1393-Merchant Shipping（Amendment And Extension）Act 2011
http://www. marine. gov. my/jlmeng/pic/article/law/ACT_1393. pdf

2. 1394号法案-2011年商船（油类污染）（修正）条例
Act 1394-Merchant Shipping（Oil Pollution）（Amendment）Act 2011
http://www. marine. gov. my/jlmeng/pic/article/law/Akta_A1394. pdf

3. 简称：2014年纳闽联邦领土法令
全称：2014年纳闽联邦领土（1953年联邦灯标税法令的扩展和修正）法令
Federal Territory Of Labuan（Extension and Modification of the Federation Light Dues Act 1953）Order 2014
http://www. marine. gov. my/jlmeng/pic/article/law/Perintah_wilayah_persekutuan_labuan_2014. pdf

4. 1984年商船（避碰规则）法令
Merchant Shipping Order（Collision Regulations），1984
http://www. marine. gov. my/jlmeng/pic/article/law/Merchant%20Shipping_Order_（Collision_Regulations）_1984. pdf

5. 2000年商船（避碰规则）（修正）法令

Merchant Shipping (Collision Regulations) (Amendment) Order 2000
http://www.marine.gov.my/jlmeng/pic/article/law/merchant%20shipping%20(collision%20regulations)%20(amendment)%20order%202000.pdf

6. 1985 年港口（劳务安全）规则
Port (Safety of Workers) Rules, 1985
http://www.marine.gov.my/jlmeng/pic/article/law/port%20(safety%20of%20workers)%20rules%20-%201985.pdf

7. 1953 年联邦港口规则
Federation Ports Rules 1953
http://www.marine.gov.my/jlmeng/pic/article/law/latest_federation%20light%20dues%20act%201953.pdf

8. 各州港口规则
State Ports Rules
http://www.marine.gov.my/jlmeng/pic/article/law/state%20port%20rules.pdf

9. 1998 年商船（修正）法案（马来文版本）
Merchant Shipping (Amendment) Act 1998 (Malay Version Only)
http://www.marine.gov.my/jlmeng/pic/article/law/akta%20perkapalan%20saudagar%20(%20pindaan%20)%201998.pdf

10. 1985 年石油（安全措施）（石油水路运输）规则
P.U (A) Petroleum (Safety Measures) (Transportation of Petroleum by Water) Regulation 1985
http://www.marine.gov.my/jlmeng/pic/article/law/petroleum_safety%20measures.pdf

11. A1316 号法案 – 2007 年商船（修正及扩展）条例
Act 1316-Merchant Shipping (Amendment & Extension) Act 2007
http://www.marine.gov.my/jlmeng/pic/article/law/Act_A1316_Merchant_Shipping_Act_2007.pdf

12. 1990 年港口（私有化）法案
Ports (Privatization) -Act 1990
http://www.marine.gov.my/jlmeng/pic/article/law/ports%20(privatization)%20act%201990.pdf

13. 1986 年槟城港（桥梁区域航行）规则

Penang Port (Navigation Within The Area Of The Brigde) Rules 1986

http://www.marine.gov.my/jlmeng/pic/article/law/penang%20port%20(navigation%20within%20the%20area%20of%20the%20brigde)%20rules%201986.pdf

14. 1999 年商船（体检）规则

P.U (A) Medical Examination Rules 1999 [Kaedah-Kaedah Perkapalan Saudagar (Pemeriksaan Perubatan) 1991]

http://www.marine.gov.my/jlmeng/pic/article/law/merchant%20shipping%20(medical%20examination)%20rules%201999.pdf

15. 简称：1984 年商船（避碰规则）法令

全称：1984 年商船（避碰规则）（马六甲海峡和新加坡海峡航行规则）法令

Merchant Shipping (Collision Regulations) (Rules Vessels Navigating Through the Straits of Malacca and Singapore) Order 1984

http://www.marine.gov.my/jlmeng/pic/article/law/P_U(A)439_1984.pdf

16. 1953 年船舶条例

Boat Rules 1953

http://www.marine.gov.my/jlmeng/pic/article/law/boat%20rules%201953.pdf

17. 515 号法案 – 1994 年商船（油类污染）条例

Act 515-Merchant Shipping (Oil Pollution) Act 1994

http://www.marine.gov.my/jlm/pic/article/law/act%20515%20%20merchant%20shipping%20(oil%20pollution)%201994.pdf

（二）国际条约

1. 海事国际条约概述

马来西亚加入的国际条约共 30 个，其中具有代表性的公约有 1982 年《联合国海洋法公约》（UNCLOS）、1974 年《国际海上人命安全公约》（SOLAS）、1973 年《国际防止船舶造成污染公约》（MARPOL）、1972 年《国际海上避碰规则公约》（COLREGS）、2006 年《国际海事劳工公约》（ML）、1969 年《国际油污损害民事责任公约》（CLC）和 1976 年《海事索赔责任限制公约》（LLMC）等。其中《联合国海洋法公约》更侧重对船旗国及其船舶的权利及义务的规范，《国际海上人命安全公约》《国际防止船舶造成污染公约》《国际海上避碰规则》《国际海事劳工公约》更关注的是船舶的技术条件和运营状况以及海上航行安全、海洋污染、船员权益保障等事项。《国际油污损害民事责任公约》和《海事索赔责任限制公约》更强调船舶海损事故中的责任分摊和赔偿等事宜。

海事国际条约梳理如下：

1. 经1988年议定书修订的1966年国际载重线公约
International Convention on Load Lines (LL), 1966 as Amended by the Protocol of 1988
http://www.imo.org/en/About/Conventions/ListOfConventions/Pages/International-Convention-on-Load-Lines.aspx

2. 1948年国际海事组织公约
Convention on the International Maritime Organization, 1948
http://www.imo.org/en/About/Conventions/ListOfConventions/Pages/Convention-on-the-International-Maritime-Organization.aspx

3. 设立国际油污损害赔偿基金公约
International Convention on the Establishment of an International Fund for Compensation for Oil Pollution Damage (FUND)
http://www.imo.org/en/About/Conventions/ListOfConventions/Pages/International-Convention-on-the-Establishment-of-an-International-Fund-for-Compensation-for-Oil-Pollution-Damage-(FUND).aspx

4. 1972年国际海上避碰规则公约
Convention on the International Regulations for Preventing Collisions at Sea (COLREG) 1972
http://www.imo.org/en/About/Conventions/ListOfConventions/Pages/COLREG.aspx

5. 经1988年议定书修订的1974年国际海上人命安全公约
International Convention for the Safety of Life at Sea (SOLAS) 1974, as amended by the Protocol of 1988
http://www.imo.org/en/About/Conventions/ListOfConventions/Pages/International-Convention-for-the-Safety-of-Life-at-Sea-(SOLAS),-1974.aspx

6. 1974年国际海上人命安全公约之1978年议定书
Protocol of 1978 relating to the International Convention for the Safety of Life at Sea 1974, as amended
http://www.imo.org/en/About/Conventions/ListOfConventions/Pages/International-Convention-for-the-Safety-of-Life-at-Sea-(SOLAS),-1974.aspx

7. 1969年国际船舶吨位丈量公约
International Convention on Tonnage Measurement of Ships, 1969
http://www.imo.org/en/About/Conventions/ListOfConventions/Pages/International-Convention-on-Tonnage-Measurement-of-Ships.aspx

8. 1976 年国际海事卫星组织公约

Convention on the International Mobile Satellite Organization (IMSO) 1976, as amended

http://www.imo.org/en/About/Conventions/ListOfConventions/Pages/Convention-on-the-International-Maritime-Satellite-Organization.aspx

9. 1976 年国际海事卫星组织业务协定

Operating Agreement on the International Mobile Satellite Organization 1976, as amended

http://www.imo.org/en/About/Conventions/ListOfConventions/Pages/Convention-on-the-International-Maritime-Satellite-Organization.aspx

10. 1978 年海员培训、发证和值班标准国际公约

International Convention on Standards of Training, Certification and Watchkeeping for Seafarers (STCW) 1978, as amended

http://www.imo.org/en/About/Conventions/ListOfConventions/Pages/International-Convention-on-Standards-of-Training,-Certification-and-Watchkeeping-for-Seafarers-(STCW).aspx

11. 1973 年防止船舶造成污染公约之 1978 年议定书,附则Ⅲ:防止海运包装有害物质污染规则

International Convention for the Prevention of Pollution from Ships (MARPOL) 73/78, Annex III: Regulations for the Prevention of Pollution by Harmful Substances Carried by Sea in Packaged Form

http://www.imo.org/en/About/Conventions/ListOfConventions/Pages/International-Convention-for-the-Prevention-of-Pollution-from-Ships-(MARPOL).aspx

12. 1971 年设立国际油污损害赔偿基金公约

International Convention on the Establishment of an International Fund for Compensation for Oil Pollution Damage (FUND) 1971

http://www.imo.org/en/About/Conventions/ListOfConventions/Pages/International-Convention-on-the-Establishment-of-an-International-Fund-for-Compensation-for-Oil-Pollution-Damage-(FUND).aspx

13. 1973 年防止船舶造成污染公约之 1978 年议定书,附则Ⅰ:防止油类污染规则

International Convention for the Prevention of Pollution from Ships (MARPOL) 73/78, Annex I: Regulations for the Prevention of Pollution by Oil

http://www.imo.org/en/About/Conventions/ListOfConventions/Pages/International-Convention-for-the-Prevention-of-Pollution-from-Ships-(MARPOL).aspx

14. 1973 年防止船舶造成污染公约之 1978 年议定书,附则Ⅱ:控制散装有毒液体

污染规则

International Convention for the Prevention of Pollution from Ships (MARPOL) 73/78, Annex II: Regulations for the Control of Pollution by Noxious Liquid Substances in Bulk

http://www.imo.org/en/About/Conventions/ListOfConventions/Pages/International-Convention-for-the-Prevention-of-Pollution-from-Ships-(MARPOL).aspx

15. 1973 年防止船舶造成污染公约之 1978 年议定书，附则 V：防止船舶垃圾污染规则

International Convention for the Prevention of Pollution from Ships (MARPOL) 73/78, Annex V: Regulations for the Prevention of Pollution by Garbage from Ships

http://www.imo.org/en/About/Conventions/ListOfConventions/Pages/International-Convention-for-the-Prevention-of-Pollution-from-Ships-(MARPOL).aspx

16. 1990 年国际油污防备、响应和合作公约

International Convention on Oil Pollution Preparedness, Response and Co-operation (OPRC) 1990

http://www.imo.org/en/About/Conventions/ListOfConventions/Pages/International-Convention-on-Oil-Pollution-Preparedness,-Response-and-Co-operation-(OPRC).aspx

17. 1973 年防止船舶造成污染公约之 1978 年议定书，附则 Ⅳ：防止船舶生活污水污染规则

International Convention for the Prevention of Pollution from Ships (MARPOL) 73/78, Annex IV: Regulations for the Prevention of Pollution by Sewage from Ships

http://www.imo.org/en/About/Conventions/ListOfConventions/Pages/International-Convention-for-the-Prevention-of-Pollution-from-Ships-(MARPOL).aspx

18. 1973 年防止船舶造成污染公约之 1978 年议定书，附则 Ⅵ：防止船舶造成空气污染规则

International Convention for the Prevention of Pollution from Ships (MARPOL) 73/78, Annex VI: Regulations for the Prevention of Air Pollution from Ships

http://www.imo.org/en/About/Conventions/ListOfConventions/Pages/International-Convention-for-the-Prevention-of-Pollution-from-Ships-(MARPOL).aspx

19. 1992 年油污损害民事责任公约

International Convention on Civil Liability for Oil Pollution Damage (CLC) 1992

http://www.imo.org/en/About/Conventions/ListOfConventions/Pages/International-Convention-on-Civil-Liability-for-Oil-Pollution-Damage-(CLC).aspx

20. 1992 年设立国际油污损害赔偿基金公约

International Convention on the Establishment of an International Fund For Compensation for Oil Pollution Damage（FUND）1992

http://www.imo.org/en/About/Conventions/ListOfConventions/Pages/International-Convention-on-the-Establishment-of-an-International-Fund-for-Compensation-for-Oil-Pollution-Damage-(FUND).aspx

21．1969 年油污损害民事责任公约之 1992 年议定书
Protocol of 1992 to amend the International Convention on Civil Liability for Oil Pollution Damage（CLC）1969
http：//www.imo.org/en/About/Conventions/ListOfConventions/Pages/International-Convention-on-Civil-Liability-for-Oil-Pollution-Damage-(CLC).aspx

22．1971 年设立国际油污损害赔偿基金公约之 1992 年议定书
Protocol of 1992 to amend the International Convention on the Establishment of an International Fund for Compensation for Oil Pollution Damage 1971
http://www.imo.org/en/About/Conventions/ListOfConventions/Pages/International-Convention-on-the-Establishment-of-an-International-Fund-for-Compensation-for-Oil-Pollution-Damage-(FUND).aspx

23．2001 年国际控制船舶有害防污系统公约
International Convention on the Control of Harmful Anti-Fouling Systems on Ships，2001
http://www.imo.org/en/About/Conventions/ListOfConventions/Pages/International-Convention-on-the-Control-of-Harmful-Anti-fouling-Systems-on-Ships-(AFS).aspx

24．2001 年国际燃油污染损害民事责任公约
The International Convention on Civil Liability for Bunker Oil Pollution Damage，2001（Bunkers Convention 2001）
http://www.imo.org/en/About/Conventions/ListOfConventions/Pages/International-Convention-on-Civil-Liability-for-Bunker-Oil-Pollution-Damage-(BUNKER).aspx

25．1976 年国际海事赔偿责任限制公约之 1996 年议定书
The International Convention for the Limitation of Liability for Maritime Claims，1976 as Amended by Protocol of 1996（LLMC Convention 1996）
http://www.imo.org/en/About/Conventions/ListOfConventions/Pages/Convention-on-Limitation-of-Liability-for-Maritime-Claims-(LLMC).aspx

26．2004 年国际船舶压载水及其沉积物控制和管理公约
International Convention for the Control and Management of Ship's Ballast Water and Sediment（BWM），2004

http://www.imo.org/en/About/Conventions/ListOfConventions/Pages/International-Convention-for-the-Control-and-Management-of-Ships-Ballast-Water-and-Sediments-(BWM).aspx

2. 国内化程序

马来西亚参加的国际条约一般要转化为国内法才能适用。但是，马来西亚立法规定有几项英国法律和国际条约在马来西亚直接适用，除非现行法律或即将生效的新订法律另有规定。1956 年《民事法令》第 5 条提供了英国法律在马来西亚某些领域应用的法律依据，包括海上运输、海上保险和一般商业法。1964 年《司法法令》第 24（b）条款规定，马来西亚高等法院对于有关海事事务和根据 1981 年英国最高法院法令下的英国高等法院司法持有一样的管辖权。此外，1950 年《海上货物运输法》《商船条例》（MSO）分别规定了统一海上客运若干规则、国际公约对于提单法案（海牙规则），以及海事索赔责任限制公约的适用。在符合诸如公共政策的情况下，倘若合同纠纷的依据法律是外国法律，马来西亚法院将沿用外国法律来确定争端的实质问题。①

三、小　结

通过对马来西亚海事管理体制和海事法律的研究，我们发现马来西亚海事管理体制是一个较为合理的有机系统，尤其马来西亚海事执法局是马来西亚海事管理体制中至关重要且不可或缺的一环。马来西亚海事执法局极具特色，它作为马来西亚唯一的海事执法机构，执行马来西亚法律、法令，履行保障海事安全的一切职责，打击和预防海上非法活动的发生，配备有足够的现代化武器用于水域巡逻，并且该局直接向首相署报告工作，具有较大实权，如拥有与内陆警察同样的管辖权等权力。

在马来西亚海事教育方面，马来西亚海事学院作为马来西亚海事教育的最高学府，最具实力且拥有丰富的教学经验，在国际航海领域也具有较高美誉度且占据一席之地。该学院也是东南亚海事职业教育的一个缩影。马来西亚海事学院注重教学实战化，注重学员综合素质的提升，注重教师的实践能力和教学方法，种种教学举措和创新确保了教学的高质量，保证了学员的适任能力，优化了师资结构并深化了校企合作。同时，该学院的订单式培养模式解决了学员就业与学费上的困难，也满足了航运企业的人才需求。

四、附录：马来西亚海事法律（国内法与国际条约）文件

（一）附录 1：1984 年商船（避碰规则）法令

Merchant Shipping (Collision Regulations) (Rules Vessels Navigating Through The Straits of Malacca and Singapore) Order 1984

---

① 摘录自马-中商务理事会，网址：http://www.mcbc.com.my/faq/shipping-law-in-malaysia，2018 年 7 月 13 日访问。

MERCHANT SHIPPING (COLLISION REGULATIONS) (RULES FOR VESSELS NAVIGATING THROUGH THE STRAITS OF MALACCA AND SINGAPORE) ORDER 1984 [1]

[P.U. (A) 439/1984]

In exercise of the powers conferred under section 252 of the Merchant Shipping Ordinance 1952, the Minister makes the following order:

1. Citation.

This Order may be cited as the **Merchant Shipping (Collision Regulations) (Rules for Vessels Navigating through the Straits of Malacca and Singapore) Order 1984.**

2. Collision regulations.

(1) The Rules for Vessels Navigating through the Straits of Malacca and Singapore as set out in Annex V of Resolution A. 375 (X) of the Assembly of the International Maritime Organization adopted on 14th November 1977 and as amended by Resolution A. 476 (XII) of the Assembly adopted on the 19th November 1981 set out in the Schedule to this Order shall constitute and have effect as the collision regulations for the purposes of the Ordinance.

(2) This Order shall be in addition to and not in substitution for the Merchant Shipping (Collision Regulations) 1984.

SCHEDULE
(Paragraph 2)
ANNEX V

RULES FOR VESSELS NAVIGATING THROUGH THE STRAITS OF MALACCA AND SINGAPORE

I. DEFINITION

For the purpose of these Rules the following definitions should apply:

1. A vessel having a draught of 15 metres or more shall be deemed to be a deep draught vessel.
2. A tanker of 150,000 dwt and above shall be deemed to be a Very Large Crude Carrier (VLCC).

NOTE — The above definitions do not prejudice the definitions of "vessel constrained by her draught" described in Rule 3 (*h*) of the International Regulations for Preventing Collisions at Sea 1972.

II. GENERAL PROVISIONS

1. Deep draught vessels and VLCCs shall allow for an Under Keel Clearance (UKC) of at least 3.5 metres at all times during the entire passage through the Straits of Malacca and Singapore and shall also take all necessary safety precautions especially when navigating through the traffic separation scheme.

---

[1] 本法条引用自 http://www.marine.gov.my/jlmeng/pic/article/law/P_U(A)439_1984.pdf。

2. Masters of deep draught vessels and VLCCs shall have particular regard to navigational constraints when planning their passage through the Straits.

3. All deep draught vessels and VLCCs navigating within the traffic separation scheme are recommended to use the pilotage service of the respective countries when they become available.

III. RULES

Rule 1 ...   (a) Deep draught vessels shall use the designated Deep Water Route (DWR) between positions 01° 09' 57" N., 103° 48' 17" E. and 01° 02' 58" N., 103° 39' 06" E. Other vessels should, as far as practicable, avoid the deep water route.

(b) Deep draught vessels are advised to use the deep water route between Buffalo Rock and Batu Berhanti.

Rule 2 ...   Deep draught vessels navigating in the deep water route shall, as far as practicable, avoid overtaking.

Rule 3 ...   All vessels navigating within the traffic separation scheme shall proceed in the appropriate traffic lane in the general direction of traffic flow for that lane and maintain as steady a course as possible consistent with safe navigation.

Rule 4 ...   In the event of an emergency or breakdown of a vessel in the traffic lane it shall, as far as practicable and safe, leave the lane by pulling out to the starboard side.

Rule 5 ...   (a) Vessels proceeding in the westbound lane of the traffic separation scheme "In the Singapore Strait" when approaching Raffles Lighthouse shall proceed with caution, taking note of the local warning system, and in compliance with Rule 18 (d) of the International Regulations for Preventing Collisions at Sea 1972 avoid impeding the safe passage of a vessel constrained by her draught and exhibiting the signals required by Rule 28, which is obliged to cross the westbound lane of the scheme in order to approach the single point mooring facility (in approximate position, latitude 1° 11' 25" N, longitude 103° 47' 30" E) from Phillip Channel.

(b) Vessels proceeding in the westbound lane of the traffic separation scheme "In the Singapore Strait" when approaching the Western Light Beacon in position 01° 12' 43" N, 103° 35' 53" E shall proceed with caution, taking note of the local warning system, and in compliance with Rule 18 (d) of the International Regulations for Preventing Collisions at Sea 1972 avoid impeding the safe passage of a vessel constrained by her draught and exhibiting the signals required by Rule her draught and exhibiting the signals required by

Rule 28, which is obliged to cross the westbound lane of the scheme in order to approach the Sultan Shoal pilot boarding ground from the eastbound lane of the scheme.

(c) A vessel proceeding in the westbound lane of the traffic separation scheme "In the Singapore Strait" which is required to avoid impeding the safe passage of a vessel constrained by her draught shall so far as practicable navigate in such a way as to avoid the development of risk of collision.

Rule 6 ... VLCCs and deep draught vessels are advised to navigate at a speed of not more than 12 knots over the ground.

Rule 7 ... All vessels navigating in the traffic separation scheme shall maintain at all times a safe speed consistent with safe navigation, shall proceed with caution, and shall be in a maximum state of manoeuvring readiness.

Rule 8 ... VLCCs and deep draught vessels navigating in the Straits of Malacca and Singapore are advised to participate in the existing voluntary ships' reporting system. Under this system, such vessels broadcast eight hours before entering the Straits/traffic separation schemes, navigational warnings giving names, deadweight tonnage, draught, speed and times of passing One Fathom Bank Lighthouse, Raffles Lighthouse and Horsburgh Lighthouse. Difficult and unwieldy tows also broadcast similar warnings giving the type, length, speed of tows and times of passing the three above-mentioned areas.

Rule 9 ... All vessels navigating in the Straits of Malacca and Singapore are requested to report by radio to the nearest shore authority any damage or malfunction of the aids to navigation in the Straits, or any aids out of position in the Straits.

Rule 10 ... Flag States, owners and operators should ensure that their vessels are adequately equipped in accordance with the appropriate international conventions/recommendations.

IV. WARNING

Mariners are warned that local traffic which could be unaware of the internationally agreed regulations and practices of seafarers, may be encountered in or near the traffic separation schemes, and should take any precautions which may be required by the ordinary practice of seamen or by the special circumstances of the case.

Made the 30th October 1984.

TAN SRI CHONG HON NYAN,
Minister of Transport

（二）附录 2：1953 年船舶条约

Boat Rules 1953

BOAT RULES 1953 [1]

[L.N. 312/1953]

ARRANGEMENT OF RULES

Rule

1. Citation and commencement.
2. Definitions.
3. Renewal of licences.
4. Production of N.R.I.C. to Port Officer.
5. Owner to furnish names on demand.
6. Boat and licence plate to be kept clean
7. Report of change, loss, damage, etc., to Port Officer.
8. Deaths, accidents and articles left in boat.
9. Limitation of number of passengers.

    Limits within which boat may ply.

10. Cargo boats carrying passengers.
11. Fishing boat not to carry passengers or cargo.

12. Manning.
13. Water-boats and bum-boats to be so marked.
14. Copy of fares and charges to be kept in the boat.
15. Owner's liability.
16. Forfeiture of a boat.
17. Loss of licence.
18. Safety equipment.
19. Revocation.

    First Schedule.
    Second Schedule.

---

[1] 本法条引用自 http://www.marine.gov.my/jlmeng/pic/article/law/boat%20rules%201953.pdf。

BOAT RULES 1953*
[L.N. 312/1953]

In exercise of the powers conferred upon him by sections 445 and 483 of the Merchant Shipping Ordinance, 1952, the High Commissioner in Council hereby makes the following Rules:

1. **Citation and commencement.**

    1) These Rules may be cited as the **Boat Rules, 1953.**

    2) These Rules shall have effect from the date appointed for the coming into force of Part XIII of the Ordinance.

2. **Definitions.**

    In these Rules:

    "Ordinance" means the Merchant Shipping Ordinance, 1952;

    "Passenger" includes any person carried by a boat, provided that a child of less than one year of age shall not be taken into account.

3. **Renewal of licences.**

    Applications for the renewal of licences for passenger, cargo and fishing boats shall be made to the Port Officer within seven days of the date of expiry shown thereon. All boats for which licences are required shall be brought to such place as the Port Officer may direct.

4. **Production of N.R.I.C. to Port Officer.**

    The owner of every passenger, cargo or fishing boat shall, at the time of application for a licence, produce his National Registration Identity Card to the Port Officer and the Port Officer shall enter the serial number of such Identity Card on the licence and in the appropriate register.

5. **Owner to furnish names on demand.**

    When any offence is alleged to have been committed against the Ordinance or any of the rules made there under the owner of any licensed boat shall furnish on demand to the Port Officer or any police officer the name and address of the person who was in charge of this boat on any specified occasion.

6. **Boat and licence plate to be kept clean.**

    The owner of a licensed boat shall keep the boat in a clean and sanitary condition and shall keep the licence number or plate of such boat clean and clearly visible to the satisfaction of the Port Officer.

As amended by L.N. 790/53, 262/55, 303/57, 361/58, 196/59.

7. **Report of change, loss, damage, etc., to Port Officer.**

   1) The owner of every licensed boat shall at once report to the Port Officer every change of his address, sale, breaking up or loss of a boat, collision or serious damage through collision or otherwise, or the laying up of a boat for repairs. The licence of such boat and the number plate shall be produced to the Port Officer at the same time.

   2) The owner of any boat not intending to renew his boat licence shall, within one week of the date of expiry thereof, notify the Port Officer in writing of such intention and give the location of his boat:

   Provided that failure to comply with this Rule may make the owner liable to payment of all arrears of licence fees due from the last expiry date, and where licence fees have been in arrears for a period of not less than two years, the Port Office may at his discretion cause the register of licences to be closed.

8. **Deaths, accidents and articles left in boat.**

   The owner, manager of boatman of every licensed boat shall immediately report to the Port Officer or nearest police station any death or accident caused by or to his boat or to a passenger or a member of the crew in his boat and shall deposit any article left in boat at the nearest police station.

9. **Limitation of number of passengers.**

   1) No licensed boat shall carry a greater number of passengers than the number allowed by its licence or under these Rules.

   2) No licensed boat shall be unduly immersed, taking into consideration the state of the weather.

   Limits within which boat may ply.

   3) No licensed boat shall ply or go beyond the limits (if any) specified in its licence and no such boat other than a fishing boat shall leave port limits without having obtained a port clearance.

10. **Cargo boats carrying passengers.**

    1) Except as provided in paragraphs (2) and (3) of this rule no passenger shall be carried in a licensed cargo boat.

    2) The Port Officer may, if he considers it in the public interest so to do and in every case with the approval of the Director of Marine, license a cargo boat to carry passengers subject to the following conditions:

       a) that not more than twelve passengers may be carried at any one time or not more than three passengers per measurement ton (whichever shall be the less);

       b) that where a cargo boat is licensed under this rule is not fully loaded with cargo, the measurement ton for the purposes of paragraph (a) shall be calculated on the gross tonnage of such boat less the weight of the cargo; and

       c) that every cargo boat licensed under this rule to carry passengers shall carry one efficient life jacket for every person the boat is licensed to carry.

3) The Port Officer may in his discretion impose such further conditions on the licence as he may consider fit having regard to the safety of the boat cargo and passengers.

4) Any persons who contravenes the provisions of this rule shall be guilty of an offence against these rules and shall, on conviction, be liable to the prescribed penalties and shall, in addition, be liable to have his licence cancelled

11. Fishing boat not to carry passengers or cargo.

No licensed fishing boat shall carry passengers or cargo.

12. Manning.

Every licensed boat when under way shall be adequately manned to the satisfaction of the Port Officer.

13. Water-boats and bum-boats to be so marked.

All water-boats and bum-boats shall have the words "Water-boat" or "Bum-boat" painted in large white letters on each side of the boat.

14. Copy of fares and charges to be kept in the boat.

1) A copy of the fares and charges payable for the use of a boat as specified in the First Schedule to these Rules shall be kept in the boat and produced for inspection when demanded.

2) No person in charge of a licensed boat or his agent shall demand more than the charge so specified.

15. Owner's liability.

The owner as well as the person in charge of a licensed boat shall be held responsible for any breach of the Rules.

16. Forfeiture of a boat.

When a Port Officer or a police officer is unable after due enquiry to find the owner of a licensed boat he may seize such boat and shall thereupon report the matter to a Court and the Court may, after directing such enquiries and taking such action as it thinks fit, and after the expiration of one month from the date of such report, make an order for the forfeiture of the boat.

17. Loss of licence.

In the event of loss or destruction of a boat licence the owner shall forthwith report such loss or destruction to the Port Officer or to the nearest police station. Penghulu or Penggawa. On production of a certified copy of such a report or a statutory declaration affirming such loss or destruction, the Port Officer shall, if he is satisfied as to the validity of the report, issue a copy of the licence upon payment of a fee of two dollars in the case of a passenger or cargo boat and fifty cents in the case of a fishing boat.

18. Safety equipment.

(1) Licensed boats, other than open boats and licensed fishing boat shall, before the granting of a licence, be equipped with the life-saving and fire-fighting equipment specified in paragraph (3) of this Rule.

(2) Where any licensed boat, other than a licensed fishing boat becomes unseaworthy or is not provided with the equipment required by paragraph (3) hereof, the licence issued in respect thereof shall cease to be valid.

(3)   (a) Every mechanically propelled boat licensed under these Rules shall carry fire-fighting appliances of the kind specified hereunder:

i) one box containing not less than two cubic feet of sand;

ii) one scoop;

iii) one foam type extinguisher of not less than two gallons capacity or one tetrachloride extinguisher of not less than one quart capacity.

a) Every boat licensed under these Rules shall carry life-saving equipment of the kind specified hereunder:

i) one efficient life-jacket for every person the boat is licensed to carry;

ii) one efficient sound signaling apparatus, either mechanically or hand operated;

iii) two life-buoys stowed in a position for quick release.

b) Every mechanically propelled boat licensed under these Rules and which may proceed beyond port limits shall, in addition,

i) fit one life-buoys with a self-igniting lights;

ii) carry one dozen red flares in a watertight container; and

iii) be fitted with an efficient mechanical or hand pump.

(4) Every fishing boat licensed under these Rules shall carry life-saving equipment of the kind specified hereunder:

Type of Fishing Boat	Safety Equipment to be carried
i)	Every sailing boat, and every boat propelled by oars or paddles which is not mechanically propelled.
ii)	Every sailing or rowing boat to which an outboard engine is fitted and whose overall length is less than 35 feet.
iii)	Every sailing or rowing boat to which an outboard engine is fitted and whose overall length is 35 feet or more.
iv)	Every fishing boat without a full permanent deck but fitted with an inboard diesel engine and whose overall length is 35 feet or less.
v)	Every fishing boat without a full permanent deck but fitted with an inboard petrol engine and whose overall length is 35 feet or less.
vi)	Every fishing boat without a full permanent deck but fitted with an inboard engine and whose overall length exceeds 35 feet but is less than 70 feet.

vii) Every fishing boat with a full permanent deck and fitted with an inboard engine and whose overall length is 35 feet or less.

viii) Every fishing boat with a full permanent deck and fitted with an inboard engine and whose overall length exceeds 35 feet but is less than 70 feet.

ix) Every fishing boat of overall length exceeding 70 feet.

NIL

NIL

1 life jacket per man

1 life jacket per man
6 red flares

1 life jacket per man
1 tetrachloride fire extinguisher
6 red flares

1 life jacket per man
1 lifebuoy
1 tetrachloride fire extinguisher
1 dozen red flares
1 mechanical or hand pump

1 life jacket per man
1 fire extinguisher
6 red flares

1 life jacket per man
1 lifebuoy
1 tetrachloride fire extinguisher
12 red flares
1 mechanical or hand pump

As per U.K. requirements for ocean-going trawlers.

19. Revocation.

The Notifications specified in the first and second columns of the Second Schedule to these Rules are hereby revoked to the extent specified in the third column of the said Schedule.

First Schedule.

(Rule 14)
BOAT FARES
JOHORE

(1) The fares to be paid for the use of a cargo boat or passenger boat:

a) between Bandar Maharani and Tanjong Agas within the Port of Muar; and
b) between Bandar Penggaram and Peserai within the Port of Batu Pahat

are specified below:

		Between 6 a.m. and 6 p.m.		Between 6 p. m. and 6 a.m.	
		$.	C.	$.	C.
(a)	Per passenger		10	...	20
(b)	Per passenger with cycle		20	...	30
(c)	Per tricycle		40	...	50
(d)	Per motorcycle	1	00	... 1	00
(e)	Per motor car or jeep	1	50	... 2	00
(f)	Per van	2	50	... 3	00
(g)	Per empty lorry	2	50	... 3	00
(h)	Per loaded lorry...	3	50	... 4	00
(i)	Per bull, buffalo or horse	1	00	... 1	50
(j)	Per bullock cart, including bullocks thereof ...	3	00	... 3	50

（三）附录 3：515 号法案——1994 年商船（油类污染）条例

LAWS OF MALAYSIA

REPRINT

Act 515

MERCHANT SHIPPING (OIL POLLUTION) ACT 1994

Incorporating all amendments up to 1 January 2006

PUBLISHED BY
THE COMMISSIONER OF LAW REVISION, MALAYSIA
UNDER THE AUTHORITY OF THE REVISION OF LAWS ACT 1968
IN COLLABORATION WITH
PERCETAKAN NASIONAL MALAYSIA BHD
2006

2

MERCHANT SHIPPING (OIL POLLUTION) ACT 1994

Date of Royal Assent ... ...   15 February 1994

Date of publication in the *Gazette* ... ...   24 February 1994

Previous Reprints

First Reprint   2002
Second Reprint   2005

LAWS OF MALAYSIA

Act 515

MERCHANT SHIPPING (OIL POLLUTION) ACT 1994 [①]

ARRANGEMENT OF SECTIONS

PART I

PRELIMINARY

Section

1. Short title and commencement
2. Interpretation

PART II

CIVIL LIABILITY FOR OIL POLLUTION

3. Liability for oil pollution
4. Exceptions from liability under section 3
5. Restriction of liability for oil pollution
6. Limitation of liability under section 3
7. Limitation actions
8. Restriction on enforcement of claims after establishment of limitation fund
9. Limitation fund outside Malaysia
10. Extinguishment of claims
11. Compulsory insurance against liability for pollution
12. Issue of certificate by Director of Marine
13. Rights of third parties against insurers
14. Government ships

---

① 本法条引用自 http://www.marine.gov.my/jlm/pic/article/law/act%20515%20-%20merchant%20shipping%20(oil%20pollution)%201994.pdf。

Part III

THE INTERNATIONAL OIL POLLUTION COMPENSATION FUND

Section

15. Interpretation
16. Legal personality of the Fund
17. Contributions by persons who receive oil
18. Power to obtain information
19. Liability of the Fund
20. (*Deleted*)
21. Extinguishment of claims
22. Subrogation and rights of recourse

Part IV

JURISDICTION AND EFFECT OF JUDGEMENTS

23. Jurisdiction and effect of judgements
24. Enforcement of judgements

Part V

ENFORCEMENT

25. Director of Marine to carry out powers and duties under this Act or regulations made thereunder
26. Power of arrest, detention and prosecution
27. Power to board and search ships

Part VI

MISCELLANEOUS

28. Offences by body corporate
29. Power to make regulations
30. Power to amend schedules

First Schedule

Second Schedule

LAWS OF MALAYSIA

Act 515

MERCHANT SHIPPING (OIL POLLUTION) ACT 1994

An Act to make provisions with respect to civil liability for oil pollution by merchant ships and for matters connected therewith.

[*6 April 1995, P.U. (B) 144/1995*]

BE IT ENACTED by the Seri Paduka Baginda Yang di-Pertuan Agong with the advice and consent of the Dewan Negara and Dewan Rakyat in Parliament assembled, and by the authority of the same, as follows:

PART I

PRELIMINARY

Short title and commencement

1. (1) This Act may be cited as the Merchant Shipping (Oil Pollution) Act 1994.

(2) This Act shall come into force on such date as the Minister may, by notification in the *Gazette*, appoint and the Minister may appoint different dates for different provisions of this Act.

Interpretation

2. (1) In this Act, unless the context otherwise requires—

"authorized officer" means a port officer as defined in section 2 of the Merchant Shipping Ordinance 1952 [*Ord. 70 of 1952*] or any authorized officer under section 25;

"Court" means the High Court in Malaya and the High Court in Sabah and Sarawak, as the case may be;

"Director of Marine" means the Director of Marine appointed under subsection 8(1) of the Merchant Shipping Ordinance 1952;

"exclusive economic zone", in relation to Malaysia, is the exclusive economic zone determined under the Exclusive Economic Zone Act 1984 [*Act 311*];

"incident" means any occurrence, or series of occurrences having the same origin, which causes pollution damage or creates a grave and imminent threat of causing such damage;

"Liability Convention" means the International Convention on Civil Liability for Oil Pollution Damage signed in London on 27 November 1992;

"Liability Convention country" means a country in respect of which the Liability Convention is in force;

"master" has the same meaning assigned to it under the Merchant Shipping Ordinance 1952;

"Minister" means the Minister charged with the responsibility for merchant shipping;

"oil", except in Part III, means any persistent hydrocarbon mineral oil such as crude oil, fuel oil, heavy diesel oil and lubricating oil, whether carried on board a ship as cargo or in the bunkers of such a ship;

"owner" means the person registered as the owner of the ship or, in the absence of registration, the person or persons owning the ship, except that in relation to a ship owned by a State and operated by a company which in that State is registered as the ship's operator, "owner" shall mean such company;

"person" means any individual or partnership or any public or private body, whether corporate or not, including a State or any of its constituent subdivisions;

Merchant Shipping (Oil Pollution) 7

"pollution damage" means—

(a) loss or damage caused outside a ship by contamination resulting from the discharge or escape of oil from the ship, wherever such discharge or escape may occur, provided that compensation for impairment of the environment other than loss of profit from such impairment shall be limited to costs and reasonable measures of reinstatement actually undertaken or to be undertaken;

(b) the costs of preventive measures and further loss or damage caused by preventive measures;

"port" means—

(a) a port or place declared to be a port under the Merchant Shipping Ordinance 1952 or under any other written law;

(b) a place prescribed as a port under the Merchant Shipping Ordinance 1960 of Sabah [*Sabah Ord. 11 of 1960*], the Merchant Shipping Ordinance 1960 of Sarawak [*Sarawak Ord. 2 of 1960*] and regulations made thereunder;

"preventive measures" means any reasonable measures taken by any person after an incident has occurred to prevent or minimize pollution damage;

"ship" means any sea going vessel and seaborne craft of any type constructed or adapted for the carriage of oil in bulk as cargo, provided that a ship capable of carrying oil and other cargoes shall be regarded as a ship only when it is actually carrying oil in bulk as cargo and during any voyage following such carriage unless it is proved that it has no residues of such carriage of oil in bulk aboard;

"terminal installation" means any site for the storage of oil in bulk which is capable of receiving oil from waterborne transportation, including any facility situated offshore and linked to any such site;

"territorial sea" means the territorial waters of Malaysia determined in accordance with the Emergency (Essential Powers) Ordinance, No. 7 of 1969 [*P.U. (A) 307A/1969*].

(2) In relation to any pollution damage resulting from the discharge or escape of any oil from a ship, references in this Act to the owner of the ship are references to the owner at the time of the incident or, if the incident consists of a series of occurrences having the same origin, at the time of the first such occurrence.

(3) For the purposes of this Act—

(a) references to any area of Malaysia include the territorial sea of Malaysia and exclusive economic zone of Malaysia and references to any area of any other Liability Convention country include the territorial sea and the exclusive economic zone of that Liability Convention country; and

(b) references to the exclusive economic zone of a country are references to the exclusive economic zone of that country established in accordance with international law, or, if such a zone has not been established, such area adjacent to the territorial sea of that country determined by that country in accordance with international law and extending not more than 200 nautical miles from the baselines from which the breadth of the territorial sea is measured.

(4) For the purposes of this Act, the ship's tonnage shall be the gross tonnage calculated in accordance with the tonnage measurement regulations contained in annex I of the International Convention on Tonnage Measurement of Ships signed in London on 23 June 1969.

PART II

CIVIL LIABILITY FOR OIL POLLUTION

Liability for oil pollution

3. (1) The owner of a ship at the time of an incident, or where the incident consists of a series of occurrences, at the time of the first occurrence, shall, except as otherwise provided for by this Act, be liable for any pollution damage caused by the ship as a result of the incident in area of Malaysia.

(2) Further, the owner of the ship shall be liable for any pollution damage caused to any area of any other Liability Convention country as a result of any incident specified in subsection (1).

(3) Where an incident involving two or more ships occurs and pollution damage results from the incident, the owners of all the ships concerned shall, unless exonerated under section 4, be jointly and severally liable for all such pollution damage which is not reasonably separable.

Exceptions from liability under section 3

4. (1) The owner of a ship from which oil has been discharged or has escaped shall not incur any liability for pollution damage under section 3 if he proves that the discharge or escape —

 (a) resulted from an act of war, hostilities, civil war, insurrection or a natural phenomenon of an exceptional, inevitable and irresistible character;

 (b) was wholly caused by an act or omission of a third party, which act or omission was done with intent to cause damage; or

 (c) was wholly caused by the negligence or wrongful act of a government or other authority responsible for the maintenance of lights or other navigational aids in the exercise of that function.

(2) Where the owner of a ship from which oil has been discharged or has escaped proves that the pollution damage resulted wholly or partially either from an act or omission done with intent to cause damage by the person who suffered the damage or from the negligence of that person, the owner may be exonerated wholly or partially from his liability to such person.

Restriction of liability for oil pollution damage

5. (1) Where an incident occurs and pollution damage results from the incident, whether or not the owner of the ship incurs a liability under section 3, the owner of the ship shall not be liable for such pollution damage otherwise than under that section.

(2) The liability for pollution damage shall not apply to—

 (a) any servant or agent of the owner of the ship or any member of the crew;

 (b) the pilot or any other person who, not being a member of the crew, performs services for the ship;

 (c) any charterer (howsoever described, including a bareboat charterer), manager or operator of the ship;

 (d) any person performing salvage operations with the consent of the owner of the ship or on the instructions of a competent public authority;

(e) any person taking preventive measures;

(f) all servants or agents of the persons mentioned in paragraphs *(c)*, *(d)* and *(e)*,

unless the pollution damage resulted from their own act or omission, committed with the intent to cause such damage, or recklessly and with the knowledge that such damage would probably result.

Limitation of liability under section 3

6. (1) Where the owner of a ship incurs a liability under section 3 in respect of any one incident, the provision relating to the limitation of liability of the owner of the ship in certain cases of loss or damage under any other written law relating to merchant shipping shall not apply to that liability.

(2) The owner of a ship who incurs a liability under section 3 may limit his liability in accordance with this Act as set out in Part I of this First Schedule.

(3) If it is proved that the pollution damage resulted from an act or omission of the owner of the ship, committed with the intent to cause such damage, or recklessly and with the knowledge that such damage would probably result, he shall not be entitled to limit his liability under subsection (2).

Limitation actions

7. (1) Where the owner of a ship has or is alleged to have incurred a liability under section 3 he may apply to the Court for the limitation of that liability to an amount determined in accordance with section 6.

(2) If on such an application the Court finds that the applicant has incurred such a liability and is entitled to limit it, the Court shall, after determining the limit of that liability and directing payment, or deposit of a bank guarantee or security into Court of the amount of that limit—

    (a) determine the amounts that would, apart from the limit, be due in respect of the liability to the persons making claims in the proceedings; and

Merchant Shipping (Oil Pollution) 11

(b) direct the distribution of the amount paid into Court (or, as the case may be, so much of it as does not exceed the liability) among the persons in proportion to their established claims, subject to subsections (3), (4), (5) and (6).

(3) No claim shall be admitted in proceedings under this section unless it is made within such time as the Court may direct or such further time as the Court may allow but such time shall not be less than six months from the date the pollution damage occurred.

(4) Where any sum has been paid in or towards satisfaction of any claim in respect of the pollution damage to which the liability extends—

(a) by the owner of a ship or any of his servants or agents or the person referred to in section 13 as "the insurer"; or

(b) by any other person,

the person who paid the sum shall, to the extent of that sum, be in the same position with respect to any distribution made in proceedings under this section as the person to whom it was paid would have been.

(5) Where the owner of a ship has voluntarily made any reasonable sacrifices or incurred any reasonable expenses to prevent or minimize pollution damage to which the liability extends or might have extended, he shall be in the same position with respect to any distribution made in proceedings under this section as if he had a claim in respect of the liability equal to the cost of the sacrifices or expenses.

(6) The Court may, on application by the owner of a ship or any other person who establishes that he may be compelled to pay at a later date, in whole or in part, any amount of compensation, with regard to which he would have enjoyed a right of subrogation under subsection (4) had the compensation been paid before the amount paid into the Court was distributed, order that a sufficient sum be set aside to enable such person to make a claim at a later date.

Restriction on enforcement of claims after establishment of limitation fund

8. Where the Court has found that a person who has incurred a liability under section 3 is entitled to limit that liability under section 6 and he has paid a sum or deposited a bank guarantee or security into the Court for a sum not less than that amount—

(a) the Court shall order the release of any ship or other property arrested in connection with the claim in respect of that liability or any bail or other security given to avoid such arrest; and

(b) no judgement or order in respect of any such claim shall be enforced, except so far as it is for costs,

if the claimant has access to the Court and if the payment or the bank guarantee or security or such part thereof as corresponds to the claim will be actually available to the claimant.

Limitation fund outside Malaysia

9. Where the event resulting in the liability of any person under section 3 has also resulted in a corresponding liability under the law of another Liability Convention country, section 8 shall apply as if the references to sections 3 and 7 include references to the corresponding provisions of that law and the references to sums paid into the Court include references to any sums secured under those provisions in respect of the liability.

Extinguishment of claims

10. No action to enforce a claim in respect of a liability incurred under section 3 shall be considered by any Court in Malaysia unless the action is commenced within three years from the date the pollution damage occurred or within six years from the date of the incident which caused the pollution damage, and where the incident consists of a series of occurrences, the six years' period shall run from the date of the first such occurrence.

Compulsory insurance against liability for pollution

11. (1) Subject to the provisions of this Act relating to Government ships, this section shall apply to any ship carrying in bulk a cargo of more than two thousand tons of oil.

(2) Any such ship shall not enter or leave a port in Malaysia or arrive at or leave a terminal installation area in any area of Malaysia or, if the ship is registered in Malaysia, it shall not enter or leave a port in any other country or a terminal installation in the territorial sea of any other country, unless there is in force a certificate complying with subsection (3) and showing that there is in force in respect of the ship a contract of insurance or other financial security satisfying the requirements of Article 7 of the Liability Convention (cover for owner's liability).

(3) The certificate shall be—

 (a) if the ship is registered in Malaysia, a certificate issued by the Director of Marine;

 (b) if the ship is registered in a Liability Convention country other than Malaysia, a certificate issued by or under the authority of the government of that country; and

 (c) if the ship is registered in a country which is not a Liability Convention country, a certificate issued by the Director of Marine or a certificate recognized for the purpose of this paragraph by regulations made under this Act.

(4) The certificate issued under paragraphs (3)(a) and (c) by the Director of Marine shall be in the national language and shall also include a translation in the English language.

(5) Any certificate required by this section to be in force in respect of a ship shall be carried in the ship and shall, on demand, be produced by the master to the Director of Marine or any authorized officer.

(6) If a ship enters or leaves, or attempts to enter or leave, a port or arrives at or leaves or attempts to arrive at or leave, a terminal installation in contravention of subsection (2), the master or the owner of the ship shall be guilty of an offence and shall be liable on conviction to a fine not exceeding fifty thousand ringgit or to imprisonment for a term not exceeding four years or to both.

(7) If a ship fails to carry or the master of a ship fails to produce a certificate as required by subsection (5) the master of the ship shall be guilty of an offence and shall be liable on conviction to a fine not exceeding ten thousand ringgit or to imprisonment for a term not exceeding one year or to both.

(8) If a ship attempts to leave a port or a terminal installation in Malaysia in contravention of this section, the ship may be detained.

Issue of certificate by Director of Marine

12. (1) Subject to subsection (2), if the Director of Marine is satisfied, on an application for such a certificate as is mentioned in section 11 in respect of a ship registered in Malaysia or any country which is not a Liability Convention country, that there will be in force in respect of the ship, throughout the period for which the certificate is to be issued, a valid contract of insurance or other financial security satisfying the requirements of Article 7 of the Liability Convention, the Director of Marine shall issue such a certificate to the owner.

(2) If the Director of Marine is of the opinion that there is a doubt whether the person providing the insurance or other financial security will be able to meet his obligations, or whether the insurance or other financial security will cover the owner's liability under section 3 in all circumstances, he may refuse to issue the certificate.

(3) The Director of Marine shall maintain a record of any certificate issued by him in respect of a ship registered in Malaysia and this shall be available for public inspection.

Rights of third parties against insurers

13. (1) Where it is alleged that the owner of a ship has incurred a liability under section 3 while there was in force a contract of insurance or other financial security to which such a certificate as is mentioned in section 11 relates, proceedings to enforce a claim in respect of the liability may be instituted against the person who provided the insurance or other financial security (referred to in this section as "the insurer").

(2) In any proceedings instituted against the insurer by virtue of this section, the insurer may invoke the defences (other than bankruptcy or winding up of the owner) which the owner himself would have been entitled to invoke, and it shall be a defence to prove that the pollution damage resulted from the wilful misconduct of the owner himself.

(3) The insurer may limit his liability in respect of claims made against him by virtue of this section in like manner and to the same extent as the owner of a ship may limit his liability under subsection 6(2) even if the owner, in accordance with subsection 6(3), is not entitled to limit his liability.

(4) Where the owner of a ship and the insurer each applies to the Court for the limitation of his liability any payment or any deposit of a bank guarantee or security into the Court in pursuance of either application shall be treated as paid or deposited also in pursuance of the other.

Government ships

14. (1) This Act shall not apply to warships or other ships owned or operated by a State and used, for the time being, only on government non-commercial service.

(2) In relation to a ship owned by a State and for the time being used for commercial purposes it shall be sufficient compliance with subsection 11(2) if there is in force a certificate issued by the appropriate authority of that State and showing that the ship is owned by that State and that any liability for pollution damage as defined in Article 1 of the Liability Convention will be met up to the limit prescribed by Article 5 thereof.

(3) Every State which is a party to the Liability Convention shall, for the purposes of any proceedings instituted in a Court in Malaysia to enforce a claim in respect of a liability incurred under section 3, be deemed to have submitted to the jurisdiction of that Court, but nothing in this subsection shall authorize the issue of execution against the property of any State.

PART III

THE INTERNATIONAL OIL POLLUTION COMPENSATION FUND

Interpretation

15. In this Part, unless the context otherwise requires—

"Fund Convention country" means a country in respect of which the Fund Convention is in force;

"Fund Convention ship" means a ship registered under the law of a Fund Convention country;

"guarantor" means any person providing insurance or other financial security to cover an owner's liability of the kind described in section 11;

"the Fund" means the International Oil Pollution Compensation Fund established by the Fund Convention;

"the Fund Convention" means the International Convention on the Establishment of an International Fund for Compensation for Oil Pollution Damage signed in London on 27 November 1992.

Legal personality of the Fund

16. (1) The Fund shall be recognized as a legal person capable of assuming rights and obligations and of being a party in legal proceedings before a Court in Malaysia.

(2) Any proceedings by or against the Fund may either be instituted by or against the Fund in its own name or be instituted by or against the Director of the Fund as the Fund's representative.

Contributions by persons who receive oil

17. (1) Contributions shall be payable annually to the Fund in respect of oil received by sea at ports or terminal installations in Malaysia.

(2) Subsection (1) applies whether or not the oil is being imported, and applies even if contributions are payable in respect of carriage of the same oil on a previous voyage.

(3) Contributions shall also be payable to the Fund in respect of oil when first received in any installation in Malaysia after having been carried by sea and discharged in a port or terminal installation in any country which is not a Fund Convention country.

(4) A person shall be liable to make contributions in respect of the oil received by him in any year if the oil so received in the year exceeds one hundred and fifty thousand tons.

Merchant Shipping (Oil Pollution)   17

(5) The contributions payable by a person for any year shall—

   (a) be of such amount as may be determined by the Assembly of the Fund under Article 12 of the Fund Convention and notified to him by the Fund;

   (b) be payable in such instalments, becoming due at such times, as may be so notified to him,

and if any amount due from him remains unpaid after the date on which it became due, it shall from then on bear interest, at a rate determined from time to time by the said Assembly, until it is paid.

(6) The Minister may, by regulations, impose on persons who are or may be liable to pay contributions under this section, obligations to give security for payment to the Director of Marine or to the Fund, and regulations under this subsection—

   (a) may contain such supplemental or incidental provisions as appear to the Minister expedient; and

   (b) may impose penalties for contravention of the regulations punishable by a fine not exceeding ten thousand ringgit.

(7) In this section, and section 18 and 19 unless the context otherwise requires—

"oil" means crude oil and fuel oil, and—

   (a) "crude oil" means any liquid hydrocarbon mixture occurring naturally in the earth whether or not treated to render it suitable for transportation, and includes—

      (i) crude oils from which distillate fractions have been removed; and

      (ii) crude oils to which distillate fractions have been added;

   (b) "fuel oil" means heavy distillates or residues from crude oil or blends of such materials intended for use as a fuel for the production of heat or power of a quality equivalent to the "American Society for Testing and Materials' Specification for Number Four Fuel Oil (Designation D 396-69)", or heavier.

18 *Laws of Malaysia* ACT 515

Power to obtain information

18. (1) For the purpose of transmitting to the Fund the names and addresses of the persons who under section 17 are liable to make contributions to the Fund for any year, and the quantity of oil in respect of which they are so liable, the Director of Marine may by notice require any person engaged in producing, treating, distributing or transporting oil to furnish such information as may be specified in the notice.

(2) A notice under this section may specify the way in which, and the time within which, it is to be complied with.

(3) In proceedings by the Fund against any person to recover any amount due under section 17, particulars contained in any list transmitted by the Director of Marine to the Fund shall, so far as those particulars are based on information obtained under this section, be admissible as evidence of the facts stated in the list; and so far as particulars which are so admissible are based on information given by the person against whom the proceedings are brought, those particulars shall be presumed to be accurate until the contrary is proved.

(4) If a person discloses any information which has been furnished to or obtained by him under this section, or in connection with the execution of this section, he shall, unless the disclosure is made—

    (a) with the consent of the person from whom the information was obtained;

    (b) in connection with the execution of this section; or

    (c) for the purposes of any legal proceedings arising out of this section or of any report of such proceedings,

be guilty of an offence and shall be liable on conviction to a fine not exceeding five thousand ringgit or to imprisonment for a term not exceeding six months or to both.

(5) A person who —

    (a) refuses or wilfully neglects to comply with a notice under this section; or

Merchant Shipping (Oil Pollution) 19

   (b) in furnishing any information in compliance with a notice under this section makes any statement which he knows to be false in a material particular, or recklessly makes any statement which is false in a material particular,

shall be guilty of an offence and shall be liable on conviction to a fine not exceeding ten thousand ringgit or to imprisonment for a term not exceeding one year or to both.

Liability of the Fund

19. (1) Save as provided under subsection (4), the Fund shall be liable for pollution damage in any area of Malaysia if the person suffering the damage has been unable to obtain full compensation under section 3—

   (a) because liability under that section is wholly exonerated by section 4;

   (b) because the owner of a ship liable for the pollution damage cannot meet his obligations in full or any insurance or other financial security provided under section 11 is insufficient to satisfy the claims; or

   (c) because the pollution damage exceeds the liability under section 3 as limited by section 6.

(2) For the purposes of this section the owner of a ship is to be treated as incapable of meeting his obligations if the obligations have not been met after all reasonable steps have been taken to pursue the legal remedies available.

(3) Expenses reasonably incurred or sacrifices reasonably made by the owner of a ship voluntarily to prevent or minimize pollution damage shall be treated as pollution damage for the purpose of this section, and accordingly he shall be in the same position with respect to claims against the Fund under this section as if he had a claim in respect of liability under section 3.

(4) The Fund shall not incur an obligation under this section if—

   (a) it proved that the pollution damage—

      (i) resulted from an act of war, hostilities, civil war or insurrection; or

(ii) was caused by oil which has been discharged or has escaped from a warship or other ship owned or operated by a State and used, at the time of the incident, only on government non-commercial service; or

(b) the claimant cannot prove that the pollution damage resulted from an incident involving one or more ships.

(5) If it is proved that the pollution damage resulted wholly or partly—

(a) from an act or omission done with intent to cause damage by the person who suffered the damage; or

(b) from the negligence of that person,

the Fund may be exonerated wholly or partly from its obligation to pay compensation to that person:

Provided that this subsection shall not apply to a claim in respect of expenses or sacrifices made voluntarily to prevent or minimize pollution damage.

(6) The Fund's liability under this section shall be subject to the limits as set out in Part II of the First Schedule.

(7) Notwithstanding any other written law evidence of any instrument issued by any organ of the Fund or of any document in the custody of the Fund, or any entry in or extract from such a document, may be given in any legal proceedings by production of a copy certified as a true copy by an official of the Fund; and any document purporting to be such a copy shall be received in evidence without proof of the official position or handwriting of the person signing the certificate.

(8) For the purpose of giving effect to the provisions of paragraphs 1, 2, 3, 6, 7 and 8 of Article 4 of the Fund Convention and Part II of the First Schedule, as the may case may be, a Court giving judgement against the Fund in proceedings under this section shall notify the Fund, and—

(a) no steps shall be taken to enforce the judgement unless and until the Court gives leave to enforce it;

(b) that leave shall not be given unless and until the Fund notifies the Court either that the amount of the claim is not to be reduced under the said provision of Article 4 or Part II of the First Schedule;

(c) in the latter case the judgement shall be enforceable only for the reduced amount.

20. (*Deleted by Act A1248*).

Extinguishment of claims

21. (1) No action to enforce a claim against the Fund under this Part shall be considered by a Court in Malaysia unless—

(a) the action is commenced; or

(b) a third party notice of an action to enforce a claim against the owner of a ship or his guarantor in respect of the pollution damage is given to the Fund,

within three years from the date the pollution damage occurred and in this subsection "third party notice" means a notice of the kind described in subsections 23(3) and (4).

(2) No action to enforce a claim against the Fund under this Part shall be considered by a Court in Malaysia unless the action is commenced within six years from the date of the incident which caused the pollution damage.

(3) (*Deleted by Act A1248*).

Subrogation and rights of recourse

22. (1) In respect of any sum paid under paragraph 19(1)*(b)* the Fund shall acquire by subrogation the rights of the recipient against the owner of a ship or his guarantor.

(2) (*Deleted by Act A1248*).

(3) In respect of any sum paid under paragraph 19(1)*(a)* or *(c)*, the Fund shall acquire by subrogation any rights of recourse or subrogation which the owner of the ship or his guarantor or any other person has in respect of his liability for the damage in question.

(4) In respect of any sum paid by a public authority in Malaysia or other State as compensation for pollution damage, that public authority or State shall acquire by subrogation any rights which the recipient has against the Fund under this Part.

PART IV

JURISDICTION AND EFFECT OF JUDGEMENTS

Jurisdiction and effect of judgements

23. (1) The jurisdiction of the High Court in relation to matters of admiralty under paragraph 24*(b)* of the Courts of Judicature Act 1964 [*Act 91*] shall extend to any claim in respect of a liability incurred under this Act, including a liability falling on the Fund under Part III.

(2) Where any oil is discharged or escapes from a ship but does not result in any pollution damage in any area of Malaysia and no preventive measures are reasonably taken to prevent or minimize such damage in that area, no Court in Malaysia shall consider an action (whether *in rem* or *in personam*) to enforce a claim arising from—

  (a) any pollution damage caused in any area of another Liability Convention country resulting from the discharge or escape;

  (b) any expenses incurred in taking preventive measures to prevent or minimize such damage in any area of another Liability Convention country; or

  (c) any damage caused by preventive measures so taken.

Merchant Shipping (Oil Pollution) 23

(3) Where the Fund has been given notice of proceedings instituted against the owner of a ship or his guarantor in respect of liability under section 3, any judgement given in the proceedings shall, after it has become final and enforceable, become binding upon the Fund in the sense that the facts and findings in the judgement may not be disputed by the Fund even if the Fund has not intervened in the proceedings.

(4) Where a person incurs a liability under the law of a Fund Convention country corresponding to Part II for damage which is partly in any area of Malaysia subsection (3) shall, for the purpose of proceedings under Part III, apply with any necessary modifications to a judgement in proceedings under that law of the said country.

Enforcement of judgements

24. (1) Subject to subsection (3), Part II of the Reciprocal Enforcement of Judgements Act 1958 [*Act 99*] shall apply to any judgement given by a Court in—

(a) a Liability Convention country to enforce a claim in respect of a liability incurred under any provision corresponding to section 3; or

(b) a Fund Convention country to enforce a claim in respect of liability incurred under any provision corresponding to section 19,

and in its application to such a judgement the said Part II shall have effect with the omission of subsections 5(2) and (3) of that Act.

(2) In respect of paragraph (1)*(b)*, no steps shall be taken to enforce such a judgement unless and until the Court in which it is registered under Part II of the Reciprocal Enforcement of Judgements Act 1958 gives leave to enforce it and—

(a) that leave shall not be given unless and until the Fund notifies the Court either that the amount of the claim is not to be reduced under paragraph 1 of Part II of the First Schedule or that it is to be reduced to a specified amount; and

(b) in the latter case the judgement shall be enforceable only for the reduced amount.

(3) For the purposes of this Act, subsection 3(2) of the Reciprocal Enforcement of Judgements Act 1958 shall apply with the following modifications:

(a) the reference to the Yang di-Pertuan Agong shall be construed as a reference to the Minister;

(b) the reference to the First Schedule shall be construed as a reference to the Second Schedule to this Act; and

(c) the High Court of the country or territory shall be deemed to be the superior court of that country or territory.

PART V

ENFORCEMENT

Director of Marine to carry out powers and duties under this Act or regulations made thereunder

25. (1) Subject to such terms and conditions as may be imposed or such directions as may be given by the Minister, it shall be the responsibility of the Director of Marine to carry out all or any of the powers and duties under this Act or any regulations made thereunder.

(2) The Director of Marine may authorize in writing any officer as he deems fit to carry out any of the powers and duties conferred on him under this Act or any regulations made thereunder.

(3) An authorized officer mentioned under subsection (2) shall be deemed to be public servants within the meaning of the Penal Code [*Act 574*].

Power of arrest, detention and prosecution

26. (1) The Director of Marine or any authorized officer may, where he has reason to believe that an offence has been committed under this Act, without a warrant—

(a) arrest any person who he has reason to believe has committed an offence under this Act; and

(b) detain any ship which he has reason to believe has been used in the commission of such an offence:

Provided that when any person has been arrested as aforesaid he shall thereafter be dealt with as provided by the Criminal Procedure Code [*Act 593*].

(2) Where a ship has been detained under subsection (1) the Director of Marine or any authorized officer may release such ship to the owner, master or agent thereof subject to sufficient security being furnished to the satisfaction of the Director of Marine or any authorized officer that the ship shall be surrendered to him on demand.

(3) The Director of Marine or any authorized officer shall have the authority to appear in court and conduct any prosecution in respect of any offence under this Act or any regulations made thereunder.

Power to board and search ships

27. (1) The Director of Marine or any authorized officer may, where he has reason to believe that an offence has been committed under this Act or any regulations made thereunder, without a warrant—

(a) board and search any ship; or

(b) enter and search any premises,

and may carry out such inspection and examination as he may consider necessary and may seize any books, papers, documents or other things found in those places which may furnish evidence of the commission of an offence under this Act or any regulations made thereunder and may make copies of, or take extracts from, any such books, papers or documents.

(2) Any person who assaults, hinders, impedes or obstructs the Director of Marine or any authorized officer in the performance of his duties under this section shall be guilty of an offence and shall be liable on conviction to a fine not exceeding five thousand ringgit or to imprisonment for a term not exceeding six months or to both.

Part VI

MISCELLANEOUS

Offences by body corporate

28. Where an offence under this Act or any regulations made thereunder has been committed by a body corporate, any person who at the time of the commission of the offence was a director, manager, secretary or other similar officer of the body corporate or any person who was purporting to act in such capacity shall, as well as such body corporate, be deemed to be guilty of that offence unless he proves that the offence was committed without his consent or connivance and that he exercised all due diligence to prevent the commission of the offence as he ought to have exercised, having regard to the nature of his functions in that capacity and to all the circumstances.

Power to make regulations

29. (1) The Minister may from time to time make such regulations as may be necessary or expedient for giving full effect to the provisions of this Act.

(2) Without prejudice to the generality of subsection (1), regulations may be made—

   (a) to prescribe the amount of fees to be paid on an application for the issue of a certificate under subsection 12(1);

   (b) to prescribe the form of the certificate to be issued under subsection 12(1) and the validity period of such certificate;

   (c) to provide for the cancellation and delivery up of a certificate issued under subsection 12(1) in such circumstances as may be prescribed by the regulations;

   (d) to provide that certificates in respect of ships registered in any, or any specified, country which is not a Liability Convention country shall, in such circumstances as may be specified in the regulations, be recognized for the purposes of paragraph 11(3)*(c)* if issued by or under the authority of the government of the country designated in

Merchant Shipping (Oil Pollution) 27

the regulations in that behalf; and the country that may be so designated may be either or both of the following, that is to say—

(i) the country in which the ship is registered; and

(ii) any country specified in the regulations for the purposes of this paragraph;

(e) to provide for the conversion of the special drawing rights referred to in this Act into the amount of money expressed in Ringgit Malaysia;

(f) to provide for any other matter which is required by any provisions of this Act to be provided for by regulations.

(3) If a person required by regulations under paragraph (2)*(c)* to deliver up a certificate fails to do so, he shall be guilty of an offence and shall be liable on conviction to a fine not exceeding five thousand ringgit.

Power to amend Schedules

30. The Minister may by order published in the *Gazette* amend, add to or vary the Schedules to this Act.

FIRST SCHEDULE

PART I

[Subsection 6(2)]

LIMITATION OF LIABILITY OF OWNER OF SHIP

The owner of a ship shall be entitled to limit his liability in respect of any one incident to an aggregate amount calculated as follows:

(a) for a ship not exceeding five thousand units of tonnage, 4,510,000 special drawing rights;

(b) for a ship with a tonnage in excess of five thousand units of tonnage, 4,510,000 special drawing rights plus an additional 631 special drawing rights for each additional unit of tonnage:

Provided however, that this aggregate amount shall not in any event exceed 89,770,00 special drawing rights.

PART II

[Subsection 19(6)]

OVERALL LIMIT ON LIABILITY OF FUND

1. (1) Except as otherwise provided in subparagraphs (2) and (3), the aggregate amount of compensation payable by the Fund shall in respect of any one incident be limited, so that the total sum of that amount and the amount of compensation actually paid under Part II of this Act for pollution damage within the scope of this Act shall not exceed 203,000,000 special drawing rights.

(2) Except as otherwise provided in subparagraph (3), the aggregate amount of compensation payable by the Fund for pollution damage resulting from a natural phenomenon of an exceptional, inevitable and irresistible character shall not exceed 203,000,000 special drawing rights.

(3) The maximum amount of compensation referred to in subparagraphs (1) and (2) shall be 300,740,000 special drawing rights with respect to any incident occurring during any period when there are three Fund Convention countries in respect of which the combined relevant quantity of oil received by persons in the territories of such countries during the preceding calendar year is not less than 600 million tons.

(4) Interest accrued on the amount paid into Court under section 7 of this Act, if any, shall not be taken into account for the computation of the maximum compensation payable by the Fund under this Act.

Merchant Shipping (Oil Pollution) 29

2. Where the amount of established claims against the Fund exceeds the aggregate amount of compensation payable under paragraph 1, the amount available shall be distributed in such a manner that the proportion between any established claim and the amount of compensation actually recovered by the claimant under this Act shall be the same for all claimants.

3. A certificate given by the Director of the Fund stating that subparagraph 1(3) is applicable to any claim under section 19 shall be conclusive evidence for the purposes of Part III of this Act.

SECOND SCHEDULE

[Subsection 24 (3)]

STATE PARTIES TO THE CIVIL LIABILITY CONVENTION

Algeria	Latvia
Angola	Liberia
Antigua and Barbuda	Lithuania
Argentina	Madagascar
Australia	Malta
Bahamas	Marshall Islands
Bahrain	Mauritius
Barbados	Mexico
Belgium	Monaco
Belize	Morocco
Brunei Darussalam	Mozambique
Bulgaria	Namibia
Cambodia	Netherlands
Cameroon	New Zealand
Canada	Nigeria
Cape Verde	Norway
Chile	Oman

China	Panama
Colombia	Papua New Guinea
Comoros	Philippines
Congo	Poland
Croatia	Portugal
Cyprus	Qatar
Denmark	Republic of Korea
Djibouti	Romania
Dominica	Russian Federation
Dominican Republic	Saint Vincent and Grenadines
Egypt	Samoa
El Salvador	Seychelles
Fiji	Sierra Leone
Finland	Singapore
France	Slovenia
Gabon	Spain
Georgia	Sri Lanka
Germany	Sweden
Ghana	Switzerland
Greece	Tonga
Grenada	Trinidad and Tobago
Guinea	Tunisia
Iceland	Turkey
India	United Arab Emirates
Indonesia	United Kingdom
Ireland	United Republic of Tanzania

Merchant Shipping (Oil Pollution) 31

Italy	Uruguay
Jamaica	Vanuatu
Japan	Venezuela
Kenya	Vietnam

STATE PARTIES TO THE FUND CONVENTION

Algeria	Liberia
Angola	Lithuania
Antigua and Barbuda	Madagascar
Argentina	Malta
Australia	Marshall Islands
Bahamas	Mauritius
Bahrain	Mexico
Barbados	Monaco
Belgium	Morocco
Belize	Mozambique
Brunei Darussalam	Namibia
Cambodia	Netherlands
Cameroon	New Zealand
Canada	Nigeria
Cape Verde	Norway
China (Hong Kong Special Administrative Region)	Oman
Colombia	Panama
Comoros	Papua New Guinea
Congo	Philippines
Croatia	Poland

Cyprus	Portugal
Denmark	Qatar
Djibouti	Republic of Korea
Dominica	Russian Federation
Dominican Republic	Saint Vincent and Grenadines
Fiji	Samoa
Finland	Seychelles
France	Sierra Leone
Gabon	Singapore
Georgia	Slovenia
Germany	Spain
Ghana	Sri Lanka
Greece	Sweden
Grenada	Tonga
Guinea	Trinidad and Tobago
Iceland	Tunisia
India	Turkey
Ireland	United Arab Emirates
Italy	United Kingdom
Jamaica	United Republic of Tanzania
Japan	Uruguay
Kenya	Vanuatu
Latvia	Venezuela

LAWS OF MALAYSIA

Act 515

MERCHANT SHIPPING (OIL POLLUTION) ACT 1994

LIST OF AMENDMENTS

Amending law	Short title	In force from
Act A1248	Merchant Shipping (Oil Pollution) (Amendment) Act 2005	15-09-2005

34

LAWS OF MALAYSIA

Act 515

MERCHANT SHIPPING (OIL POLLUTION) ACT 1994

LIST OF SECTIONS AMENDED

Section	Amending authority	In force from
2	Act A1248	15-09-2005
3	Act A1248	15-09-2005
5	Act A1248	15-09-2005
6	Act A1248	15-09-2005
11	Act A1248	15-09-2005
13	Act A1248	15-09-2005
15	Act A1248	15-09-2005
17	Act A1248	15-09-2005
19	Act A1248	15-09-2005
20	Act A1248	15-09-2005
21	Act A1248	15-09-2005
22	Act A1248	15-09-2005
24	Act A1248	15-09-2005
30	Act A1248	15-09-2005
First Schedule	Act A1248	15-09-2005
Second Schedule	Act A1248	15-09-2005

DICETAK OLEH
PERCETAKAN NASIONAL MALAYSIA BERHAD,
KUALA LUMPUR
BAGI PIHAK DAN DENGAN PERINTAH KERAJAAN MALAYSIA

第三章 印度尼西亚海事管理法律研究

印度尼西亚疆域横跨亚洲及大洋洲，由太平洋和印度洋之间约 17508 个大小岛屿组成。北部的加里曼丹岛与马来西亚接壤，新几内亚岛与巴布亚新几内亚相连。东北部面临菲律宾，东南部濒临印度洋，西南与澳大利亚相望，陆地面积约 190.4 万平方千米，海洋面积约 316.6 万平方千米（不包括专属经济区），海岸线总长 54716 千米。印度尼西亚设有雅加达首都特区、日惹特区、亚齐特区和 30 个省，共计 33 个一级行政区。印度尼西亚是名副其实的"万岛之国"。

一、海事管理体制与机构设置

印度尼西亚为了维护海洋主权，改变了过去极其分散的海事管理体制，采用了相对集中与高层协调的综合管理模式。

（一）海事管理体制

印度尼西亚采用的海事管理体制是相对集中与高层协调的综合管理模式。相对集中管理是指印度尼西亚航运、港口、船舶管理等海事事务均由交通部海运总局（Direktorat Jenderal Perhubungan Laut，简称 DJPL）负责管理；但海事执法相对比较分散，海运总局下的海洋和海岸警卫队（Kesatuan Penjagaan Laut dan Pantai Indonesia，简称 KPLP）、政治法律安全协调部下的海事安全局（Badan Keamanan Laut Republik Indonesia，简称 BAKAMLA）和海军均有权在海上巡逻执法，执法权限有所交叉。高层协调是指印度尼西亚设立的海洋事务协调部，主要负责协调统筹数个与海洋事务有关的部门，海事事务亦在其管辖权限内。

1. 中央级别的海事管理机构

印度尼西亚设立的属于中央级别的海事管理机构有海洋事务协调部、海洋事务和渔业部、海运总局、海事安全局。上述机构虽然均负责执行沿海和海洋资源法律法规，但各有其特定的职责。其中，海洋事务协调部负责协调统筹数个与发展海洋资源、兴建海洋捷运等海洋事务有关的部门。海洋事务和渔业部负责组织海洋领域的渔业事务和协助总统组织州政府的渔业事务。海运总局负责航运管理、港口管理、船舶管理等海事事务。海事安全局则隶属于政治法律安全协调部，负责制定印度尼西亚领海安全政策、监督其他机构的水上巡逻执行情况等。海运总局下设海洋和海岸警卫队，海事安全局和海军还经常一起进行演习和开展联合行动。

2. 省市级别的海事管理机构

印度尼西亚自治法赋予地方对海域的管理权限，低潮线至 4 海里内归地方政府管辖，4~12 海里范围归沿海省政府管辖。① 所以，印度尼西亚的每个省市均设有省市级的海事机构，并被授予一定权力以管理有限的海域，这些省市级海事机构在某种程度上是独立的。

（二）海运总局

海上运输部于 1960 年 12 月 31 日颁布了《海运部的就业、职责和组成法令》，该法令规定了海运部的工作范围包括海上运输领域、内河交通领域、港口区域、船舶监督和管理领域。海运部于 1967 年改制为海运总局（DJPL），隶属于交通部，后经过多次改革，根据 2000 年发布的 165 号总统令和 2001 年交通部发布的 24 号规章，现海运总局的主要职责是管理海上运输活动、港口活动，保障海上和港口的运输安全，保护群岛水域及海洋环境。②

1. 基本职责

2008 年发布的 17 号法律规定，海运总局的任务是使印度尼西亚发展成为一个高效、具有竞争力的海运国家，发展国家基础设施建设，促进国家经济增长。目前，海运总局的基本职责主要有以下几项：一是制定海运领域的相关政策、规范、程序和标准，并保证其实施；二是在海运领域进行相关的技术指导和技术评估；三是管理全国水域的运输活动；四是进行安全高效的港口管理，使港口活动确保效率并具备全球竞争力，通过监管群岛以支持国家发展；五是保障水域港口运输的安全；六是保护群岛水域及海洋环境；七是通过机构重组改革和国家监管，起到稳定社会秩序的作用。③

2. 部门架构

海运总局的最高决策机构为董事会，并设有秘书处，主要负责协调任务执行以及向海运总局内的所有部门提供技术和行政支持。

海运总局下设有五个分局：①海运交通管理局，负责制定并实施海运领域的政策、规范、标准和程序，提供技术指导和监督，对海运领域进行相关的评估并予以报告。②港口局，负责执行制定并实施港口活动的相关政策、规范、标准和程序，提供技术指导和监督，对港口设施、港口疏浚和填海的设计、开发、发展规划进行评估并予以报告。③航运和海事局，负责制定并实施船舶海运、海洋环境保护和海洋领域的相关政策与法规，提供技术指导和监督，及时进行评估并予以报告。④引航局，负责制定并实施引航领域的相关政策、规范、标准和程序，提供技术指导和监督，进行评估并予以报告。⑤海洋和海岸警卫队，负责制定并实施航运安全相关的政策、规范、标准和程序，提供技术指导和监督，在印度尼西亚管辖的海域内进行巡逻，确保航运安全，对水上基础设施、航运安全、执法和宣传领域进行评估并予以报告。下文将详细介绍航运和海事局以及海洋和海岸警卫队的具体职责。印度尼西亚海运总局部门架构如图 3-1 所示。

---

① 参见李景光、张占海《国外海洋管理与执法体制》，海洋出版社 2014 年版，第 239 页。
② 印度尼西亚海运总局的历史，参见网址：http://ditkapel.dephub.go.id//konten/show/1，2018 年 7 月 28 日访问。
③ 印度尼西亚海运总局的职能，参见网址：http://hubla.dephub.go.id/Default.aspx，2018 年 7 月 28 日访问。

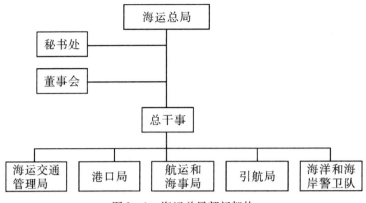

图 3-1 海运总局部门架构

3. 航运和海事局

航运和海事局作为海运总局（DJPL）下属的部门，其具体职责如下：第一，制定关于船舶的建造与适航性、船舶国籍登记、无线电技术、防止船舶污染、船舶安全管理、船舶维修保养等的认证测试和认证标准；第二，制定关于船舶的建造与适航性、船舶国籍登记、无线电技术、防止船舶污染、船舶安全管理、船舶维修保养的规则、准则、标准和程序；第三，为船舶的建造与适航性、船舶国籍登记、无线电技术、防止船舶污染、船舶安全管理、船舶维修保养等领域提供技术援助；第四，登记船舶，管理国内航运船舶的营运，签发、延期、修改、撤销许可证，签发船舶适航、防止船舶污染、船舶安全管理等相关证书；第五，确保船舶在设计、适航性、安全管理、防止污染等方面符合规定；第六，对船舶的建造与适航性、船舶国籍登记、无线电技术、防止船舶污染、船舶安全管理、船舶维修保养等方面进行评估和报告。

4. 海洋和海岸警卫队

印度尼西亚海洋和海岸警卫队（KPLP）隶属于印度尼西亚交通部海运总局（DJ-PL），主要职能是确保印度尼西亚管辖的海洋区域的航运安全。海洋和海岸警卫队的部分成员来自海军，但海洋和海岸警卫队与海军没有隶属关系，海洋和海岸警卫队经常与海军进行联合演习和联合行动。

（1）基本职责。海洋和海岸警卫队的基本职责如下：第一，制定并实施相关政策、规范、标准和程序，包括但不限于海上巡逻和安全救援、安全监督，执法和宣传，航运秩序，处理海难和水下工作，沿海和海上基础设施等领域；第二，对上述领域提供技术指导和监督；第三，在海洋和海岸警卫队管辖范围内进行执法，调查海上犯罪行为；第四，为海运总局提供技术指导和行政支持；第五，防止海洋环境污染；第六，对上述领域内的相关活动进行评估和报告。

（2）执法船舶和其他装备。海岸警卫队目前配备有7艘1级巡逻艇、14艘2级巡逻艇、40艘3级巡逻艇、数百艘4—5级巡逻艇。为了支持印度尼西亚新基地的发展，海事安全局加强巡逻艇的装备配备，确保船艇在海上作业遇到危险时能够有效保障人员安全。印度尼西亚计划至2019年将建造100艘1—3级船舶，部署在整个印度尼西亚。印度尼西亚计划在未来5年，海岸警卫队配备500艘不同规模的巡逻艇，其中将增加大约100艘1级巡逻艇和150～200艘2—5级巡逻艇。所有巡逻艇也将由以前的光纤替代为刚性充气艇。此外,印度尼西亚还将扩大巡逻区,并增加更多巡逻人员。

(三) 海事安全局

海事安全局(BAKAMLA)在2014年由印度尼西亚总统佐科·维多多(Joko Widodo)正式宣布成立,并将海事安全局归由政治法律安全协调部管辖。同时,在管理和利用海洋资源方面,政治法律安全协调部部长将与海洋部部长相协调。

海事安全局的主要负责人是从印度尼西亚海军挑选而来的,但该机构不属于印度尼西亚国家武装部队,而是一个非部级政府机构。海事安全局和印度尼西亚海军经常一起进行演习和联合行动。在搜救过程中,海事安全局还与国家搜索救援机构进行联合行动。

1. 基本职责

海事安全局的基本职责主要是:①在印度尼西亚领海和管辖范围内进行安全巡逻;②制定领海安全和管辖方面的相关国家政策;③建立安全预警系统,监督、预防领海和管辖范围内的违法行为并提起诉讼;④协同并监督相关机构的海域巡逻,为相关机构提供业务和技术支持;⑤在印度尼西亚领海和管辖范围内提供搜救援助;⑥在国防系统中执行其他任务。

2. 部门架构

海事安全局最高负责人为局长,下设有首席秘书处,按照第178号总统令第10条的规定,首席秘书处最多由三个局组成,每个局最多设立四个部门,每个部门最多设立三个子部门。海事安全局下设立有政策与战略处、操作与训练处、信息、法律与合作处,其中,政策与战略处下分为政策部门、战略部门、研究开发部门。印度尼西亚将其领海划分为三个海域,设立了西部海事区办公室、中部海事区办公室、东部海事区办公室,监管印度尼西亚海域及地方海事机构,办公室主任直接受局长管辖。印度尼西亚海事安全局部门架构如图3-2所示。

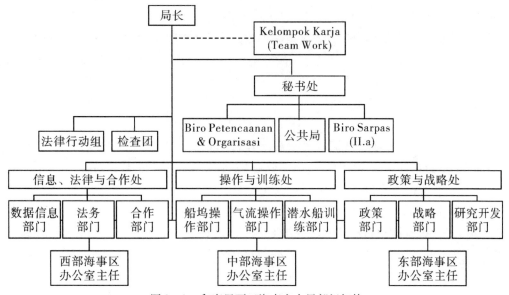

图3-2 印度尼西亚海事安全局部门架构

3. 人员情况

海事安全局（BAKAMLA）的人员包括永久雇员和委派辅员。海事安全局有 975 名安全和保安人员。其中有 242 名 A 类海事检查员，有权检查 500 总吨及以上的船舶；360 名 B 类检查员，有权检查 500 总吨以下的船舶；53 名无线电检查员，遍布整个群岛。

海事安全学院（Akademi Keselamatan and Keamanan Laut，AKKL）是海事安全局求职申请者的主要培训机构。海事安全学院的成立是由于海事安全局和海军之间的合作，该学院是准军事化教学，其学生就读 3 年后将获得文凭证书。学院位于苏拉巴亚布米莫罗的海军教育和训练发展指挥部（Kodiklatal）内，而预警系统技能实验室则位于苏腊巴亚的海军学院。

4. 执法船舶和其他装备

2015 年初，海事安全局（BAKAMLA）拥有 2000 名配员和 3 艘巡逻艇。同年，海军捐赠了 10 艘巡逻艇。但是，这些船舶仅用于非军事巡逻，因此，海事安全局对船舶做了一些调整，如拆除了大型武器。

2016 年，海事安全局在印度尼西亚东西部领海区运营 6 艘巡逻艇。2017 年又购买了 4 艘：船长 110 米和 80 米的巡逻艇各 2 艘。新船配有法医实验室，可供巡逻时立即检测可疑物体。

二、海事法律

印度尼西亚有一系列涉及海洋管理与执法的法规，其海洋法律体系比较健全。

（一）国内法

印度尼西亚主要的涉海法规有 1973 年《大陆架法》、1983 年《专属经济区法》、1990 年《自然生物资源保护法》、1996 年《领海法》、1997 年《环境管理与保护法》、2004 年《渔业法》、2007 年《国土空间规划法》、2007 年《海岸带与岛屿管理法》等。① 而在海事管理方面，主要是总统发布与海事、海港、船务、船舶事故调查相关的总统令，政府也会出台相关的行政法规。

印度尼西亚的国内法梳理如下：

1. 2008 年关于船舶事故调查第四部分第 17 号航运法

Shipping Law no. 17 Year 2008, Part Four Investigation of Ship Accidents

　　ⅰ. Article 256 follows its explanation

　　ⅱ. Article 257

http://www.indolaw.org/UU/Law%20No.%2017%20of%202008%20on%20Shipping.pdf

---

① 参见李景光、张占海《国外海洋管理与执法体制》，海洋出版社 2014 年版，239 页。

2. 1999年关于海上运输的82号政府法规

PP no. 82 of 1999 concerning Transportation in Waters；

http://translate.google.com/translate? client = tmpg&hl = en&langpair = id | en&u = http%3A//hubdat.dephub.go.id/peraturan-pemerintah/83-pp-no-82-tahun-1999-ttg-angkutan-di-perairan

3. 2000年关于海洋事务的7号政府法规

PP no. 7 of 2000 on Marine Affairs；

https://www.global-regulation.com/translation/indonesia/7223881/government-regulation-number-7-2000.html? q = PP%20no.%207%20of%202000

4. 2000年关于航海的82号政府法规

PP no. 81 Year 2000 on Navigation；

https://www.global-regulation.com/translation/indonesia/2971488/government-regulation-number-81-in-2000.html? q = PP%20no.%2081%20Year%202000

5. 2001年关于港口事务的69号政府法规

PP no. 69 of 2001 on Ports；

https://www.global-regulation.com/translation/indonesia/7223551/government-regulation-number-69-in-2001.html? q = PP%20no.%2069%20of%202001

6. 2002年关于海运的51号政府法规

PP no. 51 of 2002 concerning Shipping；

https://l.facebook.com/l.php? u = https%3A%2F%2Fwww.global-regulation.com%2Ftranslation%2Findonesia%2F7223264%2Fgovernment-regulation-number-51-in-2002.html%3Fq%3DPP%2520no.%252051%2520of%25202002&h = ATN2US7snredoOGFlaICkf1NQnCInWmFrOaGl8mDcLHHXNGzqLbmryAzmd21xHRkHCAGq6IWvqZbzVVa_ceL3UfFPrdJoBG8KEOZWgBIfINU5V5Y-T4Vg3LnZDbsuyf9Z49GzyYomK2Z_OcJ

7. 1999年关于国家运输安全委员会第105号总统令

Presidential Decree No. 105/1999 on the National Transportation Safety Committee；
(KNKT) https://l.facebook.com/l.php? u = https%3A%2F%2Fwww.global-regulation.com%2Ftranslation%2Findonesia%2F8443169%2Fpresidential-decree-number-105-in-1999.html%3Fq%3DPresidential&h = ATN2US7snredoOGFlaICkf1NQnCInWmFrOaGl8mDcLHHXNGzqLbmryAzmd21xHRkHCAGq6IWvqZbzVVa_ceL3UfFPrdJoBG8KEOZWgBIfINU5V5Y-T4Vg3LnZDbsuyf9Z49GzyYomK2Z_OcJ

8. 1998年关于船舶事故调查的1号政府法规

PP no. 1 of 1998 on the Inspection of Ship Accidents

https://www.global-regulation.com/translation/indonesia/7224946/government-regulation-no.-1-of-1998.html？q=PP%20no.%201%20of%201998

(二) 国际条约

1. 海事国际条约概述

印度尼西亚已加入《联合国海洋法公约》，加入的其他海事国际条约有22个，其中具有代表性的是1974年《国际海上人命安全公约》（SOLAS）、1966年《国际载重线公约》（LL）、1969年《国际船舶吨位丈量公约》（ICM）、1972年《国际海上避碰规则公约》（COLREGS）、1972年《国际集装箱安全公约》（CSC）、1978年《国际海员培训、发证和值班标准公约》（STCW）、1971年《特种业务客船协定》（STP）、1976年《国际海事卫星组织公约》（IMSO）、1969年《国际油污损害民事责任公约》（CLC）、1973年《国际防止船舶造成污染公约》（MARPOL）等国际条约。

2. 加入方式及国内化程序

印度尼西亚2000年第24号法律的第9、10、11条对该国加入国际条约的方式做出了规定，国际条约可通过法律或总统令批准，其中与政治、捍卫和平、国安领土安全、国家主权、人权、环境、借贷相关的国际条约需通过法律来批准，其他方面的公约可通过总统令批准。印度尼西亚加入的海事国际条约可以在国内直接适用，无须再进行国内立法转化。

三、小 结

印度尼西亚实行相对集中管理与高层协调的海事管理体制，由交通部海运总局主管海事和港口行政事务，另有海洋事务和渔业部、海事安全局等协助相关事务，同时，印度尼西亚的每个省市也设有相对独立的省市级海事机构。为了协调海洋事务管理，中央政府又设立了海洋事务协调部。但是，"多龙治海"的体制导致印度尼西亚在海事执法方面采用多机构执法，执法活动时有联合，执法权限互有交叉，这就影响到印度尼西亚的海事执法活动的效果，如各机构争相执法或推诿执法。

四、附录：印度尼西亚海事法律（国内法）文件

(一) 附录1：1998年船舶事故调查的1号政府法规

PP no. 1 of 1998 on the Inspection of Ship Accidents

PP 1 – 1998. Doc Government Regulation of Republic of Indonesia No. 1 of 1998 Concerning

The EXAMINATION of an ACCIDENT the SHIP PRESIDENT REPUBLIC of INDONESIA[①]

(PP No. 1 of 1998 on the Inspection of Ship Accidents X)

Considering: that as the implementation of the provisions of article 93 paragraph (3) of Act No. 21 of 1992 about the cruise, viewed the need to assign government regulations about examination of the Wreck of the ship; Remember: 1. Article 5 paragraph (2) of the Constitution of 1945; 2. Act No. 21 of 1992 about the voyage (State Gazette Number 98 in 1992, an additional Sheet country number 3493); Decide: Define: GOVERNMENT REGULATIONS ABOUT EXAMINATION Of THE WRECK Of THE SHIP.

CHAPTER I GENERAL PROVISIONS

Article 1

In this Regulation, the definition:

1. The inspection of the ship Accident investigation or investigation activities is an event of an accident the ship conducted by authorized government officials to find out the causes of the accident Board.

2. Snag is the Skipper or the leader ship and/or ship's officer who allegedly made a mistake or omission in the application of professional standard kepelautan which caused the accident.

3. Penal settlement was snagged the administrative sanctions imposed on the basis of the results of the decision of the Tribunal the Court of the cruise.

4. The Officers of the ship is the propagator, the engineer, and the ship's radio officer.

5. Witness is any person who can provide information to the benefit of the inspection of a ship accident events that sound myself, seen or experienced it myself, or others in authority who directly or indirectly related to a ship that was wrecked or events of the accident.

6. An expert witness is a person who has expertise in a particular field that provides information in accordance with its expertise in the examination of the advanced submarine to make light of an event of an accident the ship.

7. The Expert Advisor is the person because his expertise was appointed by snagged to accompany snagged during the follow-up inspection of the ship accident.

8. The Minister is the Minister responsible in the area of the cruise.

---

① 本法条引用自 https://www.global-regulation.com/translation/indonesia/7224946/government-regulation-no.-1-of-1998.html? q=PP%20no.%201%20of%201998。

Article 2

(1) examination of the wreck of the ship made against all accidents that occur in the territorial waters of Indonesia and Indonesia-flagged ship accidents that occur outside the territorial waters of Indonesia.

(2) an accident the ship referred to in subsection (1) include the following: a. The ship sank; b. The ship burned; c. Ship impacts; d. Ship accident which causes threatening the human soul and the loss of property; e. Ship ran aground.

Article 3

Examination of the wreck of the ship include: a. The ship accident preliminary examination; b. Examination of the advanced submarine.

CHAPTER II REPORT OF THE ACCIDENT THE SHIP

Article 4

Any person who is on board who knows the dikapalnya of an accident, subject to the limits of its ability to ship is obliged to report accidents: a. Harbour nearest port when the ship's accident happened in the territorial waters of Indonesia; b. Republic of Indonesia nearest Representative Officials and Government officials the local State authorities when the ship's accident or the first port visited after the accident the ship occurs outside the territorial waters of Indonesia.

Article 5

(1) Captain or a leader board, that: a. His ship had an accident the ship; b. Causing another vessels got an accident the ship; c. Know the other ship crashes the ship; d. Carrying crew or passengers of a ship that was wrecked ship is obliged to report the accident to the ship Harbour nearest port when the ship's accident happened in the territorial waters of Indonesia.

(2) The Skipper or the leader of the Indonesia-flagged ship had an accident the ship referred to in subsection (1) is required to report the accident to the ship's official representative of the Republic of Indonesia and the Government officials closest to the local State authorities when the ship's accident or first stopover port after the ship wreck happened is beyond the territorial waters of Indonesia.

Article 6

Further Provisions regarding the procedures and forms the contents of the ship accident report as referred to in article 4 and article 5 is set by the Minister. Chapter 7 reports on the accident of the ship reported to the Representative of the Republic of Indonesia officials referred to in article 4 of the letter b and article 5 paragraph (2), by the leadership of the representative of the Republic of Indonesia are forwarded to the Minister.

CHAPTER III SHIP ACCIDENT PRELIMINARY EXAMINATION

Article 8

(1) Preliminary examination carried out on the basis of vessel accident reports accident aboard.

(2) The preliminary examination of the accident the ship referred to in subsection (1) is executed by: a. Harbour, after receiving the accident report of Rapporteur. B. Government officials appointed by the Minister, after the Minister received the accident report the ship from the leadership of the Representative of the Republic of Indonesia and/or of the authorities the local State authorities.

Article 9

The ship accident preliminary examination referred to in article 8 undertaken for searching and/or preliminary evidence upon the occurrence of an accident the ship.

Article 10

In carrying out preliminary examination of the accident the ship, Harbour or Government officials appointed by the Minister may seek the necessary information from: a. The Captain or a leader ship; b. Officers of the ship; c. Older ships; d. The other party.

Article 11

Further Provisions regarding the procedures for preliminary examination of ship accidents as stipulated in article 8, article 9, and article 10 is set by the Minister.

Article 12

(1) The results of the preliminary examination of the accident the ship poured in the form of a news event of preliminary examination of the accident Board.

(2) The preliminary examination of accident events News the ship referred to in subsection (1) is signed by the Harbour or Government officials appointed by the Minister.

Article 13

(1) The results of the preliminary examination of the accident the ship delivered in writing to the Minister no later than thirty (30) days from the receipt of the report of the accident Board.

(2) The results of the preliminary examination of the accident the ship referred to in

subsection (1) enclosed with: a. The conclusion of the results of the preliminary examination of the accident the ship; b. Report of the accident the ship; c. Other documents required.

(3) Further Provisions regarding the procedures for making the results of the preliminary examination of the accident the ship referred to in subsection (1) and paragraph (2) is set by the Minister.

Article 14

Any costs that are required in the implementation of the preliminary examination of the accident the ship charged to income and Expenditure budget of the Ministry of transportation.

Article 15

(1) If on the basis of the results of the preliminary examination of the accident Board. The Minister argues the existence of the alleged errors and/or omissions in the standards of the profession of kepelautan performed by the Captain or a leader ship and/or officers over ship accidents aboard, then no later than within 14 (fourteen) days from the receipt of the results of the preliminary examination of the accident Board, the Minister of Justice asking for further examination of accident do Cruise ships.

(2) a request for advanced examination of the wreck of the ship referred to in subsection (1) is filed in writing accompanied by: a. Kedelakaan reports the ship; b. Results of the preliminary examination of the accident the ship; c. Conclusion the results of the preliminary examination of the accident the ship; d. Other necessary documents.

Article 16

(1) The Minister issued a letter of termination of examination of the accident the ship against ship accident preliminary examination results that are not requested examination of the advanced submarine.

(2) A letter of termination of examination of the wreck of the ship referred to in subsection (1) at least contain information on the basis of reasons not further inspection dimintakannya crash of the ship and the determination of the causes of the accident Board.

(3) The implementation of the provisions referred to in subsection (1) and paragraph (2) are governed further by a Minister.

CHAPTER IV INSPECTION ADVANCED SUBMARINE
PART ONE GENERAL

Article 17

Advanced ship accident Examination carried out by the Court of the cruise. Article 18 in carrying out follow-up examination of an accident aboard the cruise, the Court on duty: a. Examine the causes of the accident and determine the presence or absence of errors or omissions in the application of standards of the profession of kepelautan by the Captain or a leader ship and/or officers over ship accidents of ships; b. Administrative sanction dropped to Captain or a leader ship and/or officers of ships that have certificate of seafaring expertise issued by the Government of Indonesia that do errors or omissions within the standards of the profession of kepelautan.

Article 19

Administrative Sanctions referred to in the Article 6 letter b can be either: a. A warning; b. Temporary revocation of a certificate of expertise Sailors to serve in a particular position on the ship, to within 2 (two) years.

PART TWO POSITION

Article 20

Court Cruise is a government agency that is under and is responsible directly to the Minister.

Article 21

The Court Cruise is based in the capital of the Republic of Indonesia.

PART THREE MEMBERSHIP MAKEUP OF THE MEMBERSHIP OF THE COURT'S COMPOSITION

Article 22

Cruise consists of a Chairman and members, members and Secretaries of the Court.

Article 23

(1) The Court of the cruise is led by a Chairperson.

(2) The Chairman referred to in subsection (1) may be assumed by the Legal Scholar, expert on Nautika level I, level I or Teknika Bachelor of shipping.

Article 24

(1) The members of the Court of the cruise consists of some people's law degree, Nautika Expert level I, level I Teknika Expert and scholar of shipping Techniques.

(2) The number of members of the Court's Voyage referred to in subsection (1) as many

of 15 (fifteen).

Article 25
The Court Cruise helped by a Secretariat headed by a Secretary of the Court.

Article 26
(1) The Chairman, the members of the Court of Justice, and Secretary of the cruise was appointed and dismissed by the Minister.
(2) The appointment and the dismissal referred to in subsection (1) is carried out in accordance with the provisions of the applicable legislation in the field of civil servants.

Article 27
When Cruise was unable to Chief Justice in the exercise of his duties, the Minister appoints one member of the Court to be appointed as the official Cruise while the Chief Justice of the cruise.

Article 28
(1) To be appointed the Chairman and members of the Court of the cruise, a candidate must meet the requirements: a. The pious to God Almighty; b. Loyal to Pancasila and the 1945 Constitution; c. Have a working period of at least 15 (fifteen) years as a civil servant; d. Legal Scholar, expert on Nautika level I, level I or Teknika Bachelor of shipping.
(2) In addition to the provisions set forth as mentioned in subsection (1) to be appointed as the Chief Justice of the cruise, a candidate must: a. Have experience of at least 2 (two) years as a member of the Court of the cruise; b. Meet the requirements of the position in accordance with the provisions of the legislation in the field of civil servants.

Article 29
To be appointed Secretary of the Court of the cruise, a candidate must meet the requirements: a. The pious to God Almighty; b. Loyal to Pancasila and the 1945 Constitution; c. A law degree; d. Meets the requirements of the position in accordance with the provisions of the legislation in the field of civil servants.

PART FOUR TATA'S WORK IS CONSIDERED THE ESTABLISHMENT OF THE TRIBUNAL PARAGRAPH COURT CRUISE

Article 30
(1) Not later than within a period of 7 (seven) days from receipt of the request for further

examination of the wreck of the ship, the Chief Justice of the Court Tribunal formed a Cruise Voyage.

(2) The establishment of a Tribunal referred to in subsection (1) is done by pointing out some of the members of the Court's appropriate expertise required Cruise in the advanced examination of the accident Board.

Article 31

(1) The composition of the membership of the Assembly is composed of the Chairman and as a member and a member of the Tribunal.

(2) The number of members of the Tribunal must be odd and consists of at least 5 (five) persons.

(3) The members of the Tribunal as referred to in subsection (2) at least one of them is a law degree.

Article 32

(1) A Secretary seconded to the Tribunal as a logger in the Assembly.

(2) The Secretary of the Tribunal can be assumed by the Court Secretary of the Cruise or a substitute Secretary.

(3) A substitute Secretary replacing law degree and number of substitute Secretary at the Court of the cruise is limited at most 2 (two) of the Secretary's replacement. The second paragraph of article 33 Assembly not later than within a period of 30 (thirty) days since its establishment, the Tribunal should have conducted the first Assembly.

Article 34

(1) Assembly held at the seat of the Court.

(2) In the case of a specific Assembly can take place outside the seat of the Court.

(3) A hearing Tribunal that took place outside the seat of the Court's Voyage referred to in subsection (2) is made after the Chief Justice gets permit cruise.

Article 35

(1) The Council of the Assembly was held in the courtroom of the Court.

(2) The Court's Courtroom Cruise referred to in subsection (1) are arranged according to the Ordinance: a. Place tables and chairs Assembly members it is located higher than the Secretary of the Tribunal place, stuck up, witnesses, expert witnesses, and visitors; b. The place of the Secretary of the Tribunal is located in the left side of the front of the place of Assembly members; c. Place the Chair stuck, witnesses, experts and witnesses are located before the members of the Tribunal; d. Place the visitor is located behind the place is trapped; e. The national flag was placed on the right side table Assembly members and a coat of arms

placed on the top of the wall behind the counter Assembly members; f. Place among Assembly members and on-site snagged a table provided a map of the sea; g. The place referred to in letter a, letter b, letter c, letter d, letter e, letter f and were given ID.

(3) In the event the Tribunal took place outside the seat of the Court, the Tribunal courtroom preparation as possible is carried out in accordance with the provisions referred to in subsection (2).

Article 36

(1) in carrying out the Council's Assembly, the members and the Secretary of the Tribunal wearing the hearing and attributes.

(2) the implementation of the provisions referred to in subsection (1) are governed further by a Minister.

Article 37

Assembly done openly to the public.

Article 38

(1) The members of the Assembly had to resign from the Council if tied to a family relationship or a semenda to the third degree with a stuck up, or procreation despite having been divorced with a snag.

(2) If after the results of the trial have been disconnected recently known there were Assembly members affected by the provisions referred to in subsection (1), then immediately do the hearing without inviting the members of the Tribunal are concerned.

(3) If the conditions mentioned in paragraph (1) and paragraph (2) of the members of the Tribunal be fulfilled, then the Chief Justice of the cruise took the decision to increase or decrease the one member of the Tribunal so that the number of members of the Tribunal be odd, but still should not be less than 5 (five) members of the Assembly.

(4) Further Provisions regarding the procedures for resignation and the reduction or the addition of a member of the Tribunal in the discharge of the Council referred to in subsection (1), subsection (2) and paragraph (3) is set by the Minister.

Article 39

(1) In performing its duties, the trial Tribunal is calling and asking for information from snagging, witnesses, expert witnesses, conduct examinations in the field or anything else that is deemed necessary.

(2) Further Provisions regarding the procedures for calling to and request information from snagging, witness and expert witness referred to in subsection (1) is set by the Minister.

Article 40

(1) If the Tribunal viewed the absence of witnesses and/or expert witnesses in the trial caused by the case or the reasons which can be accounted for, while concerned wished to give testimony or his statement, then the Tribunal may request the concerned to provide testimony or information in writing outside the place held a hearing Tribunal.

(2) Before giving testimony or information in writing referred to in subsection (1) witnesses and/or expert witness oath or promise by way of religion and beliefs before the officials appointed by the Minister.

(3) The implementation of the provisions referred to in subsection (1) and paragraph (2) are governed further by a Minister.

Article 41

(1) In the hearing of the Tribunal, witnesses and/or expert witness before giving testimony or information to the Tribunal oath or promise menourut how religion and beliefs.

(2) In the case of witnesses and/or expert witnesses refused the oath or promise as mentioned in subsection (1), the Tribunal may consider not using testimony or information given in according to the results of the session of the Assembly.

(3) The implementation of the provisions referred to in subsection (1) and paragraph (2) are governed further by a Minister.

Article 42

In the trial Tribunal, snagged can accompanied by Expert Advisor.

Article 43

Further Provisions concerning the Assembly specified by the Minister.

Article 44

The Tribunal Trial Results

(1) The decision of the Tribunal is the decision of the Court.

(2) The decision of the Court of the cruise as mentioned in subsection (1) applied in written form.

(3) The decision of the Court of the cruise as mentioned in paragraph (1) and paragraph (2), contain: a. Head verdict which reads "for the SAKE of FAIRNESS UPON the DIVINITY of the ONE TRUE GOD"; b. The name, title, certificate of seafaring expertise, the place and date of birth, citizenship, place of residence or seat of the last trapped, witnesses and/or expert witnesses; c. Documents and data of the ship; d. Summary of the course of the proceedings; e. The presence or absence of errors or omissions committed by the Captain or a leader ship, or the ship's officer in performing the duties of his profession; f. A basis or reasons that formed the

basis of the verdict; g. Day, the date of the verdict, and the names of the members of the Assembly and the Secretary of the Tribunal.

(4) The decision of the Court of the cruise was signed by the members and the Secretary of the Tribunal.

Article 45

The Court's Decision was read by Shipping presiding in the trial open to the public.

Article 46

The Court's Decision is the final decision of the cruise.

Article 47

(1) In a period no later than 1980 (one hundred eighty) days since the establishment of the first session of the day, the Chief Justice of the Court's decision conveys the Cruise Cruise in writing to: a. The Minister accompanied the report in terms of the existence of allegations based on preliminary evidence has occurred in tort committed by government officials or other parties that are directly or indirectly related to the causes of the accident the ship; b. Snagged.

(2) The Chief Justice of a cruise can provide a copy of the results of the decision of the Court relating to Cruise in an accident the ship and/or others in need.

Article 48

(1) Administrative Sanctions set out in the decision of the Court of Justice entered into force since the signing of the Shipping News Event the implementation of court ruling by law, Shipping and Harbour Officials or Representatives of the Republic of Indonesia abroad.

(2) The Harbour or Vicarious officials of the Republic of Indonesia abroad delivered a copy of a News Event implementation of a court ruling Cruise referred to in subsection (1) to the Minister and the Chief Justice of the cruise.

PART FIVE

Article 49

Financing all the costs that are required in the implementation of the Court's duty charged on Shipping income and Expenditure budget of the Ministry of transportation.

PART SIX COACHING AND SUPERVISION

Article 50

The Chief Justice's cruise doing coaching and supervision towards the implementation of the duties and discipline of members, the Secretary for Justice and the Secretary of the cruise, a replacement.

Article 51

(1) the Chief Justice of the cruise to conduct surveillance against the operations of the Tribunal.

(2) the supervision referred to in subsection (1) shall not reduce the freedom of Assembly in completing Advanced examination of the accident Board. Article 52 in carrying out construction and supervision, the Chief Justice of a cruise can provide guidance, reprimand, and warning.

Article 53

Further Provisions regarding the implementation of coaching and supervision set up by Ministers to pay attention to ketenuan legislation in force.

CHAPTER V CRIMINAL PROVISIONS

Article 54

Every person who is on board who knows the dikapalnya of an accident the ship, within the limits of its ability did not report the accident as referred to in article 4, are convicted on the basis of the provisions of article 124 paragraph (1) of Act No. 21 of 1992 about the cruise.

Article 55

Sailors and leader ship that did not report the accident vessels referred to in article 5, are convicted on the basis of the provisions of article 127 of the Act Number 21 of 1992 about the cruise.

CHAPTER VI MISCELLANEOUS PROVISIONS

Article 56

(1) Against a decision issued by a foreign judicial bodies in the field of ship accidents regarding errors or omissions within the standards of the profession of kepelautan performed by the Captain or a leader ship and/or ship officers who are certified expertise Sailors, published

by the Government of Indonesia, conducted a follow-up inspection of the ship by accident Court cruise.

(2) Advanced Examination of an accident the ship referred to in subsection (1) is carried out in accordance with the conditions provided for in this Regulation.

Article 57

With the enactment of this Regulation, the notion of the Court's members arranged in a cruise that Government regulations it is the same with the sense of Justice of the Court referred to Cruise in the Government Regulation Number 32 in 1979 about the dismissal of civil servants.

CHAPTER VII PROVISIONS COVER

Article 58

With the introduction of government regulations, all provisions and regulations relating to the examination of existing ship accidents still continue to apply all the conflicting and/or not yet reimbursed based on government regulations.

Article 59

Peratuan with the introduction of this Government, Presidential Decree Number 32 in 1984 about the composition of the membership of the Court, stated does not apply.

Article 60

This Regulation comes into force on the date specified. In order to make everyone aware of it, ordered the enactment of this Regulation with its placement in the State Gazette of the Republic of Indonesia. Established in Jakarta on January 7, 1998 the PRESIDENT of the REPUBLIC of INDONESIA ttd. SUHARTO Enacted in Jakarta on January 7, 1998 MINISTER of STATE SECRETARY of the REPUBLIC of INDONESIA MOERDIONO ttd GAZETTE REPUBLIC of INDONESIA 1998 number 1 EXPLANATION of GOVERNMENT REGULATION of the REPUBLIC of INDONESIA number 1 in 1998 about the GENERAL conduct of the SHIP ACCIDENT INSPECTION cruise as one mode of transportation has been arranged in one unified national transportation system in Act No. 21 of 1992 about the cruise. Organizing a cruise was carried out for the purpose of realizing the provision of transportation in waters that are balanced with the level of need and the availability of transport services in the waters of a happy, secure, fast, smooth, orderly, regular, convenient, and efficient with a reasonable and affordable cost by purchasing power.

Given the significance of organizing cruises for the community, the nation and the State, Act No. 21 of 1992 about Cruise ship accidents for each mandate carried out an examination of the accident the ship by the competent authority. Inspection of the wreck of the ship is done to find out the causes of the accident the ship and/or determining the presence or absence of errors or omissions in the application of kepelautan professional standard conducted by ship or leader Nahkoda and/or officers of the ship upon the occurrence of an accident the ship. Thus, later on top of the ship accident inspection results can be taken the necessary steps to prevent the occurrence of accidents, ships with the causes of the accident. In addition, examination of the wreck of the ship was intended as a form of guidance and oversight for the energy profession kepelautan.

Inspection of the wreck of the ship include a preliminary examination and an examination of the advanced submarine wreck the ship. Preliminary examination of the accident the ship held for searching and/or preliminary evidence upon the occurrence of an accident the ship before the ship crash further examination when there is an allegation of an error or omission in the application of standards of the profession by profession, kepelautan kepelautan IE Nahkoda or leader ship and/or the officers of the ship. Advanced examination of the wreck of the vessel was done by the Court whose members consist of Cruise people expert in the field of law and kepelautan. It is intended to provide objective assessment over the presence or absence of errors or omissions in the application of kepelautan professional standard conducted by ship or leader Nahkoda and/or officers of the ship upon the occurrence of an accident the ship.

In case there are errors or omissions in the application of standards of the profession of kepelautan, then the Court Cruise based on Act No. 21 of 1992 about the cruise can give administrative sanctions. Administrative sanctions can be given a warning or temporary revocation of a certificate of seafaring skills for serving in a certain position on the ship. Government regulations regarding the inspection of ship Accidents are defined as the regulations implementing Act No. 21 of 1992.

第四章 菲律宾海事管理法律研究

菲律宾位于亚洲东南部,北隔巴士海峡与中国台湾地区遥遥相对,南和西南隔苏拉威西海、巴拉巴克海峡与印度尼西亚、马来西亚相望,西濒南中国海,东临太平洋。菲律宾总面积为 29.97 万平方千米,共有大小岛屿 7000 多个,海岸线长约 18533 千米,其中吕宋岛、棉兰老岛、萨马岛等 11 个主要岛屿占菲律宾总面积的 96%。菲律宾的陆地面积与海洋面积之比为 1∶7,是世界第二大群岛国家,也是世界上最大的海员输出国之一。

一、海事管理体制与机构设置

菲律宾负责海事管理的主要机构是菲律宾海事局(Maritime Industry Authority,简称 MARINA),辅以海岸警卫队联合执法,采用由海事局集中管理、海岸警卫队协助联合执法的海事管理体制。菲律宾海事局预算不足,开展实际检查和执法存在困难,因此,它在国家海事安全事务方面与菲律宾海岸警卫队(Philippine Coast Guard,简称 PCG)联合执法。海事局主要负责涉及船舶安全与管理的相关事务,而海岸警卫队主要负责执行海上搜救、海上执法、海上安全、海洋环境保护等工作。

(一)海事局

1972 年 6 月 1 日,菲律宾海事局根据总统办公室发布的第 474 号总统令(又被称为 1974 年航运业法律)成立,旨在使国家航运业发展、提升和监管一体化。根据生效的第 546 号行政命令,菲律宾成立了交通运输部(Department of Transportation and Communications,简称 DOTC)。在实践中,为了使政策及程序的协调一致,海事局于 1979 年 7 月 23 日隶属于交通运输部。

1. 基本职能

菲律宾海事局(MARINA)的权力在 2004 年《国内航运发展法律》及《9295 号共和国法律》的规定中得到扩充,其职能[①]主要有:

(1)登记船舶,签发、延期或修改公共交通运输业许可证。该类证书的有效期不得超过 25 年,经通知和听证,可修改、暂停或吊销任何签发给国内船舶经营人的证书和许可证或认证。

(2)设立和规划国内船舶经营人的经营航线、区域或者范围。海事局有权要求任何国内船舶经营人为了地区发展,满足海上紧急补给需求或公共利益要求,向特定的国家沿海地区、岛屿或地区提供必要的航运服务。

---

① 菲律宾海事局官网,网址:http://marina.gov.ph/about/,2018 年 6 月 20 日访问。

(3) 根据适用的公约和规章为船舶制定安全标准。海事局要求所有国内船舶经营人遵守这些船舶操作和安全标准，使船舶保持安全运营状态，符合海上人身安全标准和安全配员要求，并提供安全、充足、可靠和适当的服务。

(4) 检查所有船舶，确保其符合安全标准和其他规章。其目的是确保所有国内船舶经营人有财务能力提供并维持安全、可靠、有效、经济的客运、货运服务。

(5) 保障社会公共利益，确保其投入的新服务将对投入地产生积极影响。海事局采用并实行安全标准和其他与船舶安全相关的规章制度，确保国内船舶经营人遵守该类标准和制度；实施确保载客率和运价合理稳定的规章制度，在必要情况下可以进行干预以保护公共利益。

(6) 对任何涉及违反法律或有关当局规章制度的书面投诉进行听证和裁定。海事局对未能保持船舶处于安全运营状态或违反安全法规的国内船舶经营人处以罚款和吊销许可证的处罚，针对国内船舶经营人、托运人或托运人团体违反《9295号共和国法案》条款的书面投诉进行调查。如确定该船舶经营人、托运人或托运人团体违反该法案，经通知和听证，可处以罚款、暂停或吊销证书、许可证，也可进行其他处罚。

(7) 监督并执行已修订的《海员培训、发证和值班标准国际公约》以及相关的国际公约和协议。

2. 部门架构

菲律宾海事局的最高决策机构是董事会，行政办公室为执行机构，直属于董事会。行政办公室直接管理海事执法行动，并统筹管理下设的规划署副署长办公室、业务署副署长办公室、《海员培训、发证和值班标准公约》（STCW）执行董事办公室，以及11个海事地区办事处。其中，规划署副署长办公室主要分管财务和行政管理服务、规划和政策服务、人力开发服务、信息管理系统服务、法律服务；业务署副署长办公室负责组织管理海事安全服务、国内航运服务、海外航运服务、船坞管理服务、特许经营服务，STCW执行董事办公室主要负责海员培训、发证和值班标准公约的执行。菲律宾海事局组织架构如图4-1所示。

3. 人员情况

菲律宾海事局（MARINA）有115位技术人员，其专业包括造船工程、海事工程、机械工程、电气工程、土木工程及其他相关物理科学。

根据《国际船舶安全营运和防止污染管理规则》（ISM规则）① 的要求，从事审核合规、案例检验和执法程序的人员，都需要符合相关的教育、培训、工作经验、审核经验与能力的要求，具体要求如下：

(1) 在教育方面，工作人员需要拥有至少下述教育背景。第一，从大学、海事学院、航海学院毕业并有船舶运营经验；第二，攻读造船和海事工程专业、机械专业、电气专业、土木工程或取得其他相关物理专业学位；第三，符合《1080号共和国法律》规定资格的公务员，而且需精通审核语言。

---

① ISM规则的英文全称是 the International Management Code for the Safe Operation of Ships and for Pollution Prevention。

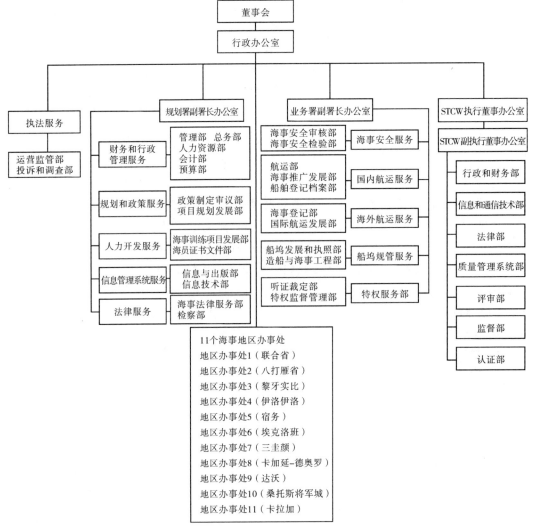

图 4-1 菲律宾海事局组织架构

（2）在培训方面，工作人员必须接受来自全国或国际认证的 ISM 发证组织的正式培训，确保至少具备下述技能：第一，认识和理解 ISM 规则、强制性法律法规、国际海事组织（IMO）、船级社和海运行业组织推荐的适用规则和标准；第二，检查、询问、评估和报告调查结果等审核技巧；第三，熟练掌握关于安全管理方面的技术和操作；第四，了解并掌握航运和船上作业知识。上述技能需通过书面、口头检验或其他可接受的考核方式来检验。

（3）在工作经验方面，工作人员需要有管理体系审核、船级检验、法定证书检验、船舶安全管理等相关工作经历，或者上述综合经验。

（4）在审核经验与能力方面，需符合有关要求。第一，对于初次或换证审核，ISM 审核员应在 ISM 主任审核员的监督下参与至少 2 次对公司和船舶的初次或换证审核；第二，对于年度或附加审核，审核员应在 ISM 主任审核员的监督下参与至少两次对公司和船舶的初次、附加、换证或年度审核，ISM 审核员参与至少 5 次公司和船舶的初次或换证审核,或者经过 ISM 主任审核员的培训,才能成为 ISM 主任审核员。

在初次和换证审核时,审核人员主要通过下述几个方面来全面评估公司和船舶是否符合 ISM 规则:一是是否符合 ISM 规则关于安全管理体系(SMS)章节的要求;二是评估公司或船舶 SMS 的工作效率,确保其符合法定和船级记录的相关规章制度;三是评估公司或船舶 SMS 的工作效率,确保其符合法定和船级记录之外的相关规章制度;四是审核是否符合 IMO、MARINA、船级社和 SMS 囊括的海运行业组织建议的安全操作。

在中期、年度和附加审核时,审核人员主要通过下述几个方面来全面评估公司和船舶是否符合 ISM 规则:一是公司或船舶 SMS 有效运行;二是公司或船舶持续符合法定和船级记录载明的相关规章制度;三是公司或船舶持续符合其他相关的规章制度,不受其他公约证书续签作出的检验影响;四是检查是否有任何严重不符项目;五是检查公司或船舶 SMS 做出的修改是否符合 ISM 规则条款。

4. 执法船舶和装备

菲律宾海域有 565 个灯塔,超过 44 个导航浮标引导船舶航行,确保船舶航行安全。菲律宾配备的船舶交通管理系统(VTMS),由雷达系统、船舶自动识别系统、VHF 电台通信系统、监控和气象预测系统、显控系统、应用系统及数据链组成。

(二)海岸警卫队

1967 年 10 月 10 日,菲律宾国会制定了《共和国第 5173 号法律》(也称菲律宾《海岸警卫法》),规定菲律宾海岸警卫队(Philippine Coast Guard,PCG)归海军管辖。2009 年,菲律宾颁布《海岸警卫队法》,同时撤销《共和国第 5173 号法律》,确立菲律宾海岸警卫队作为一个独立执法机构,是菲律宾政府的海巡武装力量,隶属于交通运输部,战时受国防部调遣。

1. 基本职能

菲律宾海事局与海岸警卫队为了进一步优化各部门的功能,于 2014 年 1 月 7 日签署了关于船舶安全检验服务的授权议定书,就国内船舶的危险货物运输、船舶安全强制功能和海上事故调查作出特别许可。① 菲律宾海岸警卫队的主要职责除了海上搜救、海上执法、海上安全、海洋环境保护等方面之外,还增加了危险货物运输管制、船舶安全强制检查和海上事故调查职能。

2. 部门架构

整个菲律宾群岛从最北端巴丹群岛的巴士古,南至塔威塔威岛,共分为 12 个海警区域,59 个海岸警卫站,共逾 190 个海岸警卫分队。菲律宾海岸警卫队总指挥为警卫队的最高长官,两名副总指挥协助总指挥分别负责日常管理和执法行动工作。海岸警卫队本部位于马尼拉,下设人事管理与档案部、情报安全与执法部、行动部、后勤部、计划与国际事务部、审计部、社区关系部、海事安全部、海洋环境保护部、船舶与飞机工程部、海上通信武器电子与信息系统部、教育培训部、海事安全和执法事务部、战略研

---

① 《菲律宾海事局与海岸警卫队授权议定书》,载菲律宾海岸警卫队官网,网址:http://www.coastguard.gov.ph/index.php/memorandums/memorandum-of-agreement/pcg-and-marina,2018 年 7 月 20 日访问。

究部。①

3. 人员情况

海岸警卫队目前共有高级警官 400 多名，在编警员 3000 多名，非在编人员 400 多名。随着菲律宾海洋经济的发展，海岸警卫队的人员也在逐渐增加，面临的挑战也层出不穷。海岸警卫队主要面向社会招募应届大学本科毕业生，对其进行海洋搜寻与救助、海洋环境保护及海洋安全管理等方面的集中培训。海岸警卫队每年还选派优秀人才前往瑞典海事大学、加拿大达尔豪西大学攻读硕士学位。菲律宾海岸警卫队还与中国、日本、意大利等国开展密切的海事交流活动和业务往来。

4. 执法船舶和装备

菲律宾配备的海事执法船舶有搜救船舶、辅助船舶、巡逻艇等装备。

（1）搜救船舶。搜救船舶配备情况如下：4 艘 San Juan 级的巡逻船，均在役，而且配有直升机平台；8 艘 Parola 级的巡逻船，是日本造船公司联合建造的全新多用途快速反应巡逻艇；4 艘 Ilocos Nort 级的巡逻船，均在役；2 艘 Bessang Pas 级巡逻艇，目前已不处于营运状态；1 艘 Agusan 级的大型巡洋舰，是美国军队辅助项目下建造的钢壳船，目前未投入使用。

（2）辅助船。辅助船配备如下：1 艘 Corregidor 级的海上事故反应/航标船；1 艘 Habagat 级的中型远洋拖轮；1 艘 Cabo Bojeador 级的航标船；1 艘 Kalinga 级的航标船，配备有直升机平台和破冰船首。

（3）巡逻艇。巡逻艇数量较多，主要有：29 艘 Swift 级的快速巡逻艇，其中有 2 艘工作受限，4 艘目前不运营；11 艘 De Havilland 系列 9209（DB - 型）的海岸巡逻艇；13 艘 103 型的武装快艇，主要用于搜救和灾害应急的海军装备；300 艘铝制 V 型船；81 艘高速快艇；50 艘橡皮艇。

（三）海事调查委员会

海事调查委员会（Board of Marine Inquiry，BMI）于 1937 年设立，现归菲律宾海岸警卫队（PCG）管辖，主要职责是认定海上事故的原因、审查对海上事故调查结果的异议、审查对海事调查特别委员会的调查结果和上诉。海事调查委员会下设海事特别调查委员会（Special Boards of Marine Inquiry，SBMI）。

1. 基本职能

海事特别调查委员会的基本职能是调查海岸警卫队各警务区域发生的小规模海上事故，以及向海事调查委员会及菲律宾海岸警卫队总指挥提交关于该事故的调查和处理报告，并提出处理意见。具体职能如下：

（1）调查海上事故中船舶所有人及高级船员的责任。

（2）调查与事故有关的高级船员的申述。

（3）审查由海事特别调查委员会或海事调查委员会进行的全部审理程序、处置或调查结果。

---

① 参见李景光、张占海《国外海洋管理与执法体制》，海洋出版社 2014 年版，第 209 页。

（4）对高级船员在业务上的违法行为、酗酒、玩忽职守或不适任等不良行为做出警告、停止业务或取消资格等处分，或者对在管理上有明显责任的船舶所有人、承运人进行处理。

2. 审理程序

海事调查委员会（BMI）由 1 名委员长、4 名委员组成，委员长须由海岸警卫队大校级军官担任，而 4 名委员包括具有正式适任资格证书的船长 2 名、司法人员 1 名、轮机员 1 名，主要职责是出席调查会议并参加审议，参加裁决书的起草并在裁决书上签字。

会议主要根据海岸警卫队最高长官的指示、确定无误的证据、海岸警卫队的海上事故报告进行审理，有举证、询问、质证等环节，对于在调查期间出现的争议，由委员长或委员根据当时情况提出决议案。经过充分审理后，海事调查委员会和海事特别调查委员会将处理意见和调查结果提交给最高长官，由其根据该会议的调查结果和处理意见做出决定，也可做出新的决定否定调查委员会的处理意见，或者命令继续调查该事故。如当事人接到最高长官的处理决定后在规定的上诉期间内没有向交通运输部提起上诉，则该决定生效。

（四）海员教育培训与服务管理体制

根据菲律宾劳动和就业部（DOLE）发布的统计数据，菲律宾是全球海员最主要的来源国，是世界上最大的海员输出国之一，在全球约 150 万海员中占比超过 25%。①

1. 海员教育培训体制

菲律宾具有较为先进合理的航海教育培训制度，采用以市场需求为导向，以企业为依托，以海员劳务输出为主要目的，进出自由的市场机制。② 海员培训多采用校企合作、订单培养的模式，即航海教育培训机构与海员外派或船员管理公司相结合，或者是航海教育培训机构、船员管理公司和航运公司三者相结合。据不完全统计，菲律宾有航海类培训机构近 150 所，本科层次加商船高级船员教育院校占 86 所，年培训能力近 50000 人次。

菲律宾的航海教育培训机构大多配备现代航海设施，校内环境也模拟成船上环境，使学员提前习惯船上的工作及生活。此外，为了培养海员的服务与服从意识，菲律宾的航海教育培训机构大多采用全封闭式和准军事化管理，在校企合作办学阶段，航运企业直接将公司的管理文化应用于教学管理上，使得学员有很强的等级观念和服务、服从意识。

2. 海员服务管理体制

菲律宾对海员服务管理的重视体现在政府制定的相关法律、政策上。菲律宾《劳工法》规定海外就业管理局（POEA）应为菲律宾海员提供发展广泛的海外雇佣计划。该计划涵盖招募和雇佣全过程，为海员提供免费的派遣服务，规范并监督中介机构和雇佣菲律宾海员从事海外工作的船公司代表的行为，并尽可能确保为海员提供受雇机会。海

---

① 《菲律宾依然是全球最大的海员输出国》，见航运界网，网址：http://www.ship.sh/news_detail.php? nid =20581，2018 年 5 月 20 日访问。
② 参见张世平、文元全《现代移民文化背景下的菲律宾航海教育与培训》，载《航海教育研究》2012 年第 4 期。

外就业管理局应当提供一个全国范围的多媒体信息渠道，使公众明确海员雇佣情况，而且海员中介机构在派遣海员之前必须为其提供专门的培训，确保其符合外派条件，并明确告知航程、到达港、索赔程序及在出现问题时如何寻求帮助。菲律宾还建立了"一站式"的海员文件处理中心，可方便快捷地处理与海员相关的各类文件、申请及认证。

虽然菲律宾没有制定单独的海员法，但政府为保护海员权益，根据本国《劳工法》和《移民劳工与海外菲律宾人法》，由海外就业管理局制定了相关规则，并根据国际条约、国外海员劳动和福利动态制定了一系列政策，以保证任何时候海外菲律宾海员都受到公平对待，包括医疗和法律协助等权益。目前，菲律宾海外就业管理局已在各国家地区建立多个地区办公室和海外派驻机构，以履行保护海员权益的职责。菲律宾外派海员最鲜明的特征就是拥有标准合同，明确双方的权利和义务。在海员劳动合同法律关系中雇佣方的权利主要包括劳动力使用权、指挥命令权；海员的权利主要包括劳动报酬请求权、人身伤亡损害赔偿请求权、休息休假权以及其他权利。标准劳动合同具有重要的意义：一是更加充分保护船员的基本权利。标准合同制度有利于限制雇佣方的行为，减少雇佣方滥用权力的行为。二是标准合同的格式和内容都是预先规定的，可以提高签订合同的效率。

3. 海员权益保障制度

菲律宾具有非常完善的劳务外派和海员保障制度，能够很好地保障海员的权益，促进海员市场的发展。在财政支持方面，菲律宾政府设立了各种基金，如海员福利基金、劳工的遣返和紧急遣返基金、海外劳工贷款保证基金、法律援助基金、为航海教育和培训而使用的 TESDA 开发基金。菲律宾政府还规定凡是海外劳工一律免征所得税，若海外劳工遇到困难，可以申请通过银行低息贷款由政府担保垫付，以后由当事人再归还政府。菲律宾政府还建立了专门为海外劳工和家属服务的医院，在体检和治病方面提供优惠。菲律宾政府一系列对海外劳工的大力支持政策，使得海员及其家属受益，对菲律宾海员输出有一定的激励作用。

菲律宾具有良好、快速、高效的劳务纠纷解决机制：首先，在有关规定中设置了明确的纠纷解决方案，使得复杂的争议解决过程明确；其次，受理机关明确，涉诉者只需向海外就业管理局提出侵权事实与诉求，海外就业管理局即可受理，即使这种诉求不应是海外就业管理局受理的，也可由海外就业管理局转交有关机关；最后，纠纷解决快捷，根据1995年《海外劳工和海外菲律宾人法》规定，对非法雇佣案件的调查应自其立案起30日内结束。

二、海事法律

历史上，菲律宾曾先后沦为西班牙和美国的殖民地，因此，菲律宾法律的发展也深受大陆法系与英美法系的影响。菲律宾不仅吸收借鉴了大陆法系和英美法系的制度，同时又根据本国情况，建立、完善了与其国情相适应的法律体系。目前，菲律宾主要的法律渊源包括宪法、法律、总统令、行政命令、备忘录通告、公告等，还有由政府部门和其他机构发布的行政规章和实施细则以及国际条约等。

（一）国内法

菲律宾关于海事管理的法律法规并不统一，分散于法律和其他政府部门立法中，主要有共和国法律、总统令、行政命令、备忘录通告、海事管理咨询、商船规则和条例。从菲律宾海事局的官方网站①中可以看到，与海事相关的共和国法律有 18 个，总统令 20 个，行政命令有 19 个。海事局颁布的有《商船规则和条例》，海事局每年还会发布多个管理咨询公告以及备忘录通告。

菲律宾的国内法梳理如下：

EXECUTIVE ORDERS

1. 314 号总统令——成立国家海事安全协调委员会，1996 年 3 月 28 日

Executive Order No. 314, Establishing a National Maritime Safety Coordinating Council, March 28, 1996

http://www.marina.gov.ph/policies/EO/eo314.pdf

2. 396 号总统令——建立菲律宾海员培训、发证和值班标准的管理制度，1997 年 1 月 30 日

Executive Order No. 396, Providing the Institutional Framework for the Administration of the Standards of Trainings, Certification and Watchkeeping for Seafarers in the Philippines, January 30, 1997

http://www.marina.gov.ph/policies/EO/eo396.pdf

3. 93 号总统令——修订 396 号总统令，1999 年 4 月 20 日

Executive Order No. 93, Amending Executive Order No. 396, Entitles "Providing the Institutional Framework for the Administration of the Standards of Training, Certification and Watchkeeping fo Seafarers in the Philippine", April 20, 1999

http://www.marina.gov.ph/policies/EO/eo93.pdf

4. 149 号总统令——进一步修订 396 号总统令，1999 年 9 月 7 日

Executive Order No. 149, Further amending Executive Order No. 396, Series of 1997, September 7, 1999

http://www.marina.gov.ph/policies/EO/eo149.pdf

5. 75 号总统令

Executive Order No. 75

http://www.marina.gov.ph/policies/EO/EO%2075.pdf

---

① 菲律宾政府官网，网址：http://marina.gov.ph/maritime-related-laws/，2018 年 7 月 27 日访问。

6. 396 号总统令——为菲律宾海员培训、发证和值班的标准管理提供制度框架
Executive Order No. 396, Providing the Institutional Framework for the Administration of the Standards of Training, Certification and Watchkeeping for Seafarers in the Philippines
http://www.marina.gov.ph/policies/EO/eo396.pdf

REPUBLIC ACT

简称：8747 号共和国法案
全称：关于要求披露 2000 年声明和计算机系统及相关产品和服务的共和国法案
Republic Act No. 8747 otherwise known as the "Philippine Year 2000 Readiness Act" issued on June 1, 1999
http://www.lawphil.net/statutes/repacts/ra1999/ra_8747_1999.html

PHILIPPINE COAST GUARD MEMORANDUM CIRCULARS

1. 关于向菲律宾籍船舶签发国际防油污证书的 06-2005 号通函
Memorandum Circular No. 06-2005, Issuance of International Oil Pollution Prevention Certificate to the Philippine Registered Vessels
http://www.coastguard.gov.ph/index.php/memorandums/12-mc/116-memorandum-circular-no-06-2005-issuance-of-international-oil-pollution-prevention-certificate-to-philippine-registered-vessels

2. 关于在菲律宾海域倾倒废物及其他有害物质的流程的 11–14 号通函
Memorandum Circular No. 11-14, Procedure for the dumping of Wastes and other harmful matter with the Philippine Maritime Jurisdiction
http://www.coastguard.gov.ph/images/philcoastguard/MC_PDF/JUNE2015/MC_11_14_Dumping.pdf

3. 关于菲律宾籍船舶船上油污应急计划的 09–14 号通函
Memorandum Circular No. 09-14, Shipboard Oil pollution Emergency Plan for Philippine Registered Vessels
http://www.coastguard.gov.ph/images/philcoastguard/MC_PDF/JUNE2015/MC_09_14_SOPEP.pdf

4. 菲律宾海警关于船舶安全执法检查的 06—12 号通函
Philippine Coast Guard Memorandum Circular Number 06-12, Vessel Safety Enforcement Inspections
http://www.coastguard.gov.ph/images/philcoastguard/MC_PDF/MC06-12.pdf

FLAG STATE ADMINISTRATION ADVISORY

1. 06 号船旗国行政公告——遵守《1992 年国际油污损害民事责任公约》,1998 年 6 月 16 日发布
Flag State Administration Advisory No. 06, Compliance with the International Convention on Civil Liability for Oil Pollution Damage, 1992, issued June 16, 1998

2. 08 号船旗国行政公告——对国内航运施行国际安全管理规则,1998 年 10 月 6 日
Flag State Administration Advisory No. 08, Implementation of the ISM Code in Domestic Shipping, October 6, 1998

3. 17 号船旗国行政公告——预防及阻止海盗行为及持械抢劫船舶,2000 年 11 月 16 日
Flag State Administration Advisory No. 17, Preventing and Supressing Acts of Piracy and Armed Robbery Against Ships, November 16, 2000

4. 18 号船旗国行政公告——搭乘公共交通安全措施,2001 年 1 月 2 日
Flag State Administration Advisory No. 18, Measures o Ensure Safety of the Riding Public, January 2, 2001

5. 22 号船旗国行政公告——强制实施 72 号公告建立禁区及安全区,2002 年 1 月 24 日
Flag State Administration Advisory No. 22, Implementation and Enforcement of the Exclusion and Safety Zones Established Under Proclamation No. 72, January 24, 2002

6. 23 号船旗国行政公告——实施国内航运货物积载保管安全措施规范,2002 年 2 月 15 日
Flag State Administration Advisory No. 23, Implementation of the Code of Safe Practice for Cargo Stowage and Securing in Domestic Shipping, February 15, 2002

7. 26 号船旗国行政公告——《1974 年国际海上人命安全公约》2000 修订版在国内生效,2002 年 7 月 28 日
Flag State Administration Advisory No. 26, Effectivity of the 2000 Amendments to the International Convention for the Safety of Life at Sea (SOLAS) 1974, as amended, July 28, 2002

8. 27 号船旗国行政公告——加强安全及安保的进一步措施,2002 年 10 月 22 日
Flag State Administration Advisory No. 27, Additional Measures to Ensure the Safety and

Security, October 22, 2002

9. 34号船旗国行政公告——重申027号行政公告关于加强我国船舶，乘客及货物安全及安保的进一步措施，2003年3月20日
Flag State Administration Advisory No. 34, Reiteration of Flag State Administration No. 027, Series of 2002 on the Additional Measures to Ensure the Safety and Security of our Ships, Their Passengers and Cargoes, March 20, 2003

10. 37号船旗国行政公告——关于实施159号备忘录公告（国家安全管理法规）的指导，2003年4月27日
Flag State Administration Advisory No. 37, Guidance on the Implementation of MARINA Memorandum Circular (MC) No. 159, otherwise known as the National Safety Management Code, April 27, 2003

11. 9号船旗国行政公告——关于实施179号备忘录公告就在菲水域作业的菲律宾船舶/渔船或暂时进行对外贸易/使用国际水域的菲律宾船舶的最低安全配员规定的指导，2003年4月28日
Flag State Administration Advisory No. 39, Guidance on the Implementation of MARINA Memorandum Circular (MC) No. 179 on the Issuance on the Minimum Safe Manning Certificate for Philippine Registered Ships/Fishing Vessels Operating in Philippine Waters or Temporarily Utilized in Overseas Trade/International Waters, April 28, 2003

12. 51号船旗国行政公告——加强国内船舶、乘客和货物安全及安保的进一步措施，2003年12月16日
Flag State Administration Advisory No. 51, Additional Measures to Ensure the Safety and Security of Our Ships, Their Passengers and Cargoes, December 16, 2003

13. 54号船旗国行政公告——实施《国际船舶和港口设施保安规则》的公认安保机构
Flag State Administration Advisory No. 54, Recognized Security Organizations in the Implementation of the International Ship and Port Facility Security (ISPS) Code

14. 57号船旗国行政公告——委任海事主管及重申国内贸易船舶的乘客和货物安保措施，2004年3月8日
Flag State Administration Advisory No. 57, Designation of Maritime Marshals and Reiteration of Security Measures on Board Passenger and Passenger-cargo Ships in the Domestic Trade, March 8, 2004

15. 2006-06 号船旗国行政公告——联合国安理会 1718 号决议关于强制执行对朝鲜民主主义人民共和国的贸易和军火禁运，2007 年 11 月 22 日
Flag State Administration Advisory No. 2006-06, UN Security Council Resolution No. 1718-Enforcement of Trade and Arms Embargo on DPRK, November 22, 2007

16. 2009-23 号船旗国行政公告——菲律宾海事局负责人指定 Pole Star 为船舶远程识别与跟踪应用服务提供商和数据中心
Flag State Administration Advisory No. 2009-23, Authority of the Undersecretary for Maritime Transport, DOTC and Officer-In-Charge, MARINA to Appoint Pole Star as Application Service Provider (ASP) and Data Center for Long-Range Identification and Tracking (LRIT) of Ships.

17. 2013-04 号船旗国行政公告
Flag State Administration Advisory No. 2013-04

18. 2017-24 号船旗国行政公告——安全管理系统之海事网络风险管理，2017 年 11 月 21 日
Flag State Administration Advisory No. 2017-24, Maritime Cyber Risk Management in Safety Management Systems, November 21, 2017
http://www.marina.gov.ph/policies/listFSAA.html

OTHERS

1. 实施 1997 年菲律宾商船法规
Implementation of the Philippine Merchant Marine Rules and Regulations (PMMRR) of 1997
http://www.marina.gov.ph/policies/pmmrr/pmmrr%201997_book.pdf

2. 1978 年菲律宾海关关税法案
Tariff and Customs Code of 1978
http://customs.gov.ph/wp-content/uploads‖10/TCCP-vol2.pdf

（二）国际条约

1. 海事国际条约概述

菲律宾目前加入的海事国际条约有 21 个，其中具有代表性的是：1974 年的《国际海上人命安全公约》（SOLAS），1966 年的《国际载重线公约》（LL），1969 年的《国际船舶吨位丈量公约》（ICM），1978 年的《国际海员培训，发证和值班标准公约》（STCW），1971 年的《特种业务客船协定》（STP），1976 年的《国际海事卫星组织公

约》(IMSO),1973 年的《国际防止船舶造成污染公约》(MARPOL),1972 年的《防止倾倒废物及其他物质污染海洋的公约》(也称"伦敦公约"),1969 年的《国际油污损害民事责任公约》(CLC),1992 年的《修正 1971 年关于设立石油污染损害赔偿国际基金的国际公约的 1992 年议定书》(FUND 议定书),1988 年的《制止危及海上航行安全非法行为公约》(SUA),1972 年的《国际海上避碰规则公约》(COLREGS),等等。

2. 加入方式及国内化程序

菲律宾 1987 年《宪法》第 21 章授予总统批准条约的权利,但需参议院以 2/3 的赞成票才能通过。1997 年 11 月 25 日公布的 459 号行政令就国际协议的协商和批准做出了明确的指示。菲律宾缔约的程序一般如下:协商、签署、批准、交换批准书。随后协议将提交联合国秘书处登记并公布,但这一步对协议在双方间的生效并非必须。协商可通过总统或其授权代表完成,这些代表被授予全权证书,在正式讨论前需向其他谈判代表出示证明。协商完成后,开封协议准备签署。该程序主要是为了验证协议,并不表示协议批准国对其批准。而批准是一项正式行为,国家经由代表确认和接收协议条约。在菲律宾,需参议院有 2/3 多数的赞成票才能通过批准。

菲律宾加入的海事国际条约自然成为国内法,组成国内法律体系的一部分,约束国家和个人,无须国内再次立法转化才适用。

三、小　结

菲律宾采用由海事局集中管理、海岸警卫队协助联合执法的海事管理体制,而菲律宾海事管理的独到之处在于其成功的海员劳务输出。菲律宾海员输出的成功原因主要有以下三点:一是菲律宾完备的航海教育和培训制度;二是专门的管理机构与健全的法律监管体制;三是完善的保障制度和后勤措施。在菲律宾良好的海事管理下,绝大多数菲律宾海员树立了以从事劳动为荣,以及为雇主服务的观念。同时,政府部门与船东国协商缔结条约,或加入国际劳工公约,使其劳务外派标准较好地与国际接轨。此外,加入国际运输劳工联合会、国际劳工组织以及其他国际性劳工协会使菲律宾海员得到了国际上的承认。

四、附录:菲律宾海事法律(国内法)文件

(一) 附录 1:菲律宾海警关于船舶安全执法检查的 06—12 号通函

Philippine Coast Guard Memorandum Circular Number 06-12, Vessel Safety Enforcement Inspections

Department of Transportation and Communications
PUNONGHIMPILAN TANODBAYBAYIN NG PILIPINAS
Headquarters Philippine Coast Guard
139 25th Street, Port Area
1018 Manila

24 August 2012

HPCG / CG-8

MEMORANDUM CIRCULAR
NUMBER.................06-12

VESSEL SAFETY ENFORCEMENT INSPECTIONS[①]

I. AUTHORITY:

A. Republic Act 9993 (Philippine Coast Guard Law of 2009)

II. REFERENCE:

A. DOTC Department Order 2012-01 dated 09 Jan 2012 entitled Mandating the Strict Implementation of Precautionary, Safety and Security Measures to Ensure Safe, Fast, Efficient and Reliable Transportation Services, the Immediate Implementation of Quick Response Protocols, and the Immediate Investigation of Transformation-Related Incidents.
B. Philippine Merchant Marine Rules and Regulation (PMMRR), as amended
C. SOLAS 74/78, as amended
D. MARPOL 73/78, as amended

III. PURPOSE:

This Memorandum Circular prescribes policies for an effective safety inspection of all Philippine-registered vessels engaged in domestic trade calling at any ports in the country to verify their continuing compliance to certain aspect of seaworthiness in accordance with applicable safety standards, rules and regulations and to safe, fast, efficient and reliable conveyance of passengers and cargoes.

IV. SCOPE:

This Memorandum Circular applies to all Philippine-registered vessels engaged in domestic trade to include fishing vessels of 3 gross tonnage and above calling at domestic ports except for ships not propelled by mechanical means wooden ships of primitive build, ships of war and troopships, Government vessels and pleasure yachts not engaged in trade.

---

① 本法条引用自 http://www.coastguard.gov.ph/images/philcoastguard/MC_PDF/MC06－12.pdf。

V. DEFINITION OF TERMS:

For the purpose of this Circular, the following words and phrases shall be defined as:

Clear Grounds – evidence that the ship, its equipment, or its crew does not correspond substantially with the requirements of the relevant maritime laws or that the master or crew members are not familiar with essential shipboard procedures relating to the safety of the ships or the prevention of marine pollution;

Deficiency – a condition found not to be in compliance with the requirements of the relevant maritime regulations;

Detention – intervention action taken by the boarding team/authority when the condition of the ship or its crew does not correspond substantially with the applicable laws to ensure that the ship will not sail until it can proceed to sea without presenting any danger to the ship or person on board, or without presenting any threat of harm to the marine environment;

Inspection Checklist – a list of documents, equipment, machinery, life-saving appliances and maritime safety devises that should be examined and evaluated by Vessel Safety Enforcement Inspectors while conducting vessel safety inspection.

More Detailed Inspection – an inspection conducted when there are clear grounds to believe that the condition of the ship, its equipment, or its crew does not correspond substantially with the particulars of the certificates.

Philippine-Registered Vessel – All vessels registered in the Philippines.

Seaworthy – ability of the vessel to withstand ordinary stress of wind, waves and other weather disturbances which the vessel might normally be expected to encounter and that the vessels is manned by competent officers and crew.

Stoppage of an Operation – formal prohibition against a ship to continue an operation due to the identified deficiency(ies) which, singly or together, render the continuation of such operation hazardous;

Sub-standard Ship – a ship whose hull, machinery, equipment or operational safety is substantially below standards required by relevant maritime laws or regulations or whose qualification of crew does not satisfy the standard manning requirements;

Valid Certificate – a certificate that has been issued by a cognizant government agency or on its behalf by a Recognized Organization which attests to the substantial compliance of ship, its equipment or crew with the required standards.

Vessel Safety Enforcement Inspection Deficiency Codes – a list of conditions of the vessel, its equipment, and crew that are not in compliance with the requirements of relevant maritime regulations and their corresponding codes that will be used to designate the specific deficiencies appearing in the checklist and EIAR.

Vessel Safety Enforcement Inspectors(VSEI) – duly trained, qualified and authorized PCG personnel task to evaluate and examine the validity of documents of the vessel and crews as well as the over-all condition of the vessel's hull, machinery

VI.　GENERAL PROVISIONS:

　　A. The inspections under this Circular shall include but not limited to the following:

　　　　1. Plans for the safe construction repair, modification or alteration of vessels;
　　　　2. Compliance to standards of materials, equipment and appliances of vessels;
　　　　3. Appropriate classification or categorization of vessels;
　　　　4. Safe manning level of vessels;
　　　　5. Compliance to loadline and stability requirements;
　　　　6. Safety management and operational systems;
　　　　7. Security plans and measures implemented by vessels;
　　　　8. Observance of proper hull and machinery conditions and maintenance;
　　　　9. Compliance to proper admeasurements of vessels, watercraft and similar conveyances.

　　B. The Vessel Safety Enforcement Inspections shall be undertaken on the basis of:

　　　　1. the initiate of the PCG
　　　　2. the request of or on the basis of information regarding a ship provided by a Government agency;
　　　　3. information regarding a ship provided by a member of a crew, a professional body, an association, a trade union or any individual with an interest in the safety of the ship, its crew and passengers, or in the protection of the marine environment.

　　C. The inspection shall also be conducted if after the vessel has been subjected to PDI and while underway, supervising events happen that would endanger continuous navigation. In which case the vessel shall be directed to immediately proceed to the nearest possible port of refuge for purposes of conducting more detaned inspection.

　　D. The PCG may suspend, hold, stop or prevent the departure of vessel to ensure compliance with the applicable safety standards, rules and regulations and to prevent it from further presenting danger to the vessel or persons on board or other vessels navigating along its route, or harm to the marine environment.

VII.　POLICIES:

A. The Vessel Safety Enforcement Inspection shall be carried out in order to assess whether the ship and/or crew, throughout its forthcoming voyage, will be able to:
   1. exercise extraordinary diligence in ensuring the safe, fast, efficient and reliable conveyance of passengers;
   2. navigate safely;
   3. maintain adequate stability and trim condition;
   4. safely handle, carry, secure and monitor the condition of the cargo;
   5. maintain all propulsion and proper steering;
   6. operate the ship's machineries safely;
   7. fight fires and prevent flooding effectively in any part of the ship, if necessary;
   8. prevent pollution of the environment;
   9. maintain adequate watertight integrity;
   10. communicate in distress situations if necessary;
   11. provide adequate life saving devices corresponding to its maximum authorized passenger and crew capacity;
   12. provide safe and healthy conditions on board;
   13. complete officer and adequate crew complement corresponding to the proper observance of appropriate periods of work and rest from work;
   14. weather condition does not merit the suspension of the voyage;
   15. required operational and emergency readiness standards of crew is met;
   16. documentations and certificates are complete and valid;
   17. sufficient training of the crew based on actual "Operational Readiness Evaluation" and
   18. other analogous circumstances.

B. The inspection shall be guided by the Vessel Safety Enforcement Inspection Checklist applicable to each type of vessel (Form F);

C. The Master or in his absence, the senior deck officer on board, should be notified on the purpose of the visit. He shall provide the Inspection Team information as to the last vessel safety inspection that took place;

D. In the event the inspection is undertaken within the last three (3) months and the corresponding report was found to be satisfactory, no further action should be taken. In case the report shows some deficiencies, the inspection should focus on the remedial actions taken by the Master on the deficiencies noted on the previous inspection. No further action shall be taken if the previous deficiencies are found to have already been rectified. In case the previous deficiencies remain uncorrected, the VSEI shall take note of the deficiencies and required the Master to rectify the same. The corresponding penalty shall be imposed for failure to correct the previously noted deficiency;

E. In the event the ships have not undergone inspection within the prescribed three-month period, the inspection shall proceed to verify all the required certificates/documents and in the conduct of inspection as warranted. If the inspection is satisfactory, the Vessel Safety Enforcement Inspection Checklist (Form F) shall be filled up. Upon completion of the inspection, the Master or senior officer on board shall be furnished with copy of the report.

F. In case the ship is not carrying valid certificates, or if the Inspectors have clear ground to believe, from general impressions or observations on board, that the condition of the ship or its equipment does not correspond substantially with the particulars of the certificates or that the master or crew is not familiar with essential shipboard procedures, a more detailed inspection should be carried out;

G. The Master shall correct the deficiency within a specified time. The Operational restriction or detention of the ship shall be imposed in the interim until the deficiencies are corrected. If minor deficiencies are found but are deemed not to endanger the ship, the passengers/crew on board and the marine environment, the vessel may be allowed to proceed to the next port of call. The vessel shall address the deficiency at the next port. Non rectification of the noted deficiency shall be a ground for holding of departure;

H. In determining whether the deficiencies are serious as to necessitate suspension, stoppage of operation or detention, the ships and/or officers and crew shall be assessed based on the ability to perform or comply, throughout intend voyage, with the following:

   1. the ship has valid documentation;
   2. the ship has satisfied the minimum Safe Manning Document or the crew requirement per its Certificate of Inspection
   3. length and nature of the intended voyage or service;
   4. whether or not the deficiency poses a danger to the ship, person on board or the environment;
   5. whether or not the appropriate periods of the crew can be observed;
   6. size and type of ship and equipment provided, and
   7. nature of cargo

I. A combination of deficiencies of a less serous nature shall also warrant the detention of the ship.

J. If a vessel is to be detained due to major deficiencies, the VSEI shall notify the MARINA and Philippine Port Authority of the detention of the vessel.

K. After the VSEI team has completed the inspection, the Master shall accomplish the Certificate of Orderly Inspection (Form B). This will be followed by the proper and courteous departure of the team.

L. The Enforcement Inspections Apprehension Reports EIAR (Form A) on ship with deficiencies/violation should be submitted to CPCG (Attention: DCS for Maritime Safety Services, CG-8), copy furnished the nearest MARINA office for the appropriate action. Same reports are also to be submitted by the VSEI Team to the District/Station and Detachment Commanders concerned.

M. Re-inspection of vessel detained by concerned VSEI, Districts/Stations and Detachments shall be conducted on the date and time requested in writing by the vessels' owner, his authorized agent or the vessel's Master for verification of the rectification of deficiencies found during the VSEI inspection. No re-inspection fee shall be collected.

N. The Master shall maintain an Inspection Record Book which shall serve as a permanent record of all deficiencies discovered in the course of every inspection.

O. A record book which the master intends to utilize as the vessel's Inspection Record Book shall be submitted to the PCG for accreditation. All entries in the registered record book shall be in chronological order and no page therein shall be removed, deleted or erased. Any correction in the entry therein shall be countersigned by the person making the correction.

P. No accreditation of Inspection Record Book shall be made unless the accreditation fee of Php 500 is fully paid. Such accreditation shall be valid for two years.

VIII. PENALTY CLAUSE:

A penalty of detention and a fine of P100,000.00 shall be imposed upon the Master or ship company for failure to correct major deficiencies that have been noted during previous inspections.

The same penalty shall be imposed for refusal to have the vessel re-inspected despite continuous findings of the existence of clear ground for inspection.

IX. SEPARABILIYT CLAUSE:

Any section or provision of this Memorandum Circular held or declared unconstitutional or invalid by a competent court, shall not affect the other sections or provisions hereof and shall continue to be enforced as if the sections or provisions so annulled or voided had never been incorporation herein.

X. RESCISSION CLAUSE:

This Memorandum Circular rescinds HPCG/CG8 MC 01-98 on Flag State Control Inspection.

XI. EFFECTIVITY:

This Memorandum Circular shall take effect fifteen (15) days after completion of publication in the Official Gazette or in a news paper or general circulation.

第四章 菲律宾海事管理法律研究

Approved by:

第五章 越南海事管理法律研究

越南位于东南亚中南半岛东部，北与中国广西、云南接壤，西与老挝、柬埔寨交界；国土狭长，呈南北走向的"S"形狭窄状，面积约33万平方千米；紧邻南海，现有90个海港、大小岛屿2600个，海岸线长3260多千米。20世纪90年代以来，越南十分重视海洋经济战略，海事活动频繁活跃。随着海权意识的增强和海洋经济的发展，越南颁布了一系列与海事相关的基本法律及大量法律文件，不断完善海事管理活动。

一、海事管理体制与机构设置

越南海事管理体制是由海事局（Vinamarine）集中管理越南的海事相关事务，在行政和商业方面监管越南航运业，但在海上事故、海上执法等方面由越南海警司令部协助其进行执法调查。

（一）海事局

越南海事局于1992年6月29日成立，1993年7月正式开始运作，其前身系重组前的越南海运公司。越南政府于1992年6月29日制定的第239/HDBT号法令和1993年2月2日制定的第31/TTg号法令，规定了越南海事局的职责和组织形式。2009年，越南政府总理颁布了《关于规定交通运输部直属越南海事局职能、任务、权限和组织机构的规定》，规定了越南海事局直属于交通运输部，实行垂直管理体制，负责对越南海上交通安全实施管理。

1. 基本职能

越南海事局的职能十分广泛，主要涵盖海事附属立法、海事执法、海事管理。越南海事局主要有以下职能：

（1）负责制定越南海洋领域的战略、规划、中长期发展计划、国家项目发展提案，起草有关海事的法律、法规和规章草案，并向交通运输部部长提交。

（2）负责制定海事相关的国家标准、技术规范和技术准则，提请部长颁布或由部长报送主管机关审定、公布；组织制定并审定、公布海事行业基本标准。

（3）组织实施上级主管机关颁布的各项法律、法规、战略、规划、计划、标准、技术规范、行业准则；根据法律法规的相关规定，在海事局的权限范围内制定海事组织和相关单位关于专业技术规范、行业准则的应用细则。

（4）组织关于海事法律的宣传教育。

（5）组织管理海港、浅水港、海岸信息系统、航道、海事信号系统、水域、船舶公司的相关海事活动。

(6) 组织管理海船①、船员、引航员和其他海事人员。

(7) 制定关于发展海运、海运服务和海运服务经营条件的法律文件草案并提交给部长,组织管理海运和海事服务。

(8) 制定关于海上安全、海事安保的各项法律法规草案并提交给部长,参与制定关于预防海域环境污染的法律法规草案;组织管理相关的海上安全和海事安保活动。

(9) 依据法律规定的权限对授权管理的海事投资项目进行管理,提请部长或由部长报请主管机关颁布有关海港和航道建设、管理和运营以及海港海事活动管理的规定;提出关于设立海事领域公共设施服务的海事收费项目、收费水平及单价的建议,提交主管部门决定。

需要注意的是,越南国内实行两套海事系统,海事局负责沿海海事行政管理,内河航道局负责内河海事行政管理。

2. 组织架构

越南海事局系越南海事监管的主管机关,监管所有与海事相关的部门。海事局由10个部门和25个地方海事局、1个海上搜救中心(MRCC)、4个搜救分中心和其他附属单位组成。越南海事局设有局长、副局长,管理总部下设的10个部门、1个海事安全信息中心、4个地方代表办公室、18个港口部门。除此之外,海上搜救和协调中心、海事安全处、海难救助公司、海事技术和培训学院等与海事相关的企业、院校亦由海事局管理。越南海事局部门架构如图5-1所示。

3. 人员情况

越南海事局在中央办公室和全国各地40家附属企业和机构拥有约30000名员工。越南海事局普通职位的工作人员需要毕业于海军设计与建筑、海事建筑、海事工程、海事安全工程、信息技术、电子通信、巡航监控等专业,并精通上述领域,具备英语B级或英语2级以上水平,持有计算机科学证书。

4. 执法船舶和其他装备

目前,越南海事局配备的海上执法装备有87艘在役船舶、3架在役飞机。海事局配备的执法船舶多数仅承担巡逻职能,其中有4艘船舶具备巡逻兼搜救功能,具备巡逻兼运输功能的船舶有5艘,搜救船舶有8艘,补给运输船仅有1艘。越南执法船舶中1000吨以上的船舶有32艘,其中有5艘4000吨船舶。越南除了执法船舶装备外,还配备了VTS自动系统、自动识别系统(AIS)、远距离识别和跟踪系统(LRIT)。此外,越南还配备了30座可用的海岸无线电站台、92座沿岸灯塔和浮标系统。

(二)海警司令部

越南海警司令部的前身为越南海警局,依据越南政府2013年8月28日颁布第96号决议,正式将"越南海洋警察局"更名为"越南海洋警察司令部",于同年10月12日生效。越南海警司令部隶属于越南国防部,年度预算直接由国家财政预算编列支付,海警司令、政委、副司令、副政委将根据国防部长建议由总理任命。

---

① 越南《海商法》第13条规定:"海船是指专用于海上活动的浮式可移动工具。不包括军事船、公务船、渔船、内河船舶、潜艇、潜航器、水上飞行器、水上仓库、移动平台、浮坞。"

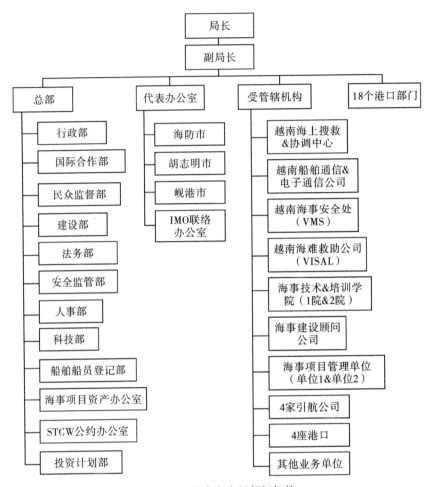

图 5-1 越南海事局部门架构

1. 基本职能

自 20 世纪 90 年代末创建以来，越南海警在维护海上安全和保护专属经济区和大陆架边界方面发挥着重要作用。它在越南与外国重叠地区的水域派遣部队，必要时为当地渔民提供保护和援助。越南海警司令部主要负责保护越南海岸线的安全，并处理以下问题：打击和防止走私，打击海盗，贩卖人口，恐怖主义活动，工业放射性和有毒废物倾倒，保护海洋环境，监督非法经营的外国渔船，海事执法，海上援助与搜救，与越南人民海军一起执行国防任务。在海上巡逻任务方面，越南海警司令部也会和越南渔业管理局的越南渔政船队联合执行勤务。

2. 组织架构

在组织架构上，越南分成 4 个地区海洋巡防区，分别是北中南三区以及靠近柬埔寨的巡防区，有 13 个职能机构、4 个禁毒特别行动组、2 个侦查组。

3. 执法船舶和装备

越南海警司令部配备的舰艇几乎均为自建，少部分为技术转移合建或外购。越南海警配备了 3 架巡防飞机、55 艘巡防船；其中，有 148 吨的胡峰级鱼雷快艇 4 艘、120 吨的巡逻艇14艘、200吨的巡逻艇13艘、280吨巡逻艇2艘、400吨的巡逻艇6艘、1200吨的巡逻搜索及拯救艇3艘、2500吨的巡逻搜索及拯救艇5艘、1400吨的打捞拖船5艘、达曼斯坦4100巡逻艇3艘。

(三) 海事调查体制

1. 法律依据

2012年9月15日，越南政府颁布的《水上交通事故调查及报告规定》正式生效。该规定主要是依据《海商法》《关于规定交通运输部直属越南海事局职能、任务、权限和组织机构的规定》以及国际海事组织2008年颁布的《国际海事事故调查规则》。①《水上交通事故调查及报告规定》第12条规定："越南海事局是事故调查的牵头单位，港务局负责组织调查在越南港口水域②内发生的事故和海事局移交的其他事故。"由此可见，法律赋予海事局负责越南港口水域外的事故调查的权力，而港务局负责港口水域内的事故调查。

2. 海事事故调查类型

《水上交通事故调查及报告规定》第10条规定，事故调查旨在查明事故原因或可能引发事故的原因、条件和环境等因素，便于寻找有效的方式以防止类似事故的发生；事故调查不在于判定责任和法律义务。海事事故调查根据调查目的的不同分为安全调查和行政调查，其中安全调查只是单纯为查明船舶及相关实施存在的问题、船员存在的疏忽等事故原因，而行政调查则是在查明事故原因的基础上判定事故责任。越南将安全调查与行政调查相分离，在以安全为中心的调查基础上，不涉及责任追究，既能保证调查过程的客观公正，又能分析查找出事故原因，防止类似事故再次发生。

二、海事法律

越南的海事活动频繁活跃。为执行1980年和1992年宪法，维护海上主权和安全，越南逐步将1982年联合国海洋法公约的规定纳入国家法律，颁布了一系列重要的基本法律，包括2003年《国界法》、2004年《国家安全法》、2008年《海警条例》、2013年《海洋法》和大量其他法律文件。

(一) 国内法

越南的最高海事法律《海商法》于1990年6月30日由国会通过（1992年1月1日执行），在2015年修订后于2017年7月1日生效。现《海商法》由20章组成，主要内

---

① 该规则要求缔约国要按照公约和规定的要求进行海事安全调查，查明原则，提出预防建议，以使海上安全程度得以提高。

② 越南《海商法》第4条规定，港口水域是指限于设立栈桥前水域、船舶掉头区、锚泊区、中转区、避风区、引航员接送区、检疫区、航道和建造其他附属工程的水域。

容包括船舶、船员、港口、海上安全、环境保护、海上运输合同、租船合同、船舶代理、引航、拖航、海难救助、海上搜救、打捞沉没财产、共同海损等,涵盖了越南海船的所有主要活动,为国家海事管理提供了法律框架。为有效执行《海商法》,各项规章制度须作为附属法例予以公布。总理办公室和交通运输部还制定了若干重要的法律文件,规定海事管理机构的具体职责及组织方式。其中,最重要的几部附属条例是:决定成立越南海事局的第 239/HDBT 号决定,规定越南海事局职责和组织形式的第 31/Ttg 号决定,规定了远洋船舶在越南登记事项的第 203/Ttg 号决定,规定了海港当局的职责和组织形式的第 639/Ttg 号决定以及规定越南登记处的职责和组织形式的第 75/Ttg 号决定。

其他与海事活动相关的法律法规还包括 1998 年《水资源法》、2003 年《水产资源法》、2008 年《石油法》《边防卫队条例》《民兵和自卫队法》《海警条例》《行政违法处罚法》《海洋法》《环境保护法》《生物多样性法》等。

越南的国内法梳理如下:

1. 越南海商法
Vietnam Maritime Code, Pursuant to the 1992 Constitution of the Socialist Republic of Vietnam, amended by Resolution No. 51/2001-QH10 dated 25 December 2001 by the National Assembly, the Legislature X, at the 10th Section
https://www.wto.org/english/thewto_e/acc_e/vnm_e/WTACCVNM43_LEG_9.pdf

2. 1998 年水资源法
Law on Water Resources, 1998 (Law No. 8/1998/QH10 of 1998)
http://extwprlegs1.fao.orgdocspdf/vie14294.pdf

3. 2003 年水产资源法
The Law on Aquatic Resources (2003)
http://www.moj.gov.vnvbpqen/lists/vn%20bn%20php%20lut/view_detail.aspx?itemid=8255

4. 1993 年石油法(2000 年和 2008 年修订)
Petroleum Law (1993, amended in 2000 and 2008)
http://extwprlegs1.fao.orgdocspdf/vie84159.pdf

5. 边防条例
Ordinance on Border Guard
http://moj.gov.vnvbpqen/lists/vn%20bn%20php%20lut/view_detail.aspx?itemid=2527

6. 2009年民兵和自卫队法

Law on Militia and Self-Defense Forces

http://www.moj.gov.vnvbpqen/Lists/Vn%20bn%20php%20lut/View_Detail.aspx? ItemID=10474

7. 行政违法处置法

Law on Handling of Administrative Violations

http://kenfoxlaw.com/faq/170-legal-docs/ip-laws-and-related-documents/13271-vietnams-law-on-handling-of-administrative-violations-.html

8. 环境保护法

Law on Environmental Protection

http://vietnamlawmagazine.vn/revised-law-on-environmental-protection-4074.html

9. 2008年生物多样性法

Law on Biodiversity

http://moj.gov.vnvbpqen/lists/vn%20bn%20php%20lut/view_detail.aspx? itemid=10503

OTHER LEGILATIONS:

1. 越南社会主义共和国海上边界线内个人、车辆和船舶活动管理法令

Decree No. 71/2015/ND-CP of September 3, 2015, On management of activities of persons, vehicles and craft in maritime boundary areas of the Socialist Republic of Vietnam

http://vietnamlawmagazine.vn/decree-no-71-2015-nd-cp-of-september-3-2015-5078.html

2. 内河船和进口海船使用年限法令

Decree No. 111/2014/NC-CP of November 20, 2014, Providing the useful life of inland waterway vessels and the useful life of vessels permitted for import

http://vietnamlawmagazine.vn/decree-no-111-2014-nd-cp-of-november-20-2014-4754.html

（二）国际条约

1. 海事国际条约概述

越南于1994年加入《联合国海洋法公约》，加入的其他海事国际条约有20个，其中具有代表性的是1965年《国际便利海上运输公约》（FAL）、1966年《国际载重线公约》（LL）、1969年《国际油污损害民事责任公约》（CLC）、1972年《国际海上避碰规则公约》（COLREGS）、1973年《国际防止船舶造成污染公约》（MARPOL）、1974年《国际海上人命安全公约》（SOLAS）、1976年《国际海事卫星组织公约》（IMSO）、1978年《国际海员培训、发证和值班标准公约》（STCW）、1979年《国际海上搜寻救

助公约》(SAR)、1988 年《制止危及海上航行安全非法行为公约》(SUA) 等。除上述国际条约外,越南还加入了《东盟便利船舶事故搜救中船舶搜索协议》《东盟多式联运框架协议》《亚洲区域反海盗及持械抢劫合作协议》。

2. 加入方式及国内化程序

越南第 108/2016/QH13 号法规定了越南批准国际条约的程序。根据该法规定,最高人民法院、最高人民检察院、国家审计署、部级机构或者政府附署机构应在其职权范围内要求国际合作,提议政府提请国家主席以国家名义进行条约谈判,或者提议总理以政府名义进行条约谈判。在提议签订条约之前,提案机构应当征求有关机构和组织的意见、外交部的审核意见和司法部的评估意见。此后,条约将被提交到国会常务委员会,由常务委员会发表意见。该意见是总统或政府决定是否签署条约的基础。

越南在《刑法》《民法》《贸易法》和《缔结加入与履行国际条约法》中都规定,国际条约和国内法律对同一问题的调整中若存在不一致的情形则优先适用国际条约,即加入的国际条约具有直接效力,无须转化即可在国内实施。

三、小　结

越南的海事管理体制是由海事局集中管理越南的海事相关事务,在海上事故、海上执法等方面由越南海警司令部协助其进行执法调查。在海事调查方面,越南 2012 年颁布的《水上交通事故调查及报告规定》正式生效,其规定与《国际海事事故调查规则》相接轨,将海事调查分为行政调查和安全调查:安全调查只是单纯为查明船舶及相关实施存在的问题、船员存在的疏忽等事故原因,而行政调查则是在查明事故原因的基础上判定事故责任。越南的海事调查在以安全为中心的调查基础上,不涉及责任追究,既能保证调查过程的客观公正,又能分析查找出事故原因,防止类似事故再次发生。

四、附录:越南海事法律(国内法)文件

(一)附录1:海警条例

5311998IND-CP 号法令

Ordinance on Marine Police

DECREE No. 53/1998/ND-CP OF JULY 21, 1998 ON THE ORGANIZATION AND

ACTIVITIES OF THE VIETNAM MARINE POLICE [1]

THE GOVERNMENT

Pursuant to the Law on Organization of the Government of September 30, 1992;

Pursuant to the Ordinance on the Vietnam Marine Police of March 28, 1998;

At the proposal of the Minister of National Defense,

DECREES:

Chapter I

GENERAL PROVISIONS

Article 1.- The Vietnam Marine Police is organized according to the Ordinance on the Vietnam Marine Police of March 28, 1998.

Its international transaction name in English is Vietnam Marine Police.

The Ministry of Defense shall directly organize, manage and direct all activities of the Vietnam Marine Police.

Article 2.- All activities of the Vietnam Marine Police must comply with the prescriptions of Vietnamese law; respect and observe the related international conventions which the Socialist Republic of Vietnam has signed or adhered to.

Article 3.- All organizations, individuals and means operating in the sea areas from the base line to the outer border line of the exclusive economic zone and the continental shelf of the Socialist Republic of Vietnam shall have to submit to the control and inspection by the Vietnam Marine Police in assuring security, order and safety and observing Vietnamese law and the related international conventions which the Socialist Republic of Vietnam has signed or adhered to.

Chapter II

ORGANIZATION AND EQUIPMENT OF VIETNAM MARINE POLICE

Article 4.- The organizational system of the Vietnam Marine Police includes:

1. The Vietnam Marine Police Department.

2. The Marine Police Sectors. The structure of a Marine Police Sector comprises Regiments, Groups and Squads of Marine Police.

3. The Training School of Marine Police.

The concrete organization, division and equipment of the Marine Police agencies and units shall be provided for by the Minister of Defense.

Article 5.- The Head of the Marine Police Department shall be appointed by the Prime Minister at the proposal of the Minister of Defense. He is assisted by a number of Deputy Department Heads to be appointed by the Minister of Defense.

The Marine Police Department has the legal person status and a seal of its own, has a budget for organization, building and operations supplied by the State budget, can open its own accounts at the State Treasury, and has its head office in Hai Phong, its permanent office in Hanoi and its representative in Ho Chi Minh City.

Article 6.- The Marine Police Sectors are organized correspondingly with the Navy Sectors. The Commander of a Marine Police Sector shall be appointed by the Minister of Defense at the proposal of the Head of the Marine Police Department.

Article 7. - The Vietnam Marine Police is supplied with the necessary means, weapons and equipment to carry out its tasks.

Article 8.- The service flag, insignia and uniform of the Vietnam Marine Police are provided for as follows:

1. Ensign:

a/ The command flag has the shape of an isosceles color marine blue, 1.5 m high, 1 m at the base, the national emblem in the center with a yellow arrow crossing in the background.

The command flag shall be hung on a mast 2.5 m high planted at the stern.

b/ The insignia has two parallel stripes, one color orange and the other color white, running from the upper edge of the hull to the water level.

The first stripe color orange lies at the end of the ship bow adjacent to the front point of the hull at $30°$ - $40°$, 0.5 m - 1 m large (depending on the size of the ship) next to the second stripe color white at a breadth of 1/4 of the first stripe.

---

[1] 本法条引用自 http://extwprlegs1.fao.orgdocspdf/vie20593.pdf。

The insignia number is depicted on either side of the ship.

c/ The ship hull is painted in marine blue, the command tower is painted in white.

On the ship hull:

+ On the stem two command stripes with the number of the ship painted in white.

+ On the stem two command stripes in white capital letters.

CANH SAT BIEN VIET NAM (upper line)

VIETNAM MARINE POLICE (lower line)

2. Service insignia.

The service insignia of the Vietnam Marine Police has the shape of a shield on a dark blue background with a 2 mm red brim and an anchor at the center flanked by two rice ears and the red lettered CSB underneath and a five-point star overhead.

3. Uniform

a/ The military badge of the Vietnam Marine Police is round in form, 33 mm in diameter, with a golden star interlaced with a dark blue anchor on a crimson background, surrounded by two rice ears, with a golden half-wheel marked with the letters CSB in red.

The military badge in service is framed by a double laurel:

+ General rank: golden double laurel

+ Colonel rank, company and non commissioned officers, rank-and-file: double laurel silver color.

b/ Rank badges and insignias of the Vietnam Marine Police shall conform with Decree No.74-HDBT of April 26, 1982 of the Council of Ministers (now the Government) concerning the "Regulations on military signs, rank badges, insignias and ceremonial uniform of the Vietnam People's Army", Decree No.78-HDBT of March 27, 1991 of the Council of Ministers (now the Government) on "Modifying and supplementing Decree No.74-HDBT of April 26, 1982" and Decree No.61-CP of October 21, 1996 of the Government on "Modifying and supplementing the regulations on the insignias, badges and ranks of professional armymen". In particular, with regard to the Vietnam Marine Police there are the following amendments and modifications:

- Background of rank badge: color dark blue

- Border of rank badge: color yellow

- Rank button: with an anchor figure and the letters CSB in red.

- Background of insignia: color dark blue, figure of insignia like figure of rank badge.

c/ The uniform of the Vietnam Marine Police comprises two categories, one for winter and the other for summer.

The Ministry of Defense shall make concrete provisions for the regime of annual equipment, style and form of tailoring.

Article 9.- While on duty the ships, boats and other means of the Vietnam Marine Police have to fly the National Flag and the Command Flag of the Marine Police; the officers and troops of the Marine Police must wear the badge and the prescribed uniform.

Chapter III

ACTIVITIES OF THE VIETNAM MARINE POLICE

Article 10.- The Vietnam Marine Police carries out its managerial function for security, order and safety and ensures the observance of the law of the Socialist Republic of Vietnam and the related international conventions which the Socialist Republic of Vietnam has signed or adhered to in the sea areas and on the continental shelf of the Socialist Republic of Vietnam.

Article 11.- The Head of the Marine Police Department is the Head of the Vietnam Marine Police. He leads and directs according to the regime of chief responsible person on the basis of ensuring the principle of democratic centralism.

The Head of the Marine Police Department has the duty to direct and organize the operations of the Vietnam Marine Police and coordinate actions with the related forces in carrying out the tasks and powers defined in the Ordinance on the Vietnam Marine Police.

The Head of the Marine Police Department shall assign responsibilities to the Deputy Heads of Department in each domain of work or each duty; he shall have to use effectively the assistant agencies and permanently educate the officers and men under his authority to raise their sense of responsibility and their standards.

Article 12.- The Marine Police Sectors shall have to carry out their tasks and powers defined in the Ordinance on the Vietnam Marine Police.

Following is the allocation of managerial powers to the Marine Police Sectors:

1. Sector 1 shall manage the sea areas and the continental shelf from the estuary of Bac Luan river in Quang Ninh province to Mui Doc in Ha Tinh province.

2. Sector 3 manages the sea areas and the continental shelf from Mui Doc in Ha Tinh province to Cu LaoXanh in Binh Dinh province.

3. Sector 4 manages the sea areas and the continental shelf from Cu Lao Xanh in Binh Dinh province to the northern bank of Dinh An estuary in Soc Trang province.

4. Sector 5 manages the sea areas and the continental shelf from the northern bank of Dinh An estuary in Soc Trang province to Ha Tien in Kien Giang province.

Article 13.- The Commander of a Marine Police Sector is the man who directly commands and organizes the direction of the Marine Police units under his authority to carry out the tasks within their scope of activity; he shall keep in touch and closely coordinate with the commanders of the units of Border Guards and the related forces in the discharge of his duty.

The Commander of a Marine Police Sector shall have to regularly educate and raise the sense of responsibility and standard of the officers and men under his authority.

Article 14.- The Commander of a Marine Police Sector shall organize and implement the regime of guard duty on each sea area, the plan of regular and irregular patrol of the Marine Police under his authority.

When detecting signs of violation of law on the sea or on orders from the higher authority, the Commander of a Marine Police Sector shall have to mobilize the forces and means under his authority to expeditiously arrive at the place where the violation occurs in order to deal with it according to his competence.

Article 15.- The officers and men of the Marine Police shall perform the duties and have concrete powers defined at the Ordinance on the Vietnam Marine Police and coordinate with the related forces on the sea in carrying out their activities in order to regularly and continuously monitor the situation on the sea, promptly detect and take cognizance of the incidents and accidents and handle them according to their competence or record them into the dossier of violation and at the same time report them urgently to their immediate higher level of command.

Article 16.- Within the internal waters, when requested, the Vietnam Marine Police shall have to coordinate and assist the other specialized forces in carrying out their tasks, and ensure the activities on the sea in conformity with the prescriptions of law; in case the Vietnam Marine Police itself detects violations of law it shall have to immediately inform the specialized forces, temporarily detain the persons and means that are caught in the act of violation, then hand them over to the competent agency to handle according to the provisions of law.

Article 17.- Within the area from the base line to the outer boundary of the exclusive economic zone and continental shelf of Vietnam, the Vietnam Marine Police shall independently carry out the tasks and powers provided for in the Ordinance on the Vietnam Marine Police. In cases of necessity, the Vietnam Marine Police may coordinate with the related specialized forces to carry out activities in order to maintain the observance of law and handle the acts of violation of law; the related branches may assign to the Vietnam Marine Police a number of given activities under its function and professional task and within the contents and scope of assignment to be defined by the Ministry of Defense and the related Ministries and branches.

Chapter IV

AWARDS AND HANDLING OF VIOLATIONS

Article 18.- Officers and men of the Marine Police with meritorious records in the implementation of their tasks shall be awarded according to the common regulations of the State.

Article 19.- Officers and men of the Marine Police who violate the provisions of this Decree and related provisions of law or who show irresponsibility and fail to accomplish their tasks shall, depending on the character and extent of the violation, be disciplined or examined for penal liability as prescribed by law.

Chapter V

IMPLEMENTATION PROVISIONS

Article 20.- This Decree takes effect on the 1st of September 1998.

Article 21.- The Minister of Defense, the Head of

the Vietnam Marine Police Department, the other Ministers, the Heads of ministerial-level agencies, the Heads of agencies attached to the Government, the Presidents of the People's Committees of the provinces and cities directly under the Central Government shall have to implement this Decree.

On behalf of the Government
Prime Minister
PHAN VAN KHAI

（二）附录 2：2012 年越南海洋法

2012 年越南海洋法
Law of the Sea of Vietnam

THE PRESIDENT	**THE SOCIALIST REPUBLIC OF VIETNAM**
	Independence-Freedom-Happiness
No. 16/2012/L-CTN	*Hanoi*, July 2, 2012

ORDER

On the promulgation of law[①]

THE PRESIDENT OF THE SOCIALIST REPUBLIC OF VIETNAM

Pursuant to Articles 103 and 106 of the 1992 Constitution of the Socialist Republic of Vietnam, which was amended and supplemented under Resolution No. 51/2001/QH10 of December 25, 2001, of the Xth National Assembly, the 10th session; Pursuant to Article 91 of the Law on Organization of the National Assembly; Pursuant to Article 57 of the Law on Promulgation of Legal Documents.

PROMULGATES:

The Law of the Sea of Vietnam,

which was passed on June 21, 2012, by the XIIIth National Assembly of the Socialist Republic of Vietnam at its 3rd session.

President of the Socialist Republic of Vietnam
TRUONG TAN SANG

---

① 本法条引用自 http://vietnamlawmagazine.vn/law-of-the-sea-of-vietnam-4895.html。

THE NATIONAL ASSEMBLY	THE SOCIALIST REPUBLIC OF VIETNAM
	Independence – Freedom – Happiness
No. 18/2012/QH13	Hanoi, June 21, 2012

LAW OF THE SEA OF VIETNAM

Pursuant to the 1992 Constitution of the Socialist Republic of Vietnam amended in accordance with Resolution No. 51/2001/QH10; The National Assembly promulgates the Law of the Sea of Vietnam.

Chapter I
GENERAL PROVISIONS

Article 1. Scope of regulation

This Law provides for the baseline, the internal waters, the territorial sea, the contiguous zone, the exclusive economic zone, the continental shelf, islands, the Paracel and Spratly archipelagos and other archipelagos under the sovereignty, sovereign rights and jurisdiction of Vietnam; operations in Vietnam's maritime zones; maritime economic development; the management and protection of the sea and islands.

Article 2. Application of law

1. The provisions of this Law shall prevail in case there are differences between the provisions of this Law and those of other laws in relation to the sovereignty and legal status of Vietnam's maritime zones.

2. In case there are differences between the provisions of this Law and those of an international treaty to which the Socialist Republic of Vietnam is a contracting party, the provisions of the international treaty shall prevail.

Article 3. Interpretation of terms

In this Law, the terms below are construed as follows:

1. The *maritime zones of Vietnam* cover the internal waters, territorial sea, contiguous zone, exclusive economic zone and continental shelf under Vietnam's sovereignty, sovereign rights and jurisdiction, determined in accordance with Vietnamese law, the treaties on boundaries and territory to which the Socialist Republic of Vietnam is a contracting party and in conformity with the 1982 United Nations Convention on the Law of the Sea.

2. The *high seas* cover all parts of the sea beyond the exclusive economic zones of Vietnam and other states, and not including the seabed and the subsoil thereof.

3. *Vessel* means a craft operating on or under the water surface, including ship, boat or another craft with or without motor.

4. *Military vessel* means a vessel of the armed forces of a state bearing external marks that

clearly manifest the nationality of that state, commanded by a navy officer serving that state, whose name appears in the list of officers or in equivalent documents. Such vessel is operated by a crew working under military orders.

5. *Vessel for official service* means a vessel that is used exclusively for the conduct of non-commercial state activities.

6. *Resources* include living and non-living resources underwater, on the seabed and the subsoil.

7. The *isobath* is the line connecting points of the same depth at sea.

Article 4. Principles of management and protection of the sea

1. The management and protection of the sea are conducted in a unified manner in accordance with Vietnamese law and in conformity with the United Nations Charter and other treaties to which the Socialist Republic of Vietnam is a contracting party.

2. Vietnamese agencies, organizations and citizens have the responsibility to safeguard the sovereignty, sovereign rights and jurisdiction of Vietnam over its maritime zones, islands and archipelagos, and protect marine resources and the marine environment.

3. The State of Vietnam settles disputes related to the sea and islands with other countries by peaceful means, in conformity with the 1982 United Nations Convention on the Law of the Sea, and international law and practices.

Article 5. Policy on the management and protection of the sea

1. To bring into full play the strength of the entire nation, take necessary measures to safeguard the sovereignty, sovereign rights and jurisdiction over the maritime zones, islands and archipelagos, protect marine resources and the marine environment, and promote the development of maritime economy.

2. To develop and implement strategies, planning and plans on the management, utilization, exploitation and protection of the maritime zones, islands and archipelagos in a sustainable manner for the sake of socio-economic development, national defense and security.

3. To encourage organizations and individuals to invest labor, materials and capital and apply scientific, technical and technological achievements in the utilization, exploitation and development of maritime economy, protection of marine resources and the marine environment and sustainable development of the marine zones suitable with the conditions of each maritime zone, meeting the requirements of national defense and security; to increase dissemination of information on the potential of and policies and law on the sea.

4. To encourage and protect fishery activities conducted by Vietnamese fishermen in Vietnam's maritime zones, protect the operation of Vietnamese organizations and citizens beyond Vietnam's maritime zones in conformity with treaties to which the Socialist Republic of Vietnam is a contracting party and international law and the laws of the coastal states concerned.

5. To make appropriate investment to ensure the operation of sea patrol and surveillance forces, improve logistic infrastructure to serve activities at sea and in islands and archipelagos

and to develop maritime human resources.

6. To implement preferential policies in favor of people living in islands and archipelagos and preferential treatment to forces engaged in the management and protection of maritime zones, islands and archipelagos.

Article 6. International cooperation on maritime matters

1. The State of Vietnam strongly promotes international cooperation on maritime matters with countries and regional and international organizations on the basis of international law and respect for independence, sovereignty and territorial integrity, equality and mutual benefit.

2. International cooperation on maritime matters includes:

a/ Maritime and oceanic surveys and researches; scientific, technical and technological applications;

b/ Climate change response, natural disaster prevention, control and warning;

c/ Protection of marine biodiversity and ecology;

d/ Prevention and combat against marine environmental pollution, treatment of waste discharged from maritime economic activities, and response to oil spill incidents;

e/ Search and rescue at sea;

f/ Prevention and combat against crimes at sea;

g/ Sustainable exploitation of marine resources and development of sea tourism.

Article 7. State management of the sea

1. The Government of Vietnam exercises nationwide state management of the sea.

2. Ministries, ministerial-level agencies and People's Committee of coastal provinces and centrally run cities shall, within the scope of their duties and competence, perform state management of the sea.

Chapter II
THE MARITIME ZONES OF VIETNAM

Article 8. Establishment of the baseline

The baseline used for measuring the breadth of Vietnam's territorial sea is the straight baseline already publicized by the Government. The Government of Vietnam shall determine and, upon approval by the National Assembly's Standing Committee, publicize the baselines in areas where baselines have not been established.

Article 9. Internal waters

The internal waters are the waters adjacent to the coast on the landward side of the baseline and constitute part of Vietnam's territory.

Article 10. Legal status of the internal waters

The State of Vietnam exercises full and absolute sovereignty over the internal waters as it does over the land territory.

Article 11. Territorial sea

The territorial sea of the Socialist Republic of Vietnam is the water area extending 12 nautical miles from the baseline.

The outer limit of the territorial sea is Vietnam's national maritime border.

Article 12. Legal status of the territorial sea

1. The State exercises full and absolute sovereignty over the territorial sea, the air space over, as well as the seabed and subsoil of the territorial sea in conformity with the 1982 United Nations Convention on the Law of the Sea.

2. Vessels of all states enjoy the right of innocent passage through Vietnam's territorial sea. Foreign military vessels exercising the right of innocent passage through Vietnam's territorial sea shall give prior notice to competent Vietnamese authorities.

3. Innocent passage of foreign vessels shall be conducted on the basis of respect for the peace, independence, sovereignty and the laws of Vietnam and treaties to which the Socialist Republic of Vietnam is a contracting party.

4. Foreign aircraft is not permitted to enter the air space over the territorial sea of Vietnam unless otherwise agreed upon by the Vietnamese Government or provided in treaties to which the Socialist Republic of Vietnam is a contracting party.

5. The State has sovereignty over all types of archaeological and historical objects in Vietnam's territorial sea.

Article 13. Contiguous zone

The contiguous zone is the sea area adjacent to and beyond the territorial sea of Vietnam, which is 12 nautical miles wide from the outer limit of the territorial sea.

Article 14. Legal status of the contiguous zone

1. The State exercises sovereign rights, jurisdiction and other rights stipulated in Article 16 of this Law over the contiguous zone.

2. The State exercises control within the contiguous zone to prevent and punish acts of infringement of the law on customs, tariff, health or immigration committed in the territory or the territorial sea of Vietnam.

Article 15. Exclusive economic zone

The exclusive economic zone is a sea area adjacent to and beyond the territorial sea of Vietnam, which integrates with the territorial sea to form a maritime zone extending to 200 nautical miles from the baseline.

Article 16. Legal status of the exclusive economic zone

1. Within the exclusive economic zone, the State of Vietnam exercises the following rights:

a/ Sovereign rights for the purpose of exploring, exploiting, managing and conserving natural resources of the waters superjacent to the seabed, of the seabed and its subsoil; as well as other activities for the economic exploitation and exploration of the zone;

b/ Jurisdiction with regard to the establishment and use of artificial islands, installations and structures at sea; as well as marine scientific research, and protection and preservation of the marine environment;

c/ Other rights and duties in conformity with international law.

2. The State of Vietnam respects freedoms of navigation and overflight, the right to lay submarine cables and pipelines and lawful uses of the sea by other states in Vietnam's exclusive economic zone in accordance with this Law and treaties to which the Socialist Republic of Vietnam is a contracting party, provided that those operations are not detrimental to the sovereign rights, jurisdiction and national maritime interests of Vietnam.

The laying of submarine cables and pipelines is subject to written consent of competent Vietnamese authorities.

3. Foreign organizations and individuals may participate in exploring, utilizing and exploiting natural resources, conducting scientific research and establishing installations and structures in the exclusive economic zone of Vietnam on the basis of treaties to which the Socialist Republic of Vietnam is a contracting party, contracts signed in accordance with the provisions of Vietnamese law or with the permission granted by the Vietnamese Government.

4. The rights related to the seabed and subsoil are exercised in accordance with Articles 17 and 18 of this Law.

Article 17. Continental shelf

The continental shelf of Vietnam is the seabed and subsoil of the submarine areas adjacent to and beyond the territorial sea of Vietnam, throughout the natural prolongation of the land territory, islands and archipelagos of Vietnam, to the outer edge of the continental margin.

Where the outer edge of the continent margin does not extend up to 200 nautical miles measured from the baseline, the continental shelf in that area extends to a distance of 200 nautical miles measured from the baseline.

Where the outer edge of the continent margin extends beyond 200 nautical miles measured from the baseline, the continental shelf in that area extends to a distance not exceeding 350 nautical miles measured from the baseline or not exceeding 100 nautical miles measured from the 2,500-metre isobath.

Article 18. Legal status of the continental shelf

1. The State of Vietnam exercises sovereign rights over its continental shelf for the purpose of exploring and exploiting natural resources.

2. The sovereign rights stipulated in Clause 1 of this Article are exclusive in the sense that no one may conduct activities of exploring the continental shelf or exploiting natural resources of the continental shelf of Vietnam without the consent of the Vietnamese Government.

3. The State of Vietnam has exclusive rights to exploit the subsoil, authorize and regulate drilling on the continental shelf for any purpose.

4. The State of Vietnam respects the right to lay submarine cables and pipelines and other lawful uses of the sea by other states on the continental shelf of Vietnam in accordance with this

Law and treaties to which the Socialist Republic of Vietnam is a contracting party, provided that those operations are not detrimental to the sovereign rights, jurisdiction and national maritime interests of Vietnam.

The laying of submarine cables and pipelines are subjected to written consent of competent Vietnamese authorities.

5. Foreign organizations and individuals are allowed to participate in exploring, using, exploiting natural resources, conducting scientific research and establishing installations and structures on the continental shelf of Vietnam on the basis of treaties to which the Socialist Republic of Vietnam is a contracting party, contracts signed in accordance with the provisions of Vietnamese law or with the permission granted by the Vietnamese Government.

Article 19. Islands and archipelagos

1. An island is a naturally formed area of land surrounded by water, which is above water at high tide.

An archipelago is a group of islands, including parts of the islands, adjacent waters and other closely related natural features.

2. Islands and archipelagos under the sovereignty of Vietnam are integral parts of Vietnam's territory.

Article 20. The internal waters, territorial seas, contiguous zones, exclusive economic zones and continental shelves of islands and archipelagos

1. Islands which can sustain human habitation or economic life of their own have internal waters, territorial seas, contiguous zones, exclusive economic zones and continental shelves.

2. Rocks which can not sustain human habitation or economic life of their own have no exclusive economic zone or continental shelf.

3. The internal waters, territorial seas, contiguous zones, exclusive economic zones and continental shelves of islands and archipelagos are determined in accordance with Articles 9, 11, 13, 14, 15 and 17 of this Law and demonstrated by maritime charts and geographical coordinates publicized by the Vietnamese Government.

Article 21. Legal status of islands and archipelagos

1. The State of Vietnam exercises sovereignty over the islands and archipelagos of Vietnam.

2. The legal status of the internal waters, territorial seas, contiguous zones, exclusive economic zones and continental shelves of islands and archipelagoes is as provided for in Articles 10, 12, 14, 16 and 18 of this Law.

Chapter III
OPERATIONS IN MARITIME ZONES OF VIETNAM

Article 22. General provisions

1. Organizations and individuals conducting operations in the maritime zones of Vietnam

shall respect Vietnam's sovereignty, territorial integrity, sovereign rights, jurisdiction and her national interests, observe the provisions of Vietnamese law and relevant international law.

2. The State of Vietnam respects and protects the legitimate rights and interests of vessels, organizations and individuals conducting operations in the maritime zones of Vietnam in conformity with the provisions of Vietnamese law and treaties to which the Socialist Republic of Vietnam is a contracting party.

Article 23. Innocent passage through the territorial sea

1. Passage through the territorial sea means the navigation of foreign vessels through the territorial sea of Vietnam for either of the following purposes:

a/ Traversing the territorial sea without entering the internal waters of Vietnam or without calling at a port facility, station or dock outside Vietnam's internal waters;

b/ Entering or leaving Vietnam's internal waters or calling at or leaving a port facility, station or dock outside Vietnam's internal waters.

2. Passage through the territorial sea must be continuous and expeditious, except in cases of maritime accidents, *force majeure* events, distress or for the purpose of rescuing people, vessels or aircraft in distress.

3. Innocent passage through the territorial sea must not be prejudicial to the peace, national defense and security of Vietnam, and maritime order and safety. The passage of a foreign vessel through the territorial sea of Vietnam shall be considered prejudicial to the peace, national defense and security of Vietnam or maritime order and safety if that vessel conducts any of the following acts:

a/ Threat or use of force against the independence, sovereignty and territorial integrity of Vietnam;

b/ Threat or use of force against the independence, sovereignty and territorial integrity of other countries; any act in violation of the fundamental principles of international law as stipulated in the United Nations Charter;

c/ Practice or exercise with any type of weapons and in any form;

d/ Collection of information detrimental to the national defense and security of Vietnam;

e/ Propaganda aimed at undermining the national defense and security of Vietnam;

f/ Launching, landing or taking on board any aircraft;

g/ Launching, landing or taking on board any military device;

h/ Loading or unloading any commodity, currency or person contrary to Vietnamese laws and regulations on customs, tariff, health or immigration;

i/ Intentionally causing serious pollution to the marine environment;

j/ Illegal fishing;

k/ Illegal conduct of research, surveys or explorations;

l/ Adversely affecting the operation of the information and communication system or other installations or structures of Vietnam;

m/ Any operation not directly related to the passage.

Article 24. Obligations while conducting innocent passage

1. Foreign organizations and individuals, while conducting innocent passage in Vietnam's territorial sea, are obliged to observe Vietnamese laws and regulations on:

a/ Safety of navigation, regulation of maritime traffic, sea lanes and traffic separation;

b/ Protection of installations and systems to ensure maritime traffic, and other installations or structures;

c/ Protection of cables and pipelines;

d/ Conservation of marine living resources;

e/ Fishing and aquaculture;

f/ Preservation of the marine environment, prevention, restriction and control of pollution thereof;

g/ Maritime scientific research and hydrographical surveys;

h/ Customs, tariff, health and immigration.

2. The captain of a foreign nuclear-powered vessel or a foreign vessel transporting radioactive, noxious or dangerous substances has the following obligations in passing through Vietnam's territorial sea:

a/ To carry sufficient technical documents related to the vessel and goods on board and documents of mandatory civil insurance;

b/ To be ready to provide competent Vietnamese authorities with all technical documents related to the vessel as well as goods on board;

c/ To fully implement the special precautionary measures established for such vessels by Vietnamese law and treaties to which the Socialist Republic of Vietnam is a contracting party;

d/ To observe decisions made by competent Vietnamese authorities on the application of the special precautionary measures, including ban of passage through Vietnam's territorial sea or forcing to leave Vietnam's territorial sea immediately in case there are clear signs or evidence of possible leakage or environmental pollution.

Article 25. Sea lanes and traffic separation in the territorial sea for innocent passage

1. The Government establishes and publicizes sea lanes and traffic separation in the territorial sea for innocent passage for the purpose of ensuring safety of navigation.

2. Foreign oil tankers, nuclear-powered vessels or vessels transporting radioactive, noxious or dangerous substances while conducting innocent passage in Vietnam's territorial sea may be required to use the sea lanes specified on a case-by-case basis.

Article 26. Suspension or restriction of innocent passage in the territorial sea

1. For the sake of safeguarding the sovereignty, national defense, security and interests or securing safety of navigation, protecting marine resources and the marine ecology, combating pollution, tackling maritime accidents or marine environmental disasters, preventing the spread of epidemics, the Government may suspend or restrict the exercise of innocent passage in

specified areas in Vietnam's territorial sea.

2. The suspension or restriction of innocent passage in specified areas in Vietnam's territorial sea in accordance with Clause 1 of this Article shall be made public domestically and internationally on the "Maritime Notice" in accordance with international maritime practice at least 15 days before the suspension or restriction takes effect or immediately after the application of such measure in case of emergency.

Article 27. Foreign military vessels and foreign vessels for official service coming to Vietnam

1. Foreign military vessels and foreign vessels for official service shall be allowed to enter the internal waters, anchor at a port facility, station or dock within the internal waters or at a port facility, station or dock outside the internal waters of Vietnam only at the invitation of the Vietnamese Government or in accordance with the agreement between competent authorities of Vietnam and the flag States.

2. Foreign military vessels and foreign vessels for official service, while being in the internal waters, ports, stations or docks within the internal waters or at the port facilities, stations or docks outside the internal waters of Vietnam, shall observe the provisions of this Law and other relevant laws and regulations and ensure that their operations conform to the invitation of the Vietnamese Government or the agreement with competent Vietnamese authorities.

Article 28. Responsibilities of foreign military vessels and foreign vessels for official service in the maritime zones of Vietnam

In case foreign military vessels violate Vietnamese laws while operating in the maritime zones of Vietnam, the Vietnamese sea patrol and surveillance forces may order them to immediately terminate their violations and, if such vessels are in Vietnam's territorial sea, to leave the territorial sea without delay. Violating vessels must observe the requests and orders of the Vietnamese sea patrol and surveillance forces.

In case a foreign military vessel or a foreign vessel for official service violates Vietnamese law or related international law while operating in Vietnam's maritime zones, its flag State shall bear responsibility for any damage caused by such vessel to Vietnam.

Article 29. Operation of foreign submarines and other underwater vehicles in Vietnam's internal waters and territorial sea

Within Vietnam's internal waters and territorial sea, foreign submarines and other foreign underwater vehicles must operate on the water surface and fly their national flags unless otherwise permitted by the Vietnamese Government or agreed upon between the Vietnamese Government and the Governments of the flag States.

Article 30. Criminal jurisdiction over foreign vessels

1. Within the scope of their mandates and responsibilities, the Vietnamese sea patrol and surveillance forces have the right to take measures such as arresting people, conducting investigation of crimes taking place on board of foreign vessels during the passage in Vietnam's territorial sea after leaving the internal waters.

2. For crimes taking place on board of foreign vessels during their passage in Vietnam's territorial sea but not immediately after leaving the internal waters, the Vietnamese sea patrol and surveillance forces have the right to arrest people and conduct investigation in the following cases:

a/ The consequence of the crime affects Vietnam;

b/ The crime committed is aimed at sabotaging the peace of Vietnam or the order in Vietnam's territorial sea;

c/ The captain of the vessel, or a diplomatic or consular official of the flag State requests assistance from competent Vietnamese authorities;

d/ To prevent acts of trafficking in persons, illicit trafficking, stockpiling or transportation of narcotics.

3. The sea patrol and surveillance forces may not take any measure on board a foreign vessel navigating in Vietnam's territorial sea for the purpose of arresting people or investigating crimes happening before the vessel enters Vietnam's territorial sea if the vessel had departed from a foreign port and only Passes through the territorial sea without going into the internal waters of Vietnam, except for the case of preventing or limiting the pollution of the marine environment or exercising the national jurisdiction prescribed at Point b, Clause 1, Article 16 of this Law.

4. The application of criminal Procedures must be in conformity with the provisions of Vietnamese law and treaties to which the Socialist Republic of Vietnam is a contracting party.

Article 31. Civil jurisdiction over foreign vessels

1. Sea patrol and surveillance forces may not force a foreign vessel passing through the territorial sea to stop or change course for the purpose of exercising civil jurisdiction over an individual aboard the vessel.

2. Sea patrol and surveillance forces may neither arrest nor apply civil measures to foreign vessels navigating in the maritime zones of Vietnam outside the internal waters, except as required in compliance with the obligations or civil liabilities borne by the vessel when passing by or in order to pass through the maritime zones of Vietnam.

3. Sea patrol and surveillance forces may apply measures, including arrest, against a foreign vessel for the purpose of exercising civil jurisdiction if the vessel is anchored in the territorial sea or passing through the territorial sea upon leaving the internal waters of Vietnam.

Article 32. Communication at ports, stations or docks of Vietnam

Organizations, individuals and vessels while staying in ports, stations or docks within the internal waters or in port facilities, stations or docks of Vietnam outside the internal waters shall communicate in accordance with the provisions of Vietnamese laws or relevant international law.

Article 33. Search and rescue

1. Individuals and vessels or flying vehicles, which are in distress or in danger at sea and in need of assistance, shall transmit SOS signals as prescribed and, as soon as the condition permits, inform the port authorities or the center for coordination of maritime search and rescue

or nearest local authorities of Vietnam for necessary assistance and guidance.

2. When noticing people or vessels in distress or in danger at sea or receiving SOS signals from people or vessels in distress at sea, all individuals and vessels shall render all possible assistance to people or vessels in distress or in danger if the actual situation allows and without causing danger to their vessels or people on board, and promptly inform such to individuals or organizations concerned.

3. The State guarantees necessary assistance in accordance with the provisions of Vietnamese law and relevant international law and in the humanitarian spirit to the people and vessels in distress or in danger at sea so that they may have quick access to search, rescue and recovery.

4. In the internal waters and territorial sea of Vietnam, the State has the exclusive rights in carrying out search and rescue activities for people and vessels in distress or in danger requiring help.

5. Competent authorities have the right to mobilize individuals and vessels operating in the maritime zones of Vietnam to join in search and rescue if the actual conditions allow and without causing danger to those individuals and vessels.

The mobilization and requests mentioned in this Article are only applied in emergency cases and only during the time necessary for search and rescue work.

6. Maritime rescue is conducted on the basis of maritime rescue contracts between the owners or captains of the vessel rendering the rescue and the vessel requiring rescue and in accordance with the provisions of Vietnamese law and relevant international law.

7. Foreign vessels entering the maritime zones of Vietnam to conduct search and rescue or to address the consequences of natural disasters or crises at the request of competent Vietnamese authorities shall abide by the provisions of Vietnamese law and treaties to which the Socialist Republic of Vietnam is a contracting party.

Article 34. Artificial islands, installations or structures at sea

1. Artificial islands, installations or structures at sea include:

a/ Drilling platforms at sea and all supporting facilities ensuring the normal and continuous operations of the drilling platforms or specialized equipment for maritime exploration, exploitation and usage;

b/ Maritime sign posts;

c/ Other installations and structures installed and used at sea.

2. The State has the jurisdiction over artificial islands, installations and structures in the exclusive economic zone and continental shelf of Vietnam, including the jurisdiction prescribed in relevant laws on customs, tax, health, security and immigration.

3. Artificial islands, installations and structures at sea and supporting facilities have a safety zone of 500 meters from the furthest point of those artificial islands, installations and structures at sea, but do not have the territorial sea or other maritime zones of their own.

4. No artificial island, installation or structure shall be constructed and no safety zone

shall be established around artificial islands, installations or structures in the locations where the existence of such artificial island, installation or structure and their safety zones may impede the use of the sea lanes recognized as essential to international maritime transport.

5. Upon expiration of usage, installations and structures at sea must be dissembled and removed from the maritime zones of Vietnam, unless otherwise permitted by competent Vietnamese authorities. In case installations or structures and their parts have not been fully removed due to technical reasons or as permitted, information regarding their location, size, shape and depth must be made available and appropriate maritime signposts or other forms of signal must be installed.

6. Information relating to the construction of artificial islands, installations and structures at sea and the establishment of safety zones around them, or the disassembling of all installations and structures and their parts must be made available to competent Vietnamese agencies and duly announced domestically and internationally, at least 15 days prior to the date of construction, establishment or disassembling of such artificial islands, installations or structures.

Article 35. Preservation and protection of marine resources and the marine environment

1. When operating in the maritime zones of Vietnam, vessels, organizations and individuals shall observe all provisions of Vietnamese laws and relevant international law relating to the preservation and protection of marine resources and the marine environment.

2. When transporting, loading or unloading goods or equipment that may cause damage to marine resources and human life, or may pollute the marine environment, vessels, organizations and individuals shall use specialized facilities and measures as prescribed to prevent and minimize the possible damage to human beings, marine resources and the environment.

3. Vessels, organizations and individuals may not discharge, sink or dump industrial waste, nuclear waste or other toxic waste in the maritime zones of Vietnam.

4. Vessels, organizations or individuals causing harmful effects to the marine resources and environment in the maritime zones of Vietnam, seaports, harbors or piers, in violation of the provisions of Vietnamese law and relevant international law, shall be dealt with in accordance with the provisions of Vietnamese law and treaties to which the Socialist Republic of Vietnam is a contracting party; those vessels, organizations or individuals are responsible for cleaning up and restoring the environment, and compensate for any damage as prescribed by law.

5. Organizations or individuals operating in the maritime zones of Vietnam are obliged to pay taxes, fees, charges and other contributions for environmental protection in accordance with the provisions of Vietnamese law and treaties to which the Socialist Republic of Vietnam is a contracting party.

Article 36. Marine scientific research

1. Foreign vessels, organizations or individuals conducting scientific research in the maritime zones of Vietnam shall obtain license from a competent State agency of Vietnam, be monitored by Vietnam, allow Vietnamese scientists to participate in the research and provide the

Vietnamese side with research materials, original specimens and related research results.

2. When conducting scientific research in the maritime zones of Vietnam, vessels, organizations or individuals shall abide by the following provisions:

a/ Research is conducted exclusively for peaceful purpose (s);

b/ Research is conducted with appropriate methods and facilities under Vietnamese law and relevant international law;

c/ Not to impede other lawful activities at sea under Vietnamese laws and relevant international law;

d/ The State of Vietnam is entitled to participate in foreign scientific research activities conducted in the maritime zones of Vietnam, to be provided with the research materials and original specimens, and to apply and use the results obtained from such scientific research or survey.

Article 37. Acts prohibited in the exclusive economic zone and on the continental shelf of Vietnam

When exercising the freedoms of navigation and overflight in the exclusive economic zone and on the continental shelf of Vietnam, organizations or individuals are not permitted to:

1. Conduct any act threatening the sovereignty, defense and security of Vietnam;
2. Conduct illegal exploitation of living resources, including illegal fishing;
3. Carry out illegal exploitation of currents, wind energy and other non-living resources;
4. Illegally construct, install and use artificial facilities or structures;
5. Conduct unlawful drilling or digging;
6. Conduct unlawful marine scientific research;
7. Pollute the marine environment;
8. Conduct piracy or armed robbery;
9. Conduct other unlawful activities under Vietnamese laws and international law.

Article 38. Ban of illegal stockpiling, use or trafficking of weapons, explosives and toxic substances

While operating in the maritime zones of Vietnam, vessels, organizations or individuals are not allowed to stockpile, use, illicitly traffic in weapons, explosives, toxic substances or other means and equipment that may cause harm to people and natural resources and pollute the marine environment.

Article 39. Ban of trafficking in persons, unlawful trafficking, transportation or stockpiling of narcotics

1. While operating in the maritime zones of Vietnam, vessels, organizations and individuals are not allowed to engage in traffic in person, or illicit transportation, stockpiling of or traffic in narcotics.

2. When there is a ground to believe that vessels, organizations or individuals are trafficking in persons or illicitly transporting, stockpiling or trafficking in narcotics, the Vietnamese sea patrol and surveillance forces are entitled to conduct search, check, arrest or to

escort them to a port, station or dock in Vietnam, or to escort or transfer them to a port, station or dock abroad in accordance with the provisions of Vietnamese law or treaties to which the Socialist Republic of Vietnam is a contracting party.

Article 40. Ban of illegal broadcasting

While operating in the maritime zones of Vietnam, vessels, organizations and individuals are not allowed to conduct illegal broadcasting or propaganda prejudicial to the national defense and security of Vietnam.

Article 41. The right of hot pursuit of foreign vessels

1. Sea patrol and surveillance forces are entitled to conduct hot pursuit of foreign vessels which violate Vietnamese laws and regulations, if such vessels are in the internal waters, territorial sea and contiguous zone of Vietnam.

The right of hot pursuit is exercised after the patrol and surveillance forces have transmitted signals requesting the violating vessel or suspected violating vessel to stop for inspection and such vessel does not cooperate. The hot pursuit may be continued outside the territorial sea or contiguous zone of Vietnam if the pursuit has not been interrupted.

2. The right of hot pursuit is also applied to acts of violation of the sovereign rights or jurisdiction of Vietnam and acts of violation within the safety zones of and in artificial islands, installations or structures in the exclusive economic zone and on the continental shelf of Vietnam.

3. The hot pursuit of Vietnamese patrol and surveillance forces terminates when the chased vessel enters the territorial sea of another state.

Chapter IV
MARITIME ECONOMIC DEVELOPMENT

Article 42. Principles of maritime economic development

Maritime economy shall be developed in a sustainable and effective manner according to the following principles:

1. Serving national socio-economic development;

2. Staying attuned to the protection of national sovereignty, defense and security, and safety and order at sea;

3. Meeting the requirements of management of marine natural resources and protection of the marine environment;

4. Promoting the socio-economic development of coastal localities and islands.

Article 43. Development of maritime economic industries

The State prioritize development of the following maritime economic industries:

1. Survey, exploration, exploitation, and processing of oil, gas, minerals and other maritime resources;

2. Maritime transportation, seaport, building and repair of seagoing vessels and other

maritime services;

3. Marine tourism and island economy;

4. Fishing, farming and processing of marine products;

5. Research, development, application, and transfer of science and technology for resource exploitation and maritime economic development;

6. Building and development of maritime human resources.

Article 44. Planning for maritime economic development

1. The planning of maritime economic development shall be based on:

a/ National strategy and master plan for socio-economic development; national strategy for environmental protection;

b/ Guidelines for a sustainable development strategy and maritime strategy;

c/ Geographic locations and features and natural characteristics or maritime zones, coastal areas and islands;

d/ Survey results on maritime resources and environment; reports on current use and forecasts of demands for maritime resource exploitation and maritime environmental protection for the country, each region and each coastal province or centrally run city;

e/ Estimated values of natural resources and vulnerability of the marine environment;

f/ Resources needed for implementing the planning.

2. Planning for maritime economic development includes:

a/ Analyzing and evaluating natural and socio-economic conditions and current state of maritime resources exploitation and use;

b/ Identifying directions, objectives and guidelines for reasonable use of resources and protection of the marine environment;

c/ Dividing maritime zones for the purpose of socio-economic development, national defense and security; identifying areas under exploitation ban or conditional exploitation, areas under special protection for the purpose of national defense, security, environmental protection, and preservation of the ecosystem, artificial islands, installations and structures at sea;

d/ Identifying locations, areas and map of areas where the sea surface, the seabed and islands are being used and developed;

e/ Identifying specifically vulnerable coastal areas, such as alluvial ground, eroding areas, protective forests, submerged land, coastal sand; identifying buffer zones and anticipating appropriate measures for management and protection;

f/ Proposing solutions and roadmap for implementing plans.

3. The Government shall formulate overall plans for developing maritime economic industries specified in Article 43 of this Law and oversee the development of the national plan for sea utilization to be submitted to the National Assembly for consideration and decision.

Article 45. Building and development of maritime economy

1. The State shall develop policies on investment in building and developing coastal economic zones and industrial clusters and developing the economy of island districts as planned

to ensure effectiveness and sustainable development.

2. The assignment of certain sea areas to organizations and individuals for marine resources exploitation and utilization shall be carried out in accordance with the regulations of the Government.

Article 46. Promotion of and incentives for investment in economic development in islands and maritime economic activities

1. The State shall prioritize investment in the building of infrastructure, networks of maritime logistics, and economic development in island districts and adopt preferential policies to improve the material and cultural lives of island residents.

2. The State shall encourage and provide tax and capital incentives and create favorable conditions for organizations and individuals to invest in exploiting the development potential and advantages of the islands.

3. The State shall provide encourage and provide tax and capital incentives and create favorable conditions for organizations and individuals to develop fisheries and other economic activities at sea and in islands; and protect people's activities at sea and in islands.

4. The Government shall detail this Article.

Chapter V
SEA PATROL AND SURVEILLANCE

Article 47. Sea patrol and surveillance forces

1. Sea patrol and surveillance forces include competent forces under the People's Army, the People's Police, and other specialized patrol and surveillance forces.

2. Militia and civil defense forces of coastal provinces and cities under central administration, guards of agencies and organizations located in coastal areas and other forces have the responsibility to participate in sea patrol and surveillance when requested by competent agencies.

Article 48. Duties and scope of responsibility of sea patrol and surveillance

1. Patrol and surveillance forces have the following duties:

a/ To protect the sovereignty, sovereign rights, jurisdiction and national interest in maritime zones and islands of Vietnam;

b/ To ensure the observance of Vietnamese law and treaties to which the Socialist Republic of Vietnam is a contracting party;

c/ To protect state assets and marine natural resources and environment;

d/ To protect, assist, search and rescue persons and vessels operating in the maritime zones and island areas of Vietnam;

e/ To deal with unlawful acts in the maritime zones and island areas of Vietnam in accordance with Vietnamese law.

2. The specific scopes of responsibility of sea patrol and surveillance forces comply with

the provisions of law.

3. The State shall ensure necessary conditions for sea patrol and surveillance forces to fulfill their assigned duties.

Article 49. Flag, uniform and badge

When on duty, vessels of sea patrol and surveillance forces must be provided with sufficient Vietnamese national flags, number signs and pennants; sea patrol and surveillance personnel shall be provided with military uniforms, uniforms of the forces and other typical signs in accordance with law.

Chapter VI
HANDLING OF VIOLATIONS

Article 50. Escort and location for settlement of violations

1. Pursuant to the provisions of law, depending on the nature and severity of violations, sea patrol and surveillance forces shall decide to handle violations on site or escort violating persons and vessels ashore or request a competent agency of the flag State or the vessel's destination country to deal with the violations.

2. When being escorted ashore for settlement, the violating persons and vessels shall be escorted to the nearest port, station or dock in the list of ports, stations or docks announced by a competent agency of Vietnam in accordance with law.

In case for the safety of life and property of persons on board, the patrol and surveillance forces may decide to escort the violating persons and vessels to the nearest port, station or dock of Vietnam or other countries in accordance with law.

Article 51. Preventive measures

1. Persons with unlawful acts may be arrested, temporarily held in custody or temporarily detained; the vessels used for the unlawful acts can be temporarily seized for the purpose of preventing unlawful acts or to secure law enforcement.

2. Arrest, temporary holding in custody, or temporary detention of persons with unlawful acts and seizure of vessels shall be made in accordance with law.

Article 52. Notice to the Ministry of Foreign Affairs

When arresting, temporarily holding in custody or temporarily detaining persons with unlawful acts or seizing foreign vessels, the sea patrol and surveillance forces or competent state agencies shall immediately give notice thereof to the Ministry of Foreign Affairs for coordination.

Article 53. Handling of violations

Agencies, organizations or individuals with unlawful acts, depending on the nature and levels, shall be dealt with by disciplining or administrative sanction, and being required to pay compensation under law in case of causing damage; the violating persons may be examined for penal liability in accordance with law.

Chapter VII
IMPLEMENTATION PROVISIONS

Article 54. Entry into effect

This Law takes effect on January 1, 2013.

Article 55. Implementation detailing and guidance

The Government shall detail and guide the implementation of articles and clauses as assigned in this Law.

This Law was passed on June 21, 2012, by the XIIIth National Assembly of the Socialist Republic of Vietnam at its 3rd session.

Chairman of the National Assembly
NGUYEN SINH HUNG

第六章 东盟五国海事管理法律对比思考

在分别介绍了东盟五国海事管理体制及其机构设置,包括海事调查体制、船员服务管理体制,以及国内海事法律体系及国际条约国内化程序之后,本章对东盟五国的海事管理体制及法律进行对比,分析相互之间的相同、差异及各自优势。

一、海事管理体制对比思考

(一) 海事管理体制的相同点

1. 海事行政与军警事务分离

东盟五国由海事部门主管水上交通安全监督和船舶、船员等方面基本海事行政管理事务,海岸警卫队或类似机构主要承担海上主权维护和刑事治安管理职责。例如,新加坡和菲律宾在海事局之外设有海岸警卫队,马来西亚直属于首相署的海事执法局,印度尼西亚隶属于政治法律安全统筹部的海事安全局,越南隶属于国防部的海警司令部与海岸警卫队类似,都属于武装警察或准军事组织。

2. 海事主管部门隶属于交通部

履行水上交通安全监督和船舶、船员等基本海事职责的海事局均隶属于交通部。例如,新加坡的海事与港务局和交通安全调查局隶属于新加坡交通部。菲律宾海事局和海岸警卫队也隶属菲律宾交通运输部,当然,海岸警卫队战时受国防部调遣。马来西亚海事局隶属于马来西亚交通部,印度尼西亚海运总局和越南海事局也隶属于交通运输部。

3. 海事行政与企业经营分离

东盟五国的海事行政机构不从事企业经营。新加坡在1996年进行海事与港口体制改革,实行政企分离的管理体制,将原新加坡海事处、新加坡国家海事局以及新加坡港务局合并,组建新加坡海事与港务局,实行海港合一、政企分离的管理体制。新加坡海事与港务局成为新加坡管理海事与港口的唯一行政主管机构,原新加坡港务局的经营职能由新成立的新加坡港务集团公司替代,实现由行政主管部门到营利性企业的转型,致力于港口经营。

(二) 海事管理体制的不同点

1. 海事和港口行政一体化

部分东盟国家采取海事行政和港口行政管理一体化的体制机制。例如,1996年改革后的新加坡海事与港务局(MPA)统一管理国家海事和港口行政工作。印度尼西亚航运、港口、船舶管理等海事事务也均由交通部海运总局负责管理。马来西亚海事局也负责管理包括海事在内的有关马来西亚航运和港口的事项,实施船舶、海员、港口设施安保、海上训练管理以及海上事故调查等。

2. 海事行政职责较为分散

东盟五国的海事行政事务大多以海事局为主，但在海事局之外往往还有其他机构行使部分海事职权或者联合履行部分海事职责。例如，新加坡在海事与港务局之外还设立交通安全调查局来负责调查海事意外和事故。菲律宾的海事调查则由菲律宾海岸警卫队及其海事调查委员会负责。印度尼西亚在交通部海运总局之外还有海洋事务协调部、海洋事务和渔业部和海事安全局。马来西亚也具有分散管理的体制特征。

（三）海事管理体制的思考

1. 需进一步完善海事公共服务理念

东盟五国具有较为先进的海事公共服务理念。以新加坡为例，新加坡海事与港务局研发港口信息应用平台和贸易信息应用平台，建设电子数据交换中心，提供"一站式"国际航运服务，积极打造全球综合海运信息平台，为海事从业者和全球客户提供全面而优质的海事及港口服务。

这种树立海事公共服务理念的做法是较为先进的。从传统海事管理的监督者、控制者的角色向服务者的角色转变，科学定位海事管理职能，海事管理的职能向"公共服务、市场监管为主，社会管理为辅"的方向发展。同时，整合建立大数据平台，建立科学的电子政务框架，加快海事电子政务建设，建设"一站式"门户网络，推进"智慧海事"进程，进一步完善海事信息系统顶层设计，完成海事系统共享数据库、船舶监管相关应用系统的建设与改造，加快推进海事综合监管指挥平台的建设。推进VTS联网进程，完善AIS信息服务平台和导航助航综合管理系统的功能。整合船舶监督信息资源，提高船舶安全监督智能化水平。

2. 缺少集中管理的海事体制

这里说的集中管理主要是指中央层面的海事行政职责尽量集中到一个机构。新加坡、马来西亚和印度尼西亚的海事行政职责较为分散，由多个部门分管不同的海事行政事务，或者共同、联合执行相同的海事行政事务，这样容易导致行政成本上升、效率下降。东盟五国可以借鉴集中管理的海事体制，由某一海事机构集中履行水上交通安全监督管理、水上交通事故调查处理、船员引航员等适任资格培训考试，以及发证管理、船舶及相关水上设施检验和登记、防止船舶污染和航海保障等行政管理和执法职责。

二、海事调查体制对比思考

海事调查是海事管理中一项比较特殊和重要的职责，是实现保障水上交通安全、保护海洋环境清洁、保护船员整体利益、维护国家海洋权益的重要体现。海事调查的工作质量直接影响着海事管理的水平。

（一）主要特点

从海事调查的体制来看，部分东盟五国的海事调查是由海事局之外的机构负责，例如，新加坡的海事意外和事故调查由独立于海事与港务局的交通安全调查局负责；菲律宾的海事调查由海岸警卫队及其海事调查委员会负责；越南海事局负责越南港口水域外的事故调查，而港务局负责港口水域内的事故调查。由海事局之外的机构负责专门对海上事故进行调查可以从制度上保障海事调查的独立性与公正性，但可能影响到海事调查的快速反应。

从海事调查的目的来看，东盟五国的海事调查具有一定的相似性，即只是就事故发生原因做分析，不直接指出责任比例，属于安全调查。海事安全调查的目的不在于确定过错、分摊责任，而是为防范风险，避免日后海上事故的再次发生。调查报告不得用于保障安全以外的其他目的，以避免相关方在调查过程中做出虚假陈述。从海事安全调查的性质来看，《国际海事调查规则》总则第 1 条、第 2 条规定："海上安全调查应和任何其他形式的调查分开，并独立于任何其他形式的调查。"东盟五国的海事调查均独立于其他民事、刑事和行政管理类型的调查，而且调查报告不判定责任比例。这种独立调查模式有利于查明事故发生的真正原因，预防类似情况再次发生。

（二）关于海事调查体制的思考

1. 完善海事安全调查法律法规

世界各主要海运国家对海事调查的管辖权基本上都采用属人主义加属地主义，即对于本国的船舶在任何海域内（包括公海和其他国家领海内）的事故都享有管辖权，因此，海事调查具有一定的国际性。从东盟五国海事调查的机制来看，这五个国家都积极吸取国际海事组织和其他先进国家在海事调查方面的先进经验，修订与国际接轨的海事调查法律法规体系，为海事调查营造了良好的法律支撑。

2. 优化海事调查队伍建设

海事调查工作具专业性、实践性、经验性，需要一支稳定的、长期从事海事调查工作的专业队伍，应该区别对待海事调查岗位与其他岗位，从事海事调查岗位工作的人员不宜频繁流动。就东盟五国的经验来看，组织一支高素质的海事调查队伍主要通过三个方面进行：一是优化选人用人机制，提高海事调查人员准入门槛，注重培养吸收专业能力强、综合素质高的人才进入海事调查部门。二是完善人才培养机制，加强对中高级海事调查人员的培养，建立权威专家、技术骨干和覆盖全员的多层次人才队伍，着力打造高素质国际型海事调查专家队伍。三是建立海事调查激励机制，保障海事调查队伍健康发展，防止队伍人才流失，保持队伍相对稳定。

三、海员服务管理体制对比思考

(一) 主要特点

东盟五国中以菲律宾的海员服务管理工作最为突出。菲律宾海员服务管理体制方面有如下几个特点:①菲律宾有着较为先进合理的航海教育和培训制度,其采用以市场需求为导向、以企业为依托、以海员劳务输出为主要目的、进出自由的市场机制,海员培训采用校企合作、订单培养的模式,保证了海员教育及培训的质量。②菲律宾有专门的服务管理机构与健全的法律监管体制,菲律宾海外就业管理局为海员提供海外雇佣计划,建立了一个全国范围的多媒体信息渠道,使公众明确海员雇用情况,规范并监督中介机构和雇佣海员的船公司的行为。③对于海外劳工一律免征所得税,还建立了专门为海外劳工和家属服务的医院,为海外劳工提供免费的法律援助,帮助被遣返的菲律宾劳工重返工作岗位等,体现对船员的关怀。

(二) 关于海员服务管理体制的思考

海员的职业具有一定特殊性,海员只能在固定的空间范围内,远离陆地和社会生活工作。因地理上的流动性及其与雇主和其他海员之间的短期合作关系使海员成为一种极不稳定的职业。因此,建立海员服务管理体制一直以来都是一个较为复杂的问题。就东盟五国的成功经验而言,主要得力于以下两个方面。

1. 重视海员教育培训

海员服务管理采用以市场需求为导向、以企业为依托、以海员劳务输出为主要目的进出自由的市场机制,海员教育培训采用订单培养模式,尽可能保证海员教育及培训的质量。同时,积极引入了发达国家的培训机构,通过与国外培训机构合作的方式开展海员培训,不但获得了发达国家对海员培训的先进理念和方法,而且使本国海员的价值取向与外国雇主所需要的价值取向趋同,便于海员融入雇主的企业文化中。国外培训机构的进入,加剧了国内各培训机构间的竞争,因而提升了国内海员培训的整体水平,从而提高了海员素质。

2. 加强海员权益保护

从立法层面考虑保障海员权益。比如,在最低从业要求、就业条件、船上生活设施标准、职业健康安全保障等方面加强海员权益保护。除此之外,还重视对于海员的人文关怀,并给予财政支持。比如,设立了专门机构为回国的劳工在国内就业方面提供方便,政府建立专门为海外劳工和家属服务的医院,在体检和治病方面提供优惠,在所有机场均为回国度假劳工提供免费市内交通服务。

四、海事法律对比思考

依法行政是海事治理现代化的重要基石,东盟五国海事法治建设成效较显著,法规标准体系较为完善。

（一）主要特点

1. 法律渊源均具有多样性

东盟五国海事管理方面的法律渊源具有多样性。例如，菲律宾海事管理的法源包括共和国法律、总统令、行政命令、商船规则和条例、备忘录通告、海事管理咨询等。新加坡除国会通过的法律之外，又制定了各种施行细则、规则、办法、规程、准则与要点等附属法规。越南主要依据《海商法》管理海事活动，除此之外，总理办公室和交通运输部制定了若干重要的法律文件，作为附属条例予以公布以使《海商法》有效施行。

2. 加入国际条约的方式具有类似性

部分东盟国家同样根据条约的种类来决定加入方式和程序。例如，印度尼西亚海事国际条约可通过总统令批准，但与政治、捍卫和平、国安及领土安全、国家主权、人权、环境、借贷相关的国际条约需通过法律来批准。

3. 国际条约国内化的方式具有差异性

东盟五国中的印度尼西亚和越南在国际条约的国内实施方面也是以并入实施为主的。菲律宾则受到美国的影响，其加入的国际条约原则上具有直接效力，无须转化即可实施。由于受到英国的影响，新加坡、马来西亚加入国际条约通常需要转化为国内法律加以实施。

（二）关于完善海事立法的思考

1. 进一步完善法律体系

就东盟五国的涉海法律法规体系而言，海事相关的法律规定大都分散于有关法律和其他政府部门立法中。这样的法律体系尽管可以涵盖较多的方面，但是必然也会存在很多漏洞，也会造成一些法律的交叉。同时，海事立法较多与国际接轨，较多的国际公约也是涉海法律体系的组成部分。因此，就完善海事立法而言，需要将这些法律法规进行系统的梳理，针对漏洞予以完善，针对重复规定进一步明确适用方法，并根据国际海事的发展及时更新。

2. 进一步协调执法工作

如前文所言，部分东盟国家海事管理方面的法律渊源具有多样性，在执法层面也没有采用集中管理的海事体制，多个机构分别行使部分海事职权或者联合履行部分海事职责。因此，在法律的执行阶段可能存在执法空隙，或者是需要联合执法的问题，这就需要通过政策或是其他方式，协调各执法部门进行执法工作，落实法律责任，保障海事制度的实施。

第七章　东盟五国海事管理体制改革建议

一、加强航运安全监管工作

保障航运安全,减少海上事故,历来是航运领域关注的重中之重。船舶安全工作直接关系到生命安全、财产安全和海洋环境。近年来,东盟五国在安全管理上面有着更多的投入,与此同时,世界兴起"以智能化管理"的安全管理新理念。新理念要求以"智能航运发展建设"为突破口,依托"智慧海事"一类先进系统的建设,推进互联网、大数据、云计算等新技术的应用,着力提升海事智能化建设水平,提高主动安全防御、预测预警和动态监控能力,推动"智能航运"的建设发展。随着经济全球化发展,海上船舶大型化、高速化趋势明显,原油、天然气等的危化品运输量不断增多,发生重大海上事故的风险增加。尽管当前航运安全已有所改善,但频频发生的各类船舶事故表明,维护安全航运仍是海事管理的重要一环,尤其是对海运频繁的东盟五国而言,安全航运是重中之重。

当下,自然环境等客观因素造成的船舶碰撞事故的发生概率已经大大降低,而视觉盲区、船员疲劳以及经验不足等人为因素成为各类事故的主因。现在世界上80%以上的船舶安全和污染事故都是人为因素直接或间接造成的。惨痛的海难事故教训让世界形成了以人为本的共识,进一步培养造就一支高素质的员工队伍十分重要。除此之外,航线密布、船舶集中、部分航道与传统渔区重叠等因素成为了航运安全中新的挑战和新的风险。目前,全世界都提倡运用风险管理分析原理,并将其贯穿到航运发展管理整个工作中。"风险管理分析"是从可能造成的后果出发去提醒人们注意的一种思维。对此,东盟五国可采用现代化新技术以及风险控制手段以避免一些危险的出现。例如,加大海运技术的投入、加大创新力度、研究现代化技术。而在安全管理工作中,东盟五国应该提倡时刻注重安全第一,重在预防的理念,确实开展风险分析活动,避免在安全管理中出现麻痹大意与失误,在问题形成之前消除问题,以达到防患于未然的目的。

(一) 提升安全技术标准

1. 掌握并有效运用安全管理新理念和规则制定新方法,重点参与目标型安全规则和技术规范制定工作

掌握并有效运用安全管理新理念和规则制定新方法,重点参与目标型安全规则和技术规范制定工作。部分东盟国家船籍港管理长期存在船舶实时动态掌握滞后、安全预警手段匮乏、安全管理体系纸质文件冗杂、信息传递梗阻等难题。整体而言,除了新加坡以外,另外的东盟国家都有很大的发展潜力。东盟部分国家在海上事故的处理问题上所采取的制度具有优势。例如,判定事故原因和判定责任分属不同机构进行。这样一来,国家在保障海上安全方面可以获得更多的经验，势必能避免更多的事故的发生。除此以外，在未来，航运安全智控可以进一步升级，面向海事、航运公司、船员、培训机构、供应商、金融、保险等各方，深度融合，构建"航运安全生态圈"，共享智能化建设带来的成果。

在规则制定方面，东盟五国应该多参考国际的形势，以国际形势引领规则的制定。例如，随着国际社会加大对绿色航运的投资力度，为航运业开辟了一个崭新的风口。谁能抓住这个机遇，谁就必将在未来的航运业占有一席之地。新法规给业界造成较大冲击的同时，也为业界带来了新的发展思路，船舶改装市场将迎来新机遇。

在国际标准研制方面，新形成的航运价值链或将为航海领域国际标准的研制带来重要机遇。一方面，资金流能够为航运相关方开展科学研究与设备研发提供重要的保障，带来更多的环保技术以支撑航运业绿色发展，这些环保技术的实践经验将逐步演化为国际标准和法规。另一方面，资金流能够帮助航运相关方加快调整产业布局与设备更新换代的步伐，更快地响应国际海事组织进行立法，在贯彻有关公约和法规的过程中尽快总结成功经验，形成国际标准解决方案。东盟五国可以考虑在绿色航运这个方面进行发展，毕竟东盟五国在拥有船只的数量上不容小觑，但是，它们在先进科技方面却还需要努力发展。因此，如果能提早关注这个"风口"，以后一定能在世界航运业中占领一席之地。

2. 加强国际事务研究与国内海事管理工作的衔接，逐步推动安全管理模式从行政规范管理向技术规范管理的转变

东盟五国应计划建立国际海事研究中心，这将是一个"服务本国、面向全球"的国际海事研究资源整合和协调的新型智囊，以"创新、务实、协作"为宗旨，努力为东盟五国和全球海运的可持续发展做出贡献。目前，东盟五国都有不少的船只和海员在世界各地，只局限于研究本国的事务已经不能满足日益增长的需求了。东盟五国更需要研究世界事务，取长补短，推动管理模式的转变。同时，国际海事研究中心也可跟踪国际海事组织的动态及其制定的各种公约和规则，在研究国际海事公约精神实质的基础上，为东盟五国参与 IMO 活动及其他类似的国际活动提供决策依据；为有关主管部门保障水路交通安全、保护海洋环境提供咨询意见，使得东盟在安全和管理方面能跟上国际的脚步。

（二）积极参与和配合国际海事组织工作

1. 进一步完善东盟五国国内履约工作机制，全面提升履约水平

东盟五国可自愿接受国际海事组织的审核，这既是对东盟五国履约能力的审核，也是对其海事监管能力、服务水平和工作成效的综合检验，有利于在将来进一步提升东盟五国海事管理水平和履约服务能力。除此以外，东盟五国还应当从多方面完善国内的履约机制制度建设，如建立履约反馈机制等，为日后全面提升履约水平打好基础。

同时，东盟五国随着其履约能力的不断提升，在未来出现新的问题时，能有针对性地去解决这些新问题；在制定国际公约的时候，也能主动提出自身经验，使得将来制定的公约可以更加优化，更加适合未来时代的发展。

2. 积极参与国际海事管理体系建设，引领规则制定工作。

东盟五国是重要的海运国家，在东南亚乃至世界范围内都有着举足轻重的地位。但是，东盟五国在国际海事管理体系中，并未参与更多的国际海事管理体系建设。虽然当前国际海事体系有其历史的必然性和合理性，但也存在很大局限性。东盟五国作为国际海事体系的参与者，应更积极地成为建设者。这就要求东盟五国在以后不仅要带头遵守国际法的现有规则，更要积极参与到制定国际法新规则的进程中去。作为海洋事务较多的国家，东盟五国必定在公约和规则的制定上有着一定的经验和教训，所以未来应该要尽可能地提出更多有用的新条款，积极发出本国声音，更好地维护本国利益。

二、构建智慧航运管理体系

近年来，随着"智慧水运""智慧物流""智慧港口"等概念相继被提出，智慧航运已成为海事管理需要面临的新考验。在现代人工智能等高新技术与航运要素的深度融合不断加快的大环境下，需要推动新技术与港航业深度融合，由依靠传统要素驱动向更加注重创新驱动转变，在这个方面，东盟五国做得稍显逊色。纵观世界，主要航运国家都在积极探索智能技术的应用方式和智能航运的发展路径，力图在"智慧航运"的风口到来之际占据下一轮产业发展的先发优势。在发达国家的推动下，2017 年 6 月，国际海事组织海上安全委员会（MSC）第 98 届会议将智能航运列为新增议题，并启动全球规范标准的讨论，世界各国争相递交提案以争夺制度性话语权。2018 年 4 月，国际标准化组织在日本就智能航运标准化等相关议题展开了讨论。东盟五国应该积极参与到这些讨论中去，取长补短，紧跟世界潮流。结合现在"5G"（第五代移动通信技术）科技创新，向数字化、智能化转型升级，是航运企业高质量发展的必由之路，数字化创新在航运领域的应用也将给行业带来质的飞跃。2019 年 6 月 11 日，香港船东协会与 E-PORTS 联合召开国际船东研讨会，主题为"智能航运——巨大变革已来"，研讨传统航运企业如何过渡到智能航运时代，探索新航运时代的船舶服务标准及企业发展机遇。E-PORTS 平台 CEO 黄启洲表示，在 5G 的环境下应该强调"船"与"岸"的联结，要从管理层面上提升港航一体化和信息化水平，做到可视化跟踪、标准化节点把控，让船舶经营管理方可以真正随时随地把控船舶在港的所有动态。未来，5G 与现代航运业尤其是港口和船舶作业的结合，将为科技助力航运业高质量发展提供新动能。东盟五国应该以此为契机，发展新时代航运科技，以求不落后于最新的科技潮流。

（一）推动航海技术发展

1. E 航海战略跟踪研究

学习先进国家经验，完善本国 E 航海发展计划，利用双、多边平台交流学习 E 航海先进技术推广应用方面的经验。E 航海技术正日益成熟，为海事领域提供更好的支持；对于东盟五国而言，应该好好利用 E 航海带来的便利。众所周知，E 航海有利于有效降低船岸值班人员的工作压力，融合海上各类信息，使信息交换更流畅，保障船舶航行安全，有效促进海上服务从传统模式向高效现代化模式转变。在海事监管方面，E 航海的一些方法和新的措施也对监管机构产生影响。就像智能船舶、无人驾驶船舶等,这些也将会给航运业和海事管理带来新的挑战。但无论如何,对东盟五国而言,这都是值得关注和学习的新的方面,因此,在将来,东盟五国应该多向技术先进的国家学习,优化本国的 E 航海系统。

目前世界各国的航海技术实施现状如下:

(1) 欧盟:ACCSEAS 系统,分析船舶密度和交通拥塞程度,有选择性地开发海上服务、船舶基本 PNT 服务和岸基通信服务等。

(2) 美国:进行 AIS 系统的推进和技术开发。进行 RBN/DGPS 系统的改进和推广。在 LRIT 方面进行了支持的工作。承担了 IALA 海上用户需求的调研和分析。

(3) 日本:对 ENSS 的深入研究,AIS 航标及虚拟航标的深入研究和应用,AIS 二进制点问的进一步应用。

2. 积极跟踪研究 GMDSS 现代化议题,推动本国 GMDSS 现代化

东盟五国在 GMDSS 现代化方面可以建立以需求为导向的服务机制,能够极大地拓宽业务范围,提高服务水平,实现通信服务的多元化。东盟五国加快 GMDSS 现代化进程的推进,能够极大地提高通信速度及通信系统的有效性和准确性,保障信息的传输质量,降低误报警率,提高搜救效率。同时,通过对新功能的拓展,也可以极大地提高失事船舶定位的准确性和信号传输的安全性,从而形成一个体系完备、功能多样、保障有力的系统。

GMDSS 现代化在世界多国都已经有了实践,为东盟五国创造了不少学习范例。因此,东盟五国应该在现有技术的基础上,加强对 GMDSS 技术的研究,更大程度地发挥现代化技术的作用。就东盟五国当前的海事管理工作而言,东盟五国应积极推动本国 GMDSS 现代化进程,认真做好通航要素采集系统的建设和维护工作,稳步推进通航要素数据库的开发开放和应用,严格落实工作责任,保证通航环境数据的全面准确。东盟五国在未来还可以着手的工作包括开发建设水上无线电管理信息系统、完成项目审批手续及招标工作、研究解决水上无线电通信信号监测的技术难题,为水上无线电通信秩序治理提供支持。

(二) 促进海运便利

1. 实行"单一窗口",加快船舶证书电子化、船岸交互信息传输系统等技术研究和项目建设的进程

船舶证书电子化作为新生的新技术,存在着很大的机遇,也面临着不小的挑战。目前存在的一些问题及应采取的对策如下。

(1) 电子证书管理标准问题及对策。目前,电子证书还是只有少数国家和认可组织开始使用,虽然出台了电子证书的使用指南,但具体的技术细节还需要各个海事组织成员自行开发。因此,东盟五国可以互相承认对方的电子证书,至于具体的技术细节,再由东盟五国合力进行研发。但是,相关国家和组织对电子签证和唯一跟踪码也并未细化要求。在实际操作中,每个成员会根据自身情况应用不同技术,这就导致各个成员之间存在技术壁垒,电子签证和唯一跟踪码一样样式繁多。如果每个船旗国或认可组织都出台一个验证网站和跟踪码样式，将会给证书的检查和验证带来不便。对此，针对各个组织应用的技术不一致的问题，技术不同，跟踪码形式不一样，最终反映到证书变成签发形式和验证方式不一样。但是殊途同归，最终都是要利用网站或者客户端实现调阅、验证证书。东盟五国可以建立统一的查阅、验证平台，对各个东盟五国和认可组织的接口进行整合，最终利用同一出口输出，便于证书的查阅和验证。

（2）各船旗国信息化、电子化发展的差距问题及对策。近年来，随着东盟五国的经济快速增长，社会信息化、电子化发展也越来越完善，这为实施电子化办公提供了便利条件。但我们仍要看到，在一些欠发达地区，网络管理还不完善，一些船旗国不能有效建立和维护船舶电子数据，一些港口的网络不能覆盖，这样电子证书就无法替代纸质证书。最明显的就是东盟四国的马来西亚、印度尼西亚、菲律宾、越南与新加坡之间的差距。新加坡的信息化和电子化程度高，因而电子管理等都比较完善，而且其余的四国还在发展的阶段，因此，可以建议新加坡等电子管理发展较为完善的国家在数据库建设、港口信息化建设等方面给予一定的政策倾斜和帮助，帮助东盟四国实施证书的电子化。

（3）存量船基数大、数据库建立困难的问题及对策。虽然新的船舶大多能够实现电子数据建立档案，但是很多存量船舶的证书是以纸质材料建立的档案，甚至有些船舶经多次买卖后纸质档案都已经不全。每艘船舶的数据种类繁多，重新建立电子数据库需要耗费大量的人力、物力和财力。对此，对于存量船基数庞大的问题，可以用"新船新办法，老船老方法"来逐步解决。在新建船舶或者已有电子档案的现有船舶先推广实行电子证书，而老船分船型、船龄等有梯度地逐步实行。随着时间的迁移，一方面，老旧船舶逐步退出市场，存量船数量有所下降；另一方面，降低了短时间内大量纸质数据转换成电子数据所需要的成本。这对于东盟五国的现状处理是一个很好的方法。由于东盟五国在海洋上的事务都有很悠久的历史，所以船舶数量、品类等都存在各自复杂的状况，因此，如果可以逐步实现电子数据管理，那么在管理上必定能提升效率。

2. 推广实践经验，推动区域统一标准的建立

目前，东盟五国在许多方面都按照其国内法进行海事管理。就智慧航运管理体系而言，东盟五国已经开始向先进国家学习，并计划在国内开始进行试点。例如，将信息流与业务数据进行有机整合，通过网络摄像头等物联网设备，与海事业务系统相结合，达到两者相辅相成的效果。相信在未来，东盟五国将积累更多的实践经验，这些实践经验既值得在东盟内部交流，又可向全球各国进行推广介绍。与此同时，国际上的一些经验反馈也能为东盟五国提供有益启示，从而有利于其不断完善各自的做法。

3. 深化东盟五国之间的合作，推动区域统一标准的建立

目前，东盟五国在许多方面仍然按照其国内法运行，这自然是无可厚非的。但是，如果希望区域内的海事问题的解决能够变得更加高效和完善，日后应当建立更多联系，然后在这些联系的基础上，订立共同标准，使一些原本复杂的问题简单化，加快海事问题解决的速度。同时，将本国及区域关于海事管理的标准和经验积极向国际社会推广介绍，争取在后续示范项目的标准制定、系统建设等方面体现本国技术与标准，推动区域统一标准的建立。

（三）应对船舶智能化发展的新问题

1. 重视智能船舶发展，为未来参与新规则和新标准的制定提供实践基础

近年来，智能船舶在优化船舶航行、控制燃油消耗、降低成本、提高收益、保护环境等方面都具有重大意义，成为了全球航运的大势所趋，这对东盟五国也不例外。因此，东盟五国需要关注和跟踪国内外船舶智能化技术应用发展动态，研判船舶智能化发展对海上安全、环境保护和海上安保等方面的国际规则和标准带来的影响。

有些国家已经开始了 MASS（自主航行船）的试航，较小的无人船已经投入使用。对于操作烦琐或存在危险的船舶，如溢油应急船、消防船和救援船，无人操作是一种特别有吸引力的选择，自动化具有巨大潜力来避免人员伤亡，同时能够节约大量成本。为保证 MASS 的安全运营，IMO 海上安全委员会（MSC）正在探索如何将安全、稳定且环境良好的 MASS 运营纳入 IMO 法规中。2019 年 6 月，MSC 会议通过了一套关于自主航行船舶试航的初步指南，要求在试航时至少应具备相关法律所规定的安全和环保等级。这对东盟五国的海事管理而言，也将是一个需要不断提升的过程，在管理过程中需要不断积累经验，以期在未来新规则和新标准的制定中占据有利地位。

2. 在海事管理体系中积极引入数字化技术支持

尽管目前智慧航运管理体系还没有跟上智能船舶的发展脚步，但是智能船舶的诞生势必促使智慧航运管理体系的发展，并且必然会促使智慧航运管理体系的改革。所以，东盟五国应在海事管理体系中积极引入数字化技术支持。

以东盟五国海事应急监管为例，它主要包括区内搜寻和救助问题，引入数字化技术支持后可以采取以下措施：一是使海员可以在遇险后使用卫星功能发送求救信息；二是用海事高频基站设备对全区内河流域覆盖实现语音录制和现场还原等功能；三是使用应急响应服务并结合 3D 技术实现船舶重建和场景模拟。这些措施可以提高搜救效率，使事故损失最小化。

从部分国家的先进经验来看，东盟五国在积极引入数字化技术支持后，可以实现对船舶的动静态监管、对航道的智能化监管、对锚地安全生产作业的可视化监管；也可以与 5G + AR（增强现实）相结合，依托 5G 宽带、高速率、海量接入特性，结合高性能 AR 智能监控系统，实现空中巡检、智能监控、机器人巡逻等人工智能运作方式；还可以更进一步完善海事监控指挥体系，提供实时信息监控、实时海事信息的快速传递、共享和综合管理，达到海事管理精细化、实时化的深度目标。

随着全球硫排放限额进一步降低，互联网和航运业的进一步融合给海事环保监管提出了新问题和新挑战。根据统计，目前船舶污染防控主要分为动力监测、排放废气监测、燃料检测三方面。在引入数字化技术支持后，东盟五国也可以利用可视化软件对监测数据进行处理和分析，为船舶污染防控提供解决方案。

三、强化绿色航运监管

全球气候问题成为各项事务的重中之重。各国航运业开始考虑通过电力驱动船舶、风能船和零碳航运等创新解决方案力求减少其对环境及海洋的影响。联合国内部专门负责海上航行安全和防止船舶造成海洋污染的国际海事组织（IMO），针对船舶污染防控陆续制定出台了各类新公约、新规范，并根据实际发展进行适时修订。其中，国际海事组织技术合作司执行副司长 Chris Trelawny 说，为支持联合国 2030 年可持续发展目标，减少温室气体排放和减少船舶燃油含硫量已成为近年来国际海事组织的工作重点。而东盟五国的航运业也在绿色航运方面加大了投入，并设定了新的环境目标，绿色航运正成为关键趋势的扭转要素。

要实现绿色航运，需要行业与监管机构、港口管理当局和政府共同协作，落实和解决船舶污染防治、零排放航运及其他新兴环境问题，确保推动绿色航运发展和创新，建设绿色交通始终是海洋运输从业者追求的目标和践行的使命。近年来，东盟五国通过优化交通运输结构、加强生态保护和污染综合防治、推进资源节约循环利用、提升综合治理能力，把绿色发展理念融入了交通运输发展的全过程和各方面，行业的生态良好程度和环境保护水平逐年提升。例如，即使在新冠肺炎疫情流行期间，新加坡依然严格执行 IMO 2020 限硫令对船舶燃料油的合规性检查。据报道，新加坡船舶及港口管理局在 2020 年第一季度共开展 326 次港口国监控和船旗国监控检查，并扣押两艘使用不合规燃料的船舶；第一季度在停靠新加坡港口的船舶中，除安装开环式脱硫塔并在靠港时使用合规燃油的船舶外，约 96% 的船舶都使用了合规燃油。由此可见，绿色航运将是东盟五国航运发展的一个重要的方向。

（一）船舶污染防治

1. 开展对国际排放控制区、特别敏感海区和特殊区域设置的研究，并制定对策建议

国际排放控制区的设立存在着阻碍，受到国际公约和国际法的限制，目前世界各国国内法划定的排放控制区受到了极大的制约，所设定的排放控制区基本难以达到原有目的。这是因为无害通过权的存在，除现有标准外，不应对外国船只的设计、建设等提出要求。然而，在现有标准下，外国船只会产生巨大的污染，东盟五国都有着广阔的海域面积，其必然会受到很大的污染和影响。所以，东盟五国应该尽快共同研究和协商，协议建立国际排放控制区，减少船舶污染。

2. 推动清洁能源的技术研发和在船使用，推动东盟五国国内标准国际化

据报道，一艘使用 3.5% 含硫量燃料油中大型集装箱船会排放大量的 PM 2.5（细颗粒物），因此，急需清洁能源的研发。LNG 是目前很流行的一种清洁能源，但普及度还不够高，需要东盟五国政府从财政和政策上进行补贴。除此之外，还可以使用生物燃料，如生物液化天然气（Bio-LNG）作为一种过渡性燃料具有巨大的潜力，可以逐渐取代化石燃料。其他被认为可以替代传统燃料的合成燃料包括甲醇、氢和氨。如果使用可再生电力（即通过电解生产氢）生产可持续的燃料，那么，这些燃料可以有效地减少甚至消除航运业的排放。虽然目前替代燃料在经济上没有竞争力，但从中长期来看，随着替代燃料价格的下降、使用量的增加和技术的改进，替代燃料有望成为可行的选择。除此之外，太阳能动力、新型天然气内燃机和岸电站也是发展的趋势之一。所以，东盟五国应该多交流多合作，尤其是像新加坡这样的发达国家可以提供更多先进的技术给其他东盟国家,共同促进新能源、绿色能源的使用,共同保护环境。

3. 深化溢油应急处置和有毒有害物质应急处置的双、多边合作

对于溢油应急处置和有毒有害物质应急处置,东盟五国可以建立相应的应急处理措施,如应急信息系统、应急决策系统、应急处理保障机制、船舶油污损害赔偿机制、增强实战经验等。

(二) 温室气体减排

1. 推动国际社会制定科学合理的船舶能效措施和温室气体减排机制

船舶能效管理的目的就是尽可能地提高能源(燃油)的使用效率,从而有效地防止大气污染,降低大气中二氧化碳等温室气体的排放量,控制和减少全球的温室效应。对此,东盟五国在未来可以采取一些相应的措施:一是合理使用经济航速;二是加强低速下的主机管理;三是合理下调主机汽缸油注油量;四是优化航线设计;五是优化压载水操作;六是重载回航时适当调整吃水差,以提高船舶螺旋桨的效率;七是主机加装ALPHA电子注油器;八是使用节能型船壳油漆。对东盟五国而言,提高能源利用率,除了可以减少环境污染,也可以节约能源支出,能节省下一笔可观的支出。

2. 积极参与海运温室气体减排国际合作和示范项目,进一步建立健全本国海运低碳发展的战略、法规、政策和标准

针对国家间海运温室气体减排,IMO 公布的国际海运温室气体减排初步战略包括愿景、减排力度、指导原则、短中长期减排措施等一系列要素,这是 IMO 启动温室气体减排谈判 20 年来具有里程碑意义的成果,展示了 IMO 引领国际海运业应对气候变化的决心,明确了未来海运业的低碳发展方向。东盟五国在将来应该积极参与减排的国际合作和项目,一方面,要紧跟 IMO 的脚步,学习先进的技术和方法;另一方面,积极配合项目的实施,主动履行合作的约定,促进温室气体减排。东盟五国可采取如下的具体措施:从短期看,东盟五国可完善能效框架、研发高效能技术、制定能效指标、制订海运减排国家计划、传播速度优化和降速、减少港口排放、研发替代低碳或零碳燃油等。从中期看,可以实施替代低碳或零碳燃油项目、实施提高能效措施、完善市场机制等其他创新及减排机制、技术合作和能力建设等。从长期看,可以开发和使用零碳燃油,鼓励全面实施其他创新减排机制。因此,东盟五国应该积极践行这些减排措施和政策,合力减少温室气体的排放。例如,改进船舶设计、供应岸电、新能源利用、降低船舶航速、提高装卸货效率、严格控制制冷气体泄漏、排放交易体系、将强制性 CO_2 因素纳入到港口费中去等的措施。

(三) 新兴环境问题的积极应对

1. 深入研究压载水公约、拆船公约、极地规则等新公约要求,持续跟踪并积极参与配套导则的制定和修订

东盟五国可以从新公约入手,面对新兴的环境问题,制定新的配套规则。

首先是压载水公约。压载水是控制船舶纵倾、横倾、吃水、稳性或应力而在船上加装的水及其悬浮物。在船舶航行、装载货物过程中,需要常常排放或吸入淡水或海水,以实时调整船上压载水量,保障船舶安全平稳运行。该公约的核心要求是在公约实施初期,船舶需要通过置换压载水的方式来缓解压载水携带有害水生物和病原体入侵的情况。其具体要求为船舶需要在距离最近陆地 200 海里、水深超过 200 米的区域对船上携带的压载水按照公约要求的方式进行大洋海水置换。按照公约规定的时间表,所有船舶在 2024 年 9 月 8 日之后都需要安装压载水管理系统,或者使用岸基压载水管理系统对船舶携带的压载水进行处理,从而最终消除上面提到的这些危害。

其次是拆船公约。这是有关拆解船舶的公约,其具体要求:①对供应商和建造业,不能含有危害物质。②对航运业,按规定建造维修拆解船舶。③对拆船业,符合环保要求,接受监管机关的监督。

再次是极地规则。极地规则要求拟在极地水域营运的船舶具备其船旗国签发的有效极地船舶证书。船舶需要进行风险评估,包括在极地水域营运的预期环境条件及风险。

最后是应对相关规则的挑战。一方面,极地规则在保护船舶、船员和环境方面缺乏强硬措施,而理想的状态是在上述方面的标准要远远高于现行规则的最低标准。另一方面,沿岸国的法规可能保留对于渔船和国内商船的现有要求,而此类船舶并不在目前极地规则的适用范围之内。此外,极地规则建议船舶"不要在北极水域使用或运载重油",然而该建议并无法律约束力。

2. 开展新公约宣传,引导国内产业向绿色无害化全面升级,推动相关技术和装备的研发,探索与周边国家履约合作的可行性

为确保船舶及其结构、设备、系统和材料等公约规定的配套导则要求,应引导造船界、航运界、制造业向绿色无害化全面升级,鼓励新造船、营运船在公约生效前提前履约。东盟五国应该主动进行技术和设备研发,使得将来绿色无害化的设想成为实际。同时,应该积极探索与周边各国履约合作,无论是东盟内部的国家,还是非东盟国家,都应该尽力合作,共同促进绿色无害化的发展。

3. 关注黑炭、重油使用等极地水域环境保护问题,提升国际规则、最佳实践与技术指南制定的引导能力

在未来,东盟五国应该同时关注极地水域的环境问题。虽然东盟五国并不是极地的沿岸国,但是全球的环境系统是一体的,东盟五国都应该注意自己国内的船舶在保护环境方面的问题。

目前,黑炭的污染现状触目惊心,尽管来自陆地柴油机的全球黑炭排放量比来自船舶引擎的高出约 20 倍,但在很多繁忙的港口和沿海地区,船舶污染造成的健康和环境影响非常大。据了解,如果黑炭沉降到冰雪表面,就可降低表面反照率,从而有可能加速冰雪消融,因此,黑炭研究已成为当前北极科学研究的热点。随着海冰消退,北极地区的船舶交通量预计在未来几十年内将出现大幅增长,而当黑炭颗粒落在雪和冰上,会加速融化过程。

我们目前可利用溢油回收系统、吸收剂、分散剂、凝油剂、焚烧等解决重油污染。对此,政府应对采用新能源船替代能源的集装箱支线船,对老旧船舶的淘汰给予适当的税收等方面的政策减免,以降低航运、新能源和替代能源企业减排的绿色成本。事实上,即使在北欧,为了引导船舶接受越来越严格的排放标准,政府也不得不出台一些让利措施。例如,芬兰政府就决定在未来两年航道费减半,并减少或停止收取其他一些来自船东的税费。中国香港也采取类似措施,船舶使用不超过0.5%含硫量燃油时可减免50%的港口设施费用。美国洛杉矶和长滩港的有关自愿减速方案规定,在一年中,如果一支船队有90%或更多的船舶满足了减速要求,可在来年获得15%的停靠费率折扣。

为有效控制船舶柴油机的污染排放,一些环保研究团队提出如下建议:加快世界各国新生产船舶柴油机排放标准的制定和升级工作,尽快颁布实施船舶柴油机排放标准;建立船舶柴油机排放年检制度,制定相关标准,重点加强对在用船舶柴油机烟度排放的日常监督管理;应加强船舶在港口区域的排放控制;船舶柴油供应渠道复杂且油品质量参差不齐,既直接影响颗粒物的排放,也影响到船舶柴油机排放控制技术的进步,应采取有效措施,建立有效的船用柴油监督管理机制。

目前,燃油-LNG双燃料发动机、纯LNG发动机以及可以安全实现重油与低硫油转换使用的发动机等产品的技术都已较成熟。欧美日等国家和地区的企业在选择性催化还原(SCR)系统、排气再循环(EGR)装置和废气洗涤器研制方面的技术走在前面。SCR是一种后处理技术,它能有效削减移动源的氮氧化物的排放。在较理想的运营环境下,闭环SCR系统可实现氮氧化物减排90%以上。柴油颗粒物捕集器(DPF)也是一种后处理装置,主要用于PM减排。当使用超低硫燃料时,DPF技术最高可实现PM减排90%以及碳氢化合物和一氧化碳减排60%~90%。有些研究员表示,要进一步减少船舶大气污染物的排放,只在改变发动机结构上动脑筋是不现实的,理性的措施是安装SCR系统、EGR装置以及废气洗涤器等附加装置来降低硫排放。

发动机和附加装置到位后,船舶降低速度航行可进一步实现减排。船舶降速减排潜力取决于降速幅度、燃料类型和发动机性能,通常速度降低10%可实现每海里降低燃料消耗15%~20%。美国一些港口已认识到船舶减速的减排效果,并开始鼓励船舶自愿降低速度从而减少污染排放。美国洛杉矶和长滩港实施的自愿减速方案很有效,两个港口都将减速区从港口外20海里扩展至40海里。

附录：相关国际条约

1. International Convention for the Unification of Certain Rules of Law Relating to Collision between Vessels 1910

《1910 年关于统一船舶碰撞若干法律规定的国际公约》

2. International Convention for the Unification of Certain Rules of Law Relating to Assistance and Salvage at Sea 1910

《1910 年关于统一海难救助若干法律规定的国际公约》

3. International Convention for the Unification of Certain Rules of Law relating to Bills of Lading 1924（Hague Rules）

《1924 年关于统一提单若干法律规定的国际公约》（海牙规则）

4. Protocol to Amend the International Convention for the Unification of Certain Rules of Law Relating to Bills of Lading 1968 Visby Rules（Visby Rules）

《1968 年关于修订统一提单若干法律规定的国际公约的议定书》（维斯比规则）

5. Convention for the Suppression of Unlawful Acts against the Safety of Maritime Navigation 1988

《1988 年制止危及海上航行安全的非法行为的公约》

6. Provisions of the Protocol for the Suppression of Unlawful Acts against the Safety of Fixed Platforms Located on the Continental Shelf 1988

《1988 年制止危及大陆架固定式平台安全的非法行为的议定书》

7. International Convention on Civil Liability for Oil Pollution Damage 1992

《1992 年国际油污民事责任公约》

8. International Convention on the Establishment of an International Fund for Compensation for Oil Pollution Damage 1992

《1992 年设立国际油污损害赔偿基金公约》

9. International Convention for the Prevention of Pollution from Ships, 1973 as modified by the Protocol of 1978 relating thereto（MARPOL 73/78）

《1973 年防止船舶污染国际公约 1978 年议定书》（MARPOL 73/78）

10. International Convention for the Control and Management of Ships' Ballast Water and Sediments 2004

《2004 年国际船舶压载水和沉积物控制与管理公约》

11. International Convention on Oil Pollution Preparedness, Response and Co-operation 1990（OPRC 1990）

《1990 年国际油污防备、反应和合作公约》

12. Convention on Limitation of Liability for Maritime Claims 1976

《1976年海事索赔责任限制公约》

13. International Convention on Civil Liability for Bunker Oil Pollution Damage 2001 (BUNKER 2001)

《2001年国际燃料油污染损害民事责任公约》

14. Maritime Labour Convention 2006

《2006年国际海事劳工公约》

15. Nairobi International Convention on the Removal of Wrecks 2007

《2007年内罗毕国际船舶残骸清除公约》

16. International Convention for the Safety of Life at Sea

《国际海上人命安全公约》

17. International Convention on Tonnage Measurement of Ships 1969 (TONNAGE 69)

《1969年国际船舶吨位丈量公约》

18. Convention on the International Regulations for Preventing Collisions at Sea 1972 (COLREG 72)

《1972年国际海上避碰规则公约》

19. International Convention for the Safety of Life at Sea 1974 (SOLAS 74)

《1974年国际海上人命安全公约》(SOLAS 74)

20. International Convention on Standards of Training, Certification and Watchkeeping for Seafarers 1978 (STCW 78)

《1978年海员培训、发证和值班标准国际公约》

21. Protocol of 1988 relating to the International Convention on Load Lines 1966 [LL PROT (HSSC) 88] (LL88)

《1966年国际载重线公约1988年议定书》

22. Merchant Shipping (Maritime Labour Convention)

《商船条例》(《国际海事劳工公约》)

23. International Convention on the Control of Harmful Anti-fouling Systems on Ships 2001 (AFS 2001)

《2001年国际控制船舶有害防污底系统公约》

24. Convention on the International Maritime Organization, 1948

《1948年国际海事组织公约》

25. International Convention on the Establishment of an International Fund for Compensation for Oil Pollution Damage (FUND)

《设立国际油污损害赔偿基金国际公约》

26. International Convention for the Safety of Life at Sea (SOLAS) 1974, as amended by the Protocol of 1988

《1974年国际海上人命安全公约1988年议定书》

27. Protocol of 1978 relating to the International Convention for the Safety of Life at Sea 1974, as amended

《1974年国际海上人命安全公约1978年议定书》

28. Convention on the International Mobile Satellite Organization (IMSO) 1976, as amended

《1976年国际海事卫星组织公约》

29. Operating Agreement on the International Mobile Satellite Organization 1976, as amended

《1979年国际海事卫星组织业务协定》

30. International Convention for the Prevention of Pollution from Ships (MARPOL) 73/78, Annex Ⅲ: Regulations for the Prevention of Pollution by Harmful Substances Carried by Sea in Packaged Form

《国际防止船舶污染公约》附则Ⅲ：防止海运包装有害物质污染规则

31. International Convention on the Establishment of an International Fund for Compensation for Oil Pollution Damage (FUND) 1971

《1971年关于设立国际油污损害赔偿基金国际公约》

32. International Convention for the Prevention of Pollution from Ships (MARPOL) 73/78, Annex Ⅰ: Regulations for the Prevention of Pollution by Oil

《国际防止船舶污染公约》附则Ⅰ：防止油类污染规则

33. International Convention for the Prevention of Pollution from Ships (MARPOL) 73/78, Annex Ⅱ: Regulations for the Control of Pollution by Noxious Liquid Substances in Bulk

《国际防止船舶污染公约》附则Ⅱ：控制散装有毒液体物质污染规则

34. International Convention for the Prevention of Pollution from Ships (MARPOL) 73/78, Annex Ⅴ: Regulations for the Prevention of Pollution by Garbage from Ships

《国际防止船舶污染公约》附则Ⅴ：防止船舶垃圾污染规则

35. International Convention for the Prevention of Pollution from Ships (MARPOL) 73/78, Annex Ⅳ: Regulations for the Prevention of Pollution by Sewage from Ships

《国际防止船舶污染公约》附则Ⅳ：防止船舶生活污水污染规则

36. Amendments Adopted in November 1991 to the Convention of the International Maritime Organization

《国际海事组织公约1991年修正案》

37. International Convention for the Prevention of Pollution from Ships (MARPOL) 73/78, Annex Ⅵ: Regulations for the Prevention of Air Pollution from Ships

《国际防止船舶污染公约》附则Ⅵ：防止船舶造成空气污染规则

38. Protocol of 1992 to amend the International Convention on Civil Liability for Oil Pollution Damage (CLC) 1969

《1969年国际油污损害民事责任公约1992年议定书》

39. Protocol of 1992 to amend the International Convention on the Establishment of an International Fund for Compensation for Oil Pollution Damage 1971

《1971年关于设立国际油污损害赔偿基金国际公约1992年议定书》

40. The International Convention for the Limitation of Liability for Maritime Claims, 1976 as Amended by Protocol of 1996 (LLMC Convention 1996)

《1976年海事索赔责任限制公约1996年议定书》

41. International Convention for the Control and Management of Ship's Ballast Water and Sediment (BWM), 2004

《2004年国际船舶压载水和沉积物控制与管理公约》

后　　记

　　本书课题组通过对东盟五国实地考察调研、专家访谈、法律数据库查询等方式，调查并收集了东盟五国海事管理法律框架体系及主要法律制度的资料，并分别从海事管理体制与架构、国际公约和国内法律等方面，梳理出东盟五国在海事管理方面的科学理念、成功经验和存在问题，通过分析研究，对东盟五国海事管理法律的完善提出了若干建议。

　　由于时间、资料等方面的限制，以及笔者能力水平所限，本研究报告仅聚焦于东盟的新加坡、马来西亚、印度尼西亚、菲律宾和越南这五个有代表性的国家，而且没有覆盖海事管理法律的全部要素。这些欠缺都有待在以后的研究中不断予以完善。

　　在课题研究期间，众多单位和个人为课题组提供了大量的资源和信息，可以说，没有他们的无私奉献和帮助，研究报告难以如期完成。对此，我们表示衷心感谢！尤其要特别感谢广东省高级人民法院、广州海事法院、广东恒福律师事务所、广州市航运法学研究会和广州航海学院等单位专家给予的中肯建议和专业指导。